International Trade and the Successful Intermediary

International Trade and the Successful Intermediary

DAVIDE GIOVANNI PAPA
and
LORNA ELLIOTT

GOWER

Published by
Ashgate Publishing Limited
Wey Court East
Union Road
Farnham
Surrey GU9 7PT
England

Ashgate Publishing Company
Suite 420
101 Cherry Street
Burlington,
VT 05401-4405
USA

www.gowerpublishing.com

British Library Cataloguing in Publication Data
Papa, Davide Giovanni.
   International trade and the successful intermediary.
   1. International trade--Finance. 2. Commission merchants.
   3. Export sales contracts.
   I. Title II. Elliott, Lorna.
   658.8'4-dc22

   ISBN: 978-0-566-08934-3 (hbk)
   ISBN: 978-0-566-09223-7 (ebk)

Library of Congress Cataloging-in-Publication Data
Papa, Davide Giovanni.
   International trade and the successful intermediary / by Davide Giovanni Papa and Lorna Elliott.
      p. cm.
   Includes index.
   ISBN 978-0-566-08934-3 (hardback) -- ISBN 978-0-566-09223-7 (ebook) 1. International trade. 2. Businesspeople. 3. Entrepreneurship. I. Elliott, Lorna. II. Title.
   HF1379.P364 2009
   658.8'4--dc22

                                                                                    2009024523

Reprinted 2011

Printed and bound in Great Britain by the
MPG Books Group, UK

Contents

Preface

This book has been written to provide an in-depth insight into the importation and exportation of commodities and how an intermediary can secure commission within these transactions. For this reason it is aimed at novice intermediaries who are yet to close a deal, as well as intermediaries who have been trading for some time. Some of these more seasoned intermediaries may have been close to closing a deal, but want to understand why these deals have fallen through; others may have been circumvented in a deal that closed successfully, thereby missing out on commission payments.

Many intermediaries consider that by signing a confidentiality document their commission will be protected and they trust that a supplier or buyer will pay commission to them when the deal closes. In the real world of business, this is pure fantasy. This book explains how intermediaries can control a deal from the outset while remaining compliant with the rules and procedures of international trade. Most importantly, it reveals how to guarantee that commissions are paid while managing other intermediaries involved in the trade.

In order to become an effective intermediary, the international trader needs to know a little about law, finance, rules of agency and delivery. While subject matter is available from higher learning institutions, the whole process cannot be learned effectively from a classroom. *International Trade and the Successful Intermediary* presents the trading process as a whole, incorporating rules, laws and the personal trading experience – both the adventures and misadventures – of an intermediary with over twenty years' experience.

Due to intellectual property restrictions the actual wording of UCP600 and Incoterms is not used. However UCP600 and Incoterms are explained in order to demonstrate their purpose in the international trading arena. Rules that are specific to the USA's internal code of practice (UCC or Uniform Commercial

Code) are not addressed because they are mostly relevant for interstate business rather than the international trading arena. Knowledge of UCP600 letter of credit rules alone will not assist the intermediary as matters relating to letters of credit are governed internally by the financial institution in question. This publication deals only with the important aspects as they relate to the practice of trading in appropriate and exportable goods.

Similarly, having knowledge of the applicable commercial laws is not sufficient. However, do not be intimidated by bankers, lawyers, sellers, buyers, accountants or other individuals when you start to trade. You are the professional intermediary – they are not – and they will often attempt to learn specific details about methods of trading from you. The way in which you reply will demonstrate that you are in control, not them.

Don't worry if you do not absorb everything at first. Read the publication quickly to get a general idea of the methods and then read it again, after which the trading protocol should become clear. The rest is up to you, the trader, and your own ability and experience.

Finally, get that documentary letter of credit into your account. Banks will not acknowledge your existence until you do. Once the funds are in your control financial institutions will be more willing to help you. It is your role to tell them what you want: they are obliged to follow the rules of UCP600. You are the freelance agent: they are bound to perform in strict accordance with their ICC Mandate. Banks who perform without adhering to such rules are subject to substantial fines.

Remember there are no trading secrets in the import/export business, just strict and safe trading procedures.

Davide G. Papa
February 2009

1

The Intermediary – An Introduction

Davide Giovanni Papa, CEO of FTN Exporting and author of this book, has twenty years' experience as an intermediary both in practice as a trader and as a teacher of theory to others. In 1994 FTN Exporting, and its dealings with a certain sugar trade, was the subject of a major editorial in the *Australian Sunday Herald*. Two weeks after the article was published the sugar deal collapsed into a litigious mess but, as far as everyone else was concerned, FTN Exporting had made a huge amount of money from the deal.

After three months of negotiation Davide Papa had secured a UCP500 Non-cumulative Revolving Letter of Credit from the end buyer's bank, the Bank of China in New York, to the value of $6,000,000, for a contracted supply of sugar worth more than $120,000,000 over two years. It eventually came to light that a simple misunderstanding caused the collapse of the deal in its entirety. That misunderstanding didn't become apparent until some time later when Davide Papa sought to educate himself as to what exactly had gone wrong.

The meaning of the terms 'buyer' and 'seller' were proving to be problematic and it was this one anomaly that held the secret to successful trading as an intermediary. The term 'buyer' or 'seller' could indeed mean the 'end buyer' or 'supplier' as well as the 'buyer/seller,' who is also an intermediary. This meant that mandate holders, brokers, agents, next-door neighbours, the bus driver, their dog – and even end buyers and suppliers – were all using the term 'seller' or 'buyer'.

For the first six years of trading this simple fact had not been evident to FTN Exporting, nor to anyone else for that matter, because no publication spelt out the different meanings of these terms. Even today these issues have not been addressed sufficiently and remain a major issue of contention with the majority of internet traders. For example, Tom who drives a taxi for a living in England can offer goods as a seller in the same internet thread as the corporate lawyer from New York who is acting as a buyer for those very same goods.

So what went wrong with the sugar deal? FTN had accepted an offer from another 'seller' and not a 'supplier'. This 'seller' was another intermediary from California who insisted, over a period of several months, that they had the sugar in their immediate control. To make matters worse he was offering unverified goods to FTN that he had only been told about by another dubious intermediary. This created a very dangerous precedent in that FTN Exporting had accepted an offer for a product that never existed. But the worst was still to come. The US intermediary thought he was acting appropriately and with good intent.

Unfortunately for him the law doesn't see it that way and although FTN managed to appease the end buyer to the extent that fraud charges were avoided, the same could not be said for the US intermediary who apparently fled to Mexico and has never been seen or heard of again. The golden rule of trading is this: never offer goods to anyone unless you have verified personally that the goods are genuine. Never!

Without the requisite knowledge of correct trading procedures, you are simply wasting your time by attempting to trade. The vast majority of traders you will see on the internet don't know how to close a deal. Most don't even know how to start a deal correctly let alone bring one to a successful conclusion. Davide Papa then realized that intermediaries needed to know what had happened in order to avoid being caught in the same situation. Since the sugar deal, intermediaries from all over the world have asked him for his advice on all aspects of international trade. In terms of the methodology of trading internationally intermediaries must use the same laws, rules and procedures as end buyers and suppliers.

FTN Exporting receives hundreds of offers by email each week, of which 99 per cent are deleted as either inappropriate or unworkable. Anyone attempting to do business with these types of intermediaries will also be unable to close a deal or collect a cent in commissions, no matter how long they trade for or how hard they try. There is one exception, which is if the intermediary happens to be related to someone who owns a factory producing exportable products. Perhaps they have a relative who is an export manager who works for the supplier, or they are friendly with the procurement manager in the end buyer's corporation. In this sense there will always be a handful of intermediaries who purport to have secured commissions in a deal simply by passing information down a long line of individual traders, but in our experience they are usually either lying or are related to one of the principals.

Since the collapse of the sugar deal and armed with these new insights Davide Papa has spent years educating others about procedural matters, during which time the import/export arena has changed beyond recognition. Telex and facsimile machines have been replaced with the internet. For a short while this new method of doing business was a godsend: you could chat online and send countless replies without having to spend thousands of dollars per month on phone bills.

Alas, with the inception of the internet another explosion soon followed. The calm order provided by a regimented trading arena was replaced with a frenzy of untrained intermediaries, to whom no guidance in the complex realm of international trade was available. The trading protocol of intermediaries had come crashing down overnight as the internet phenomenon grew and yet nobody could tell the difference: intermediaries were jumping on board a 'damaged and floundering vessel' at an unstoppable rate.

Those in 'the know' acknowledge that there has not been a proper intermediary trading market for some years. The internet has destroyed what was a reasonably viable market, although small, which existed when facsimile and telex trading reigned supreme. It wasn't uncommon for an intermediary occasionally to get to a contract closing stage and even to documentary letter of credit (DLC) stage back then. There were problems with procedures and ill-informed traders, but it was very expensive to trade in such an environment because of the high cost of telecommunications expenses. A fax from a hotel out of Switzerland sent by an intermediary chasing gold would cost 50 dollars per page. One trader would often send FTN ten faxes over a three- or four-day period. In effect these expenses allowed only the serious traders to compete.

The internet changed all that. Nowadays 'traders' can work from an internet café from which they could attempt to sell 100 million dollars worth of crude oil (not that they ever would!). Anyone can buy a second-hand computer for a few hundred dollars and can send hundreds of simultaneous emails at literally no cost. The result? Suppliers can't be bothered to reply to dubious purchase offers or requests for quotes. Similarly end buyers won't reply to equally stupid offers. As a result the only people 'trading' are all those misguided intermediaries chasing each other's tails for deals that are, for the most part, incorrect or fake. Add to this the plethora of scam emails and the like and you have what amounts to a 'circus managed by clowns' rather than a serious trading environment. FTN Exporting has seen thousands upon thousands of worthless offers and contracts being touted by intermediaries who obviously have no idea what they are doing, evidenced by the fact that they use terminology such as 'LOI', 'BCL', 'ICPO' and 'POP'. The reasons why these terms are inappropriate for intermediary use, and their correct usage in international trade procedures will be explained in this book.

The following text provides a comprehensive grounding for use by intermediaries dealing in international commodities. Such intermediaries now ostensibly number in excess of at least a million traders who, for the most part, are chasing dreams and will never close a commodity transaction due to their ignorance as to how the industry works. This book seeks to address a widespread lack of knowledge in this very specialized field, which is simply not available elsewhere.

Formal education on the subject of international trade is widely available but is without exception approached from the viewpoint of importers, exporters and manufacturers. Intermediaries are forced to extract and adopt trading methods from this information. *International Trade and the Successful Intermediary* provides the underlying trading principles that will remain relevant even when banking and delivery rules are amended in the future. For the first time, there is a uniform trading regime for global intermediary use, and which is applicable not only to the intermediary involved in international trade but also in any type of commercial business activity. This is especially the case when as consumer you are dealing with individuals or companies who serve principals.

The following chapters are also intended to be a useful resource and guide to dealing in commodities for those in related industries, such as international banking and finance, stockbrokers and shipping and distribution entities. End buyers and suppliers could also benefit from this publication by gaining an understanding of the role of the intermediary and why they need to adopt certain procedures in order to close a deal safely and properly for the benefit of everyone involved. The overall premise of this publication, however, is to provide the intermediary with the requisite insight to be able to trade in a safe international trading environment. There are no short cuts in this business and only two viable options: trade correctly or don't trade at all.

With the introduction of the UCP600 banking rules in July 2007 all global intermediaries, end buyers and suppliers are reacquainting themselves with trading procedures in light of the new developments. Indeed UCP600 has irrevocably changed the trading environment again, bringing with it important and exciting changes to the way intermediaries need to do business. UCP600 will, it is assumed, be the applicable banking doctrine for the next ten or more years and its introduction has made the playing field level for everyone. As a result of their novelty, some of the issues relating to these new provisions are considered theoretically at this stage.

The success or failure of any international trade intermediary depends on a variety of factors including sourcing ability, intelligence, persistence and of course, luck. Luck notwithstanding, if the trading methods contained within this book are used correctly, the intermediary still has a far better chance of closing an import/export transaction than someone who doesn't follow these rules; rules that define the trading methods that all intermediaries should use if they want to trade in exportable commodities.

A Rare Insight

There are countless private independent import/export commodity intermediaries worldwide trading from home on a daily basis. It is questionable as to whether any of them are closing any deals at all. So why are so many internet traders wasting their time on deals that simply cannot be closed? The truth is that even experienced intermediaries who apply the rules of international trade find it difficult to source genuine goods and secure a contract of sale for goods. So how are all those internet traders going to succeed using ambiguous and flawed procedures that cannot work? The simple answer is – they don't!

There are intermediaries on the internet offering to buy and sell crude oil, sugar, cement and many other products at unbelievable prices and in quantities that boggle the mind. The irony is that there is a vast quantity of information available regarding export and import transactions, procedures and rules of trade for corporate use by end buyers and suppliers, yet intermediaries do not realize that these are the very same rules they should be following in their own trading practices. For as long as they continue to use flawed procedures these intermediaries will not see a cent in commissions. Misguided intermediaries have begun to trade following the blind edicts of other misguided intermediaries, and so the cycle continues.

International trade is the world's biggest industry: California alone has operated yearly import/export oriented financial instruments worth a trillion dollars. Followed by China and Europe, intermediaries in the United States are perhaps the most prolific traders on earth and as such this publication pays particular attention to their requirements. There is in fact a genuine need for intermediaries. Intermediaries can source end buyer and suppliers, adding valuable financial input to countries dependent on economic growth and which export bulk or heavily manufactured value added goods. Further markets are created that otherwise could have been lost to favour only the biggest exporters, such as those supported and promoted by cash-rich government trade agencies.

In the aforementioned sugar deal the end buyer was secured with the involvement of a few other intermediaries. Intermediaries are allowed to deal in commodities by securing the required funds by way of a transferable letter of credit.

Intermediaries who are united in their methods of trading can also help others find a source of supply, either directly or with the assistance of others within their group. The intermediary 'buyer/seller' must secure goods from the supplier directly. If an offer to sell goods originates from another intermediary the buyer/seller must verify it all the way to the supplier or there is no deal.

By using safe trading procedures there is absolutely nothing – not in practice nor in the law – that would prevent a private home-based intermediary in most countries from closing a deal. The intermediary in question has to be a highly skilled and intelligent individual with an understanding as to how to apply good business principles, who is able to read and write in English reasonably well and have a good grasp of basic arithmetic. Most of the intermediaries on the internet today lack some or all of the minimum requirements. By analogy there should be plenty of room for good import/export intermediaries to trade effectively, but only if everyone works to the same rules and procedures.

Even while writing this, FTN Exporting received an 'agency agreement' to sign protecting the interests of an 'intermediary'. Someone claiming to be a doctor of philosophy asked FTN Exporting to sign an agreement stating that 'upon contracts being signed' for goods being offered FTN is to pay their commission. When that person was reminded that no commission is payable until delivery has been successfully recorded, they fired a barrage of email insults for three days. Such scams are easy traps for the unwary intermediary.

Recent Changes

In July 2007 the trading environment irrevocably changed as all the major banks around the world implemented the new UCP600 banking rules, which bring with them important and exciting changes to the way intermediaries need to do business. Trillions of dollars annually change hands worldwide in international commodity transactions and a uniform application serves to ensure that a small part of these activities can be reserved to those intermediaries who have learned how to trade within the realm of this instrument. This new and vigorous protocol is implemented globally in an effort to restore the once respected position of the international trade intermediary.

What the intermediary requires today is not just a set of guiding rules and procedures but also the knowledge required to identify when they are dealing with an intermediate buyer or seller as opposed to an 'end buyer' and/or 'supplier' of goods. More importantly the intermediary has to have the ability to identify false offerings as opposed to a real supply of goods.

For example, offers that FTN has rejected years earlier still turn up in the FTN Exporting email inbox, sent by sellers and buyers alike from all over the globe. An offer rejected by one person could simultaneously be adopted by another as being entirely genuine. At FTN Exporting we call these 'perpetual offers orbiting the planet'. Once an intermediary gets hold of one of these perpetual offers it can circle the globe for years, even though the goods being offered simply no longer exist. Although this is a serious problem there are many other minefields that could land the unsuspecting intermediary in serious legal difficulties unless he adopts sound trading procedures.

Even using the trading method described in this book it is still very difficult to earn 500,000 or even just 500 dollars in commissions for closing one deal. Regardless of the amount of commission involved, the procedures are exactly the same. Therefore there is no point exerting considerable efforts over a trade that will only earn a meagre amount of money: if an intermediary has to work this hard to secure commission, the reward may as well be substantial. If you are thinking about or attempting to trade in import/export deals, or if you have been trading already for some time and getting nowhere using flawed 'LOI', 'BCL', 'ICPO' and 'POP' procedures, as found mostly on the internet, then why not at least attempt to close a deal using proper trading rules?

A Better Trading Environment

Global laws and rules allow intermediaries to trade as a 'buyer/seller' and, in the same way that corporate traders apply UCP600 and Incoterms 2000 in their own deals, intermediaries who use these rules and the mechanisms can do so favourably in their own transactions. That is not to say, however, that closing an export deal successfully is easy. It takes a great deal of effort and skill. Rewards can indeed be great but only if you know what you are doing. Nonetheless, UCP600 now offers well-versed intermediaries a better method of closing commodity deals than the procedures that existed previously.

Litigation permeates all areas of life and international trade is no exception. Two parties argue the merits of a sales contract often drawn up by their own lawyers. Even highly skilled and well-paid lawyers are not always right in the ways they apply the laws of trade. If this is the case for end buyers and suppliers then what chance has an intermediary in conducting such business safely, when clear trading information is so hard to find? By following the guidance and the rules outlined in this book the intermediary is only trading with the safe principles of trade, the very same as those used by good exporters, importers and international banks.

Even many of our own trained intermediaries, who have paid for tuition over the past few years, have given up trading altogether after learning the true nature of what is required. The message here is clear: if you are not in it for the long haul then learning to grasp the fundamentals offered in this publication is a futile exercise. There are no shortcuts in international trade.

Do not be surprised that most other traders will not understand the procedures you are about to learn. Some traders may even attempt to persuade you otherwise but these challenges will usually be very short lived. Remember, the majority of genuine end buyers and suppliers will understand your procedures if you trade only using the safe methods outlined in this book. The last thing you want, after a long period of trading correctly, is for a potentially viable deal to land in your lap and you let your guard down. Trivial mistakes can usually be sorted out so long as the foundations of the trade are sound: anything less than using strict trading procedures will lead you into precarious situations and even potential legal difficulties.

2

The Correct Trading Rules

What is set out in this chapter will play an important part in learning the business, but may not be easy to comprehend the first time around. Read these passages again once you reach halfway into the book, and then again when you have finished reading it. This self-assessment will test your knowledge as to how well you have understood the trading process. Being able fully to understand and interpret every aspect of the procedure in this text means that you are ready to trade as a well informed and effective international trade intermediary.

A Trade between End Buyer and Supplier Only

When intermediaries are NOT involved in a deal, an end buyer contacts a supplier directly. Often this begins with an informal discussion, in which the end buyer seeks a quote for the goods required. The end buyer communicates interest in the quote and confirms their interest to the supplier. The supplier issues an offer. The end buyer, within a stated validity period, accepts the offer at which point both parties usually also agree to become legally bound to each other. The 'acceptance' of the offer is communicated to the supplier who, in turn, issues a draft copy of the contract of sale. The end buyer considers the terms and conditions of the contract and when all is in order a final contract is furnished, that has been signed by the supplier. The end buyer signs the contract and returns it; most often in hardcopy form via a courier (although the transaction would still be valid if service was by email or facsimile copy of the contract). A short time thereafter the end buyer advises their bank to issue a financial instrument to the supplier for the payment of goods, in accordance with the terms and conditions agreed between the supplier and the end buyer. The supplier accepts the financial instrument, and their accepting bank now indicates this acceptance to the end buyer's issuing bank. The financial instrument is now handled by the respective banks, each representing and protecting the interests of their clients, and each guarantees their irrevocable commitment to perform as per the issuance rules (terms and conditions of which are apparent on the credit). The supplier and end buyer also perform as per the terms and conditions of the contract. Sometimes the supplier accepts the credit and provides a 'performance guarantee' (PG) for the end buyer, although most times PG issuance is not a requirement.

If required the supplier issues the performance guarantee, which the end buyer accepts and notifies the supplier of the acceptance. The supplier now ships the goods to raise the required delivery documents, which must be acquired once the goods are loaded on board ship (that is, in an FOB or CIF type of deal). The delivery documents are collected and forwarded to the end buyer or the end buyer's bank for presentation. The bank looks at the documents (at sight). If all is in order (if they are 'clean') the issuing bank allows 'collection' of the credit to proceed. The ship heads for the destination country and port as stated on the contract. Upon arrival at the destination port, the goods are unloaded. The end buyer holding title to the goods now presents the title and other delivery documents to customs, and pays the imports taxes and other charges as required under Incoterms 2000 FOB or CIF delivery rules. The end buyer now obtains 'possession' of the goods and arranges for the goods to be delivered to their place of business. The issuing bank that advises the financial instrument is in fact looking after the interests of the end buyer. The accepting bank looks after the interests of the supplier at collection time. The banks themselves earn commission and charge fees, while acting under a regime of agency. In effect banks are also conducting business as intermediaries. The advising bank, depending on its active status, is said to be looking after the interests of the intermediary.

The Intermediary in International Trade

An intermediary is defined as:

> *Intermediary (n): Person acting between parties, a mediator.*

As an international trade intermediary you are going to attempt to close an import/export deal using only acceptable international rules of trade. You will follow the same laws and doctrines used by corporate entities and global banks, following strict agency guidelines as apparent in most countries that are similar to those provided under English law.

Intermediaries in the USA are called 'brokers'. In most other countries around the world you are known as an 'agent' or intermediary. Specifically you are an independent primary intermediary agent (PIA) acting as an intermediate buyer/seller and from hereon for ease of use the abbreviation PIA will generally be used.

As the PIA you'll need to learn the principles of international trade and the rules relating to financial instruments. If you do not, you will be leaving yourself vulnerable to dangerous and costly mistakes. Entering into a contract that cannot be closed, providing banks with letters of credit that cannot be used, attempting to secure commissions that will never be gained, and bluffing your way in a deal are all situations that must be avoided at all times.

If you do not want to take up the mantle of the PIA, as buyer/seller, then you can be a sourcing intermediary (SI) so long as you remain attached to an honourable and trusted buyer/seller (PIA). That is not to say that everyone can be a sourcing intermediary: it takes special skills to source suppliers and end buyers effectively, and in any event if you are going to align yourself with a buyer/seller then you should at least have a grasp of the major elements of an import/export deal. Knowledge of the fundamental rules will enable you to monitor the activities of your buyer/seller to ensure that your interests are being protected.

A buyer/seller, on the other hand, has to have many other skills than just sourcing goods and buyers for those goods. He must also be able to research as well as close an import/export deal and to solve problems as and when they arise during the trade. Ironically, a buyer/seller may not be very good at sourcing goods or finding end buyers. Thus buyers/sellers always welcome associations or affiliations with good sourcing intermediaries. For example, an excellent and very successful car salesperson who is only an employee may not have the ability to set up and manage their own car showroom because being a principal has responsibilities that affect the entire transaction. The salesperson can simply leave anytime and take up another sales job in a different car showroom.

The main concern as a sourcing intermediary is finding a good teacher to whom you can attach yourself, as securing commission payments is the ultimate concern. The sourcing intermediary's activities are simply to verify that goods being offered are genuine, or to find out whether an end buyer's intent to purchase goods is real, and to communicate these findings to their buyer/seller who then works together with the sourcing intermediary to close the deal. The sourcing intermediary also guides the buyer/seller in relation to the other intermediaries involved in the string contract. In effect the sourcing intermediary closest in proximity to the buyer/seller develops a special relationship with that person and is responsible for keeping all the other intermediaries informed as to the progress of the deal, and the commissions being protected. The sourcing intermediary becomes the primary intermediary (PI) of the buyer/seller.

This book is mainly concerned with how to trade as a buyer/seller: the activities of sourcing intermediaries are incorporated within the sphere of the buyer/seller role. Once you grasp the basic trading premise the rest can be learned over time as you gain confidence and experience.

It is assumed that most readers of this book are yet to close their first deal. Thus, when an intermediary is involved in a first time deal as the middle controlling buyer/seller the credit should be issued with a transferable status. Where for instance a buyer/seller makes an offer to sell goods to a potential end buyer, the offer must state that payment is required as a bank issued transferable instrument. First time intermediaries must not accept a non-transferable credit from an end buyer. Intermediaries cannot use financial instruments such as SLC (Standby Letter of Credit), SWIFT, T/T (Telegraphic Transfer), MTN 100 (Medium Term Notes) and so on, or a document called a 'Bank Guarantee' (BG).

Once the documents have been correctly presented (known as 'clean presentation') the work of the buyer/seller is said to be complete, even if the goods are still on board ship at the port of loading. In general, if you are not prepared to act in the above buyer/seller position but expect others to trade in this position and secure commissions for you because you have simply passed information along a line of other traders with the same mindset, then forget about trading all together.

As a buyer/seller you will attempt to buy goods from a supplier in one country and sell them to an end buyer in another country. In doing so you will attempt to secure commission for your efforts and possibly for the efforts of those other traders who have assisted you in closing the deal. This is the true definition of the business of an international trade intermediary. You conduct your business as a buyer of exportable goods from a supplier in one country that you have personally verified as being genuine. You are then, within the same transaction, going to become a seller of those sourced goods to an end buyer from another country that you have personally secured and/or verified as genuine.

The competent buyer/seller knows how to close an import export deal. Anyone can trade in the position of a buyer/seller but, if like most on the internet you are bluffing your way, then you are wasting your time and will never close a commodity sale and purchase deal. Similarly as a sourcing intermediary you must be sure that the buyer/seller to whom you attach yourself is in fact proficient in international trading procedures. An intermediary buyer/seller will attempt to 'buy' goods from a supplier for resale by using the end buyer's funds. Then they resell the same goods to the end buyer at a higher price, using a strict set of rules. The profit the buyer/seller makes is the difference between the buying price and the selling price and is termed 'commission'.

If an end buyer were dealing directly with a supplier then the end buyer would still need to pay the supplier – the owner of the goods – in the supplier's country. There is no difference when an intermediary is involved. An end buyer may need to provide both financial capability and other related documents to the supplier upfront before contracts are agreed, because the end buyer is not just obtaining title to the goods but is also taking possession of them. Intermediaries also need to show that they have the financial capacity to enter into the transaction but they use a different method to do so. Unlike the end buyer the intermediary buyer/seller is not taking delivery of the goods but only the title or delivery documents relating to them. The intermediary needs only the documentary title to be able to transfer the interest or ownership of the goods to the end buyer. This prompts the big question: why should an end buyer use an intermediary?

As an end buyer, there are several advantages to using an intermediary. The end buyer can avoid having to disclose proof of financial capability and other problematic documents upfront. This is particularly relevant in circumstances in which, for example, an end buyer has an excellent credit rating or available collateral to borrow large amounts of funds from a bank, but who in turn may be cash poor to buy 500,000 dollars' worth of goods. Given that credit is often based on personal bank lending policies, which are complicated and time-consuming affairs, getting a bank to approve a loan on the off-chance that there might be a purchase of goods is not practical – especially in international commodity trading which is notoriously tainted with countless false offerings.

This is not the case where it becomes apparent that goods are genuinely offered at a very good price.

An end buyer dealing with an intermediary can enter into a deal stage by stage: obtain prices, quotes and even an offer to consider before entering into a contract. A supplier, on the other hand, may make immediate demands regarding financial capabilities, and even refuse to provide vital information about the transaction unless and until such matters are addressed first. This alone is a very good reason for using an intermediary.

Other issues of concern are language barriers and knowledge and understanding of safe trading practices, procedures and local customs. It may be that the end buyer is looking to secure goods at more cost effective prices in order to resell them, or to offset a local competitor's price. Intermediaries will be able to research suppliers and may obtain several different prices for the same goods, which is something that very few end buyers have time to do themselves. It is not uncommon for end buyers to allocate large amounts of personal funds to buy exportable products just before the end of the fiscal year in order to reduce or defer taxation liabilities.

So we have seen that there are useful roles for well-informed intermediaries. The ability of the intermediary to source and secure products, and then close a deal while providing sound advice regarding the intricacies of the trade, is attractive to both end buyers and suppliers alike. Unfortunately there are very few such intermediaries in today's internet-driven trading environment.

There is a lot that an intermediary has to understand about trading in commodities, especially when it comes to handling and transacting with financial instruments. The funds used to pay for the goods are not like cash, but more akin to a guarantee. This comes not from the end buyer directly but from their bank, following a very special set of issuance rules (UCP600). The bank will guarantee the payment for the goods being purchased: the guarantee is to the supplier and not the end buyer (who then becomes beholden to their bankers). The intermediary cannot obtain a DLC and use it for their own purchases like cash. Certain conditions must prevail after which the ability to transfer a large part of the credit value to the supplier is initiated, leaving a small portion behind as commission. Upon correct presentation of the relevant 'delivery' documents to the buyer's bank the issuing bank will allow collection of the 'guarantee' to occur, using another set of rules known as the 'Uniform Rules of Collection, publication 522' or URC 522. One of the conditions required for collection on the financial instrument is that the delivery documents must be produced.

The intermediary transfers the portion of the purchase price to the supplier who in turn provides the intermediary with the required delivery documents. The intermediary swaps the supplier's invoice with their own to reflect the end buyer's purchase price and all the documents are usually sent to the end buyer's bank, the issuing bank (there is no difference in the final result between an end buyer dealing directly with a supplier, or whether an intermediary is involved – the only thing that changes is the process). Documents are checked and, if all is in order as per the stipulations made on the credit, the issuing bank allows collection to occur. The supplier gets paid but the ship hasn't even left the loading port: the intermediary has dealt only in documents and not physical goods. Since the intermediary has asked for a confirmed credit (whereas a supplier doing business with a past client may not) then the delivery documents do not even need to go to the issuing bank. This is because the confirmed credit allows the intermediary's advising bank to check and accept the documents there and then, as agent to the issuing bank. The advising bank allows collection to occur and then seeks reimbursement of the payment with the issuing bank, as per the reimbursement rules of UCP600.

When the documents are presented to the bank for the purpose of allowing payment on the credit it is known as 'presentation'. Once presentation has been successful the 'collection' upon the financial instrument can take place. As has already been seen the intermediary provides the link between the end buyer and the supplier so it is the buyer/seller's duty – as per quotations, offers and the eventual contract – to perform on two sides of the deal – the end buyer's and supplier's sides. The buyer/seller is working with two sets of documents as though both deals are independent of each other. This means that the middle controlling buyer/seller has to work with two quotations, two offers and two contracts at the same time from both sides of the deal, while ensuring information from one side of the fence never crosses over to the other side. Intermediaries have great problems in understanding this concept.

Under UCP600 the buyer/seller has to produce and present documents, and initiate payment procedures, as per these rules. Trying to facilitate the deal any other way will cause delays or even the collapse of the deal. It is bad practice to include within the terms of the contract provisions relating to how the DLC should be presented. To do this is essentially to attempt to add the bank to the contract as a third party. This makes for a poorly drafted and perhaps invalid contract, but more importantly the bank's obligations are clearly stated under UCP600. They cannot avoid those obligations so it is an exercise in futility to attempt to change standard practices.

A successful international trade intermediary trades in the position of 'buyer/seller'. When sourcing intermediaries are involved in a trade they are attached to the buyer/seller, who is the principal intermediary agent controlling the whole deal.

The following is a summary that shows how a deal is conducted with a buyer/seller or a PIA. An informal discussion often takes place during which the end buyer obtains a quote for the goods he needs to buy from a sourcing intermediary (as obtained from the PIA, the controlling buyer/seller, who is acting in the position of seller on this side of the deal). The end buyer communicates interest in the quotation and confirms this interest to the seller (the PIA) via the same intermediary path, who in turn does the same with their supplier, as the buyer of these goods. The supplier issues an offer to *the PIA as the buyer*. The same buyer now reverts back to the position of *the PIA as the seller* and makes up their own offer to the end buyer, which is similar to their own terms and conditions with their supplier. The offer is passed via the sourcing intermediaries the seller is protecting, so that they all remain informed as to the progress of the deal at hand. The final sourcing intermediary hands over the original offer to the end buyer, unmarked, which discloses among other things the details of the seller. The end buyer, within a stated validity period accepts the offer, which the sourcing intermediaries pass back to the seller. The seller and end buyer now agree to become legally bound to each other. The PIA (the buyer/seller) issues an IPG (Intermediaries Personal Protection Guarantee) to the intermediaries whose commission the PIA is protecting.

The 'acceptance' of the offer is also communicated to the supplier from the buyer, who in turn issues a draft copy of the contract of sale. The buyer reverts back to the position of seller and as seller uses their own contract model that is much more suited to their own needs. The contract is sent once more via the seller's protected intermediaries to the end buyer. The end buyer considers the terms and conditions on the draft contract and when all is in order a final contract is furnished, signed by the seller. Similarly the seller again reverts back to the position of a buyer and returns their signed contract to the supplier. The end buyer signs the contract and returns it, most often in hardcopy by courier (although the transaction still continues if it is based on the issuance of an email or facsimile copy contract directly to the seller). The seller goes through the same process with their supplier. A short time thereafter the end buyer advises their bank to issue a transferable financial instrument to the seller, who in turn as buyer issues a portion of the credit as non-transferable to their supplier for the payment of goods (in accordance with their contracting terms and conditions).

The supplier accepts the financial instrument and their accepting bank now indicates this to the advising bank of the intermediary, the buyer/seller. The matter of the financial instrument is now handled by the respective banks that each represent, and which protect the interests of their own clients. Each guarantees their irrevocable commitment to perform as per the rules of issuance (the terms and conditions on the credit). The supplier to the buyer, and end buyer to the seller, must also perform as per their own contracting terms and conditions. Thus the primary intermediary, the controlling buyer/seller, has a deal with the end buyer that is entirely independent of the deal with the supplier. Two separate contracts are in play. One side never crosses over to the other.

The seller provides the performance guarantee, if required, which is formally accepted by the end buyer. The supplier now ships the goods to produce the required delivery documents (which happens once the goods are loaded on board ship) in an FOB or CIF type of deal. The 'delivery' documents are collected and forwarded to the buyer's bank, the advising bank. The buyer/seller checks that all is in order, changes the supplier's invoice to a seller's invoice recording the correct selling price of the goods sold to the end buyer, and instructs their bank to send the documents to the end buyer or the end buyer's bank for presentation. The end buyer's bank looks at the documents ('at sight'). If all is in order ('clean') the issuing bank allows 'collection' of the credit to proceed to their seller. The seller's portion is retained in their account as commission: the rest of the available funds are made ready for collection by the supplier. The ship is allowed to slip its moorings, and heads for the destination country and port as defined on the contract. The goods are unloaded on arrival at the destination port. The end buyer holding title to the goods (as provided by the seller), now presents the title and other delivery documents to customs and pays all the import taxes and other charges as defined under Incoterms 2000 FOB or CIF delivery rules. The end buyer now obtains 'possession' of the goods and arranges for the goods to be delivered to their place of business. The buyer/seller distributes the commission to their protected intermediaries from the amount held in their account by issuing an in-house SLC (as supported by the previously issued IPG).

As can be seen from the above outlines, intermediaries must trade in the same manner as an end buyer doing business with a supplier directly. There will always be situations in which variables will apply, but the underlying rules and order of the stages must be preserved at all times.

3

PIA: The Primary Intermediary Agent

As a primary intermediary agent (PIA) you are neither an end buyer nor a supplier. As already demonstrated you are an independent private buyer and seller of commodities who buys goods from a supplier that you have personally sourced and secured. In purchasing the goods you are securing the documentary title to them, which, like the physical goods themselves, is a tangible, saleable and negotiable instrument. You then resell these same goods to an end buyer you have also sourced and secured – whether on your own or using other sourcing intermediaries to assist you.

The priority is always to ensure you have personally sourced or verified the goods being offered from a supplier, and to secure these goods immediately, or have the ability to secure those goods at a later time from the sourced supplier as a buyer. The second stage is to find an end buyer to whom you can resell the goods. Many internet traders look for end buyers first, and then go hunting for the goods they require. This is completely inappropriate: if you think you can secure the goods, if you think that the goods someone else is offering you are real, if you think the goods offered are from a direct supplier, then you have not secured any goods and accordingly you should not offer any goods for resale in the first place. You must secure the goods first and be 100 per cent sure of their immediate or later availability before attempting to source an end buyer. Remember:

> *Supplier First, Buyer Second: You Must Never Deviate from this Order*

The International Chamber of Commerce and other publications often use only the words 'buyer' and 'seller' but if this book were only to refer to 'buyers' and 'sellers' it would be impossible to explain the trading premise without it becoming very confusing. For example, the buyer issues the credit to the seller who in turn as buyer transfers the credit to their seller who turns out not to be the actual seller of the goods the previous seller had offered, who now earnestly goes hunting for a real seller of the goods they had offered only to be confronted with another false seller. In the meantime one of the sellers is arguing with the buyer, but not the buyer who issued the credit; and so forth and so on. Confused? So are we!

For the sake of clarity, here are the three parties to a transaction and a brief description of their role:

1. The PIA is a buyer/seller – a person who buys goods from one side and resells to another. They cannot be only a buyer or a seller and must be both buyer and seller. This may not be apparent to others involved in the deal. To the buyer's side of the deal all the way to the principal end buyer the PIA is the seller. All the way to the supplier, the PIA is a buyer. Only the PIA understands that they are controlling a deal as a united buyer/seller.

2. A supplier may be a seller but a seller may not always be a supplier. The supplier is one who owns the goods or who actually manufactures the goods being sought.

3. An end buyer may be a buyer, but a buyer may not be an end buyer. An end buyer is the person actually paying for the goods with their money and is the one who will take final possession of the goods being purchased from you.

A buyer/seller never takes possession of goods nor uses their own money to pay for goods. The buyer/seller only uses the funds of the end buyer to secure the title of the goods from the supplier in order to pass title to those goods to the end buyer. Therefore the buyer/seller is an intermediary, the type of sourcing intermediary who also knows how to close a deal.

The PIA is an intermediary in the first instance and a principal in the second instance. The end buyer is a principal, as is the supplier. Initially everyone else in a deal is considered to be a sourcing intermediary belonging to either the buyer's side or the seller's side. A sourcing intermediary who does not have the added burden of closing a deal never belongs to both sides simultaneously.

That role is exclusively reserved for one buyer/seller in any string contract. Anyone trying to earn commission from a deal is an intermediary.

When the PIA has been identified and is dealing with two other principals it is at that point of the deal that the PIA stops being a sourcing intermediary and becomes the third principal. The PIA is still defined as an intermediate buyer/seller but is also regarded as a principal among other agents or intermediaries involved in the same deal. The PIA becomes the principal because they have forced every other intermediary all the way to the supplier on one side and all the way to the end buyer on the other side to 'step back'. This leaves the PIA to close the deal between two other principals. The PIA is in the middle and in full control of the deal. Nobody is able to cross over from one side to another. This prevents anyone from being able to circumvent anyone else. If nobody is able to circumvent the PIA, then nobody else that the PIA is protecting in a string contract is capable of being circumvented either. It really is that simple.

Avoiding Circumvention

The PIA is not only a skilled buyer/seller but also acts as a 'door stop' by preventing the whole trading group from being circumvented. This further demonstrates the importance of the position. As the PIA expect that you are going to come up against resistance when declaring the buyer's/seller's position in a string contract. The PIA becomes immediately identifiable as the 'buyer' of the goods being offered on one side of the fence leading to the supplier. If there are intermediaries along the way to the supplier the PIA must ensure they step back. In return the PIA guarantees to look after their interest in the deal by collecting and protecting each intermediary's commission. Even if the position just before the supplier is met with another misguided seller, the PIA will endeavour to persuade the seller to step back as well by issuing a commission pay order. The PIA is a buyer on that side of the fence and won't be dictated to by anyone. Remember, if the PIA cannot verify the supplier there is no deal.

Once the supply of goods have been assured with the provision of a quotation the same process starts again, except this time the PIA is identified as the seller of the goods to the end buyer. Intermediaries on the end buyer's side may think someone else is going to protect their commission, but the PIA takes control to avoid wasted efforts and misinformed attempts. The PIA offers to protect all commissions on the end buyer's side and in return everyone will be required to step back. In effect the PIA has taken control of the whole deal and is protecting everyone's commission on both sides of the fence because the PIA is the buyer/seller. The PIA is in full control of the deal. The mechanism needed to eliminate the risk of circumvention is in place.

The PIA becomes the controlling person between the two principals. The PIA is also a principal head of an implied agency, looking after the interests of all other intermediaries who are assisting the PIA with the deal at hand. If there are any anticipated difficulties with the PIA reaching this position the PIA must ascertain this at the earliest possibility and if the situation cannot be resolved, treat the proposal as non-workable (at FTN Exporting we call this 'RF' or Rubbish Fodder) and move onto the next potential transaction. The PIA will not waste time on deals that cannot be closed and will learn how to identify such deals quickly. This is achieved by asking questions at an early stage and becomes more instinctive with knowledge and experience. When the PIA officially starts to trade, the majority of their dealings will be purely gaining this experience as at first it is normal to confront many RF deals.

Even if there are other intermediaries, buyers or sellers in between the principals, the PIA is the controlling middle person who takes care of the interests of all the others involved so long as the PIA is able to eventually deal only with the principals.

Read the following introductions and see whether you can ascertain who the principals are:

> 'Hello PIA, I am Jack. I am interested in buying the goods you are offering.'

> 'Hello PIA, I am Jack. My client is interested in buying the goods you are offering.'

> 'Hello PIA, I am Jenny the Seller offering goods for you to purchase.'

> 'Hello PIA, I am Jenny. I can help you to find goods to purchase.'

Unless as the PIA you know you are dealing with the end buyer or supplier, you are very likely to be dealing with other intermediaries and as such cannot enter into a legally-binding transaction with these entities. So how do you know who these people are? The PIA can only test the viability of each proposed transaction to decide whether or not to proceed. If the PIA proceeds, then they take care of all the intermediaries' interests and close the transaction with the end principals. If the intermediaries are not prepared to disclose their principals to the PIA there is no deal, and the PIA moves on to the next email/facsimile enquiry.

In three of the examples mentioned previously, the PIA is dealing with intermediaries. Only one of the enquiries might be a potential end buyer. The PIA will test the above buyers and sellers to ascertain the viability or otherwise of their proposals. They will start with the trader's enquiry that began:

> 'Hello PIA, I am Jack. I am interested in buying the goods you are offering.'

The PIA needs to ascertain if the above 'buyer' is an intermediary buyer or end buyer and in the first instance would ask: 'Are you the buyer taking possession and paying for the goods?' The PIA would only then continue with the trade as appropriate depending on the answer given.

A buyer claiming to be the person taking possession of the goods at the port of unloading is the end buyer. A person who only purports to be able to pay for the goods is an intermediary seller attempting to transfer a credit to the PIA – who cannot accept it because the PIA will not be able to transfer the credit a second time.

A buyer/seller must never state anything but the fact that they wish to buy or wish to sell goods. Terms such as: 'We are buyers and have clients' or 'we have secured as sellers …' mean nothing. A genuine and well informed trader must state in the first instance that they are offering goods, or purchasing goods as a buyer or seller, because the PIA understands that if this buyer or seller is not the end principal, then the PIA may be able to cause this buyer or seller to 'step back'. The PIA must simply test the veracity of the above enquiries to establish as quickly as possible whether the sellers or buyers are either genuine principals themselves, or will lead to securing genuine principals. The PIA must not get excited when they receive initial enquiries, but should simply test each enquiry to see whether it might lead to the start of a potentially viable deal.

This example should act as a warning. There are millions and millions of traders worldwide, especially from Europe and the USA, all claiming to be either 'buyers' or 'sellers'. In reality they are nothing more than misguided sourcing intermediaries who have no idea what the buyer/seller position really entails, and many of whom have no idea how to trade correctly. The PIA will need to undertake a rigorous search to find and secure a principal: this is an unavoidable part of dealing as an intermediary. Such efforts are not a waste of time but rather provide invaluable lessons in how to identify these types of misguided dealers. If any intermediaries do not believe that they must step back to expose the end players in a deal, then the PIA simply walks away.

So how does a PIA go about judging the merits of each of these enquiries? The reality is there is no set method. The PIA may choose to be gentle or abrupt in the testing of this information – either way it is imperative to ascertain the viability of each enquiry while reassuring others of their good intent. It isn't easy to convince others to step back: after all, they don't know the PIA. However, the PIA will identify a 'RF' deal from the information provided and will be able to evaluate whether further effort is needed to initiate the 'stepping back' process. In an intermediary trade, it is very important that there is only one buyer/seller. If there are any more buyer/sellers in a string contract than just the PIA, the deal will fall apart because the credit cannot be transferred more than once. In addition, the PIA must also know that the end buyer and the supplier are both real principals and not just intermediaries and once their genuine status is established, the other intermediaries in the deal 'step back' to allow the PIA to close the deal directly and effectively with both principals.

'Stepping back' is a term created for this book. Without exception the PIA will not trade with any other intermediary unless they step back. Therefore the PIA will always ask for a firm quotation or offer before attempting any stepping back operation. It is these documents that will expose the viability of a deal in the first instance.

Spending a few minutes, a few hours or even a day testing viability is fine, but spending weeks on a deal which finally collapses into a mess is not. By conducting a little due diligence the PIA will soon ascertain whether the enquiry is flawed or has potential. Once you know what you are looking for it is easy to spot flawed enquiries. While the internet is not considered a vital tool in the closure of a deal it is a great tool for conducting research and due diligence.

In essence weeks turns into months and years, in which the intermediary practises their trade. Although each deal may be unworkable and poorly offered, the intermediary is in fact honing their skills at due diligence and effective research. As the months become years the intermediary aligns themselves with real suppliers and end buyers, all the while increasing their expertise. When a genuine deal presents itself, the intermediary will know how to close it and earn commission because of their prior training and practice in testing enquiries, which are skills that can only be learned while trading.

A few minutes spent researching a seemingly viable enquiry could save the PIA weeks of effort trying to facilitate a deal that eventually collapses. A PIA receives an enquiry, for example, stating, 'We are sellers of crude oil, please furnish us with LOI or email stating the API grade, Specification and Quantity needed.' This type of enquiry is not worth pursuing as, given the lack of specific information, there is no way of conducting due diligence. The PIA is unsure of the intent of the enquiry. The PIA could purposefully provide misleading information as to API grade, specification and quantity. If the reply states that supply is possible, then the PIA has revealed a 'RF' trader. This approach is to be used sparingly. If the supply proves to be real, the PIA looks incompetent for providing information that was inaccurate and ironically the supplier could mark the PIA as a suspect trader.

Here's another example of a typical enquiry:

> 'Hello PIA, I am Jack Wells from International Oil Corp USA.'

The PIA has an immediate opportunity to conduct online due diligence before answering the enquiry. By typing 'Jack Wells, International Oil' and 'International Oil Corp' into a search engine any results may identify whether this is a supplier, end buyer or another intermediary. If nothing comes up, by implication, it is an intermediary making the enquiry unless there is information to the contrary.

> 'Hello I am FTN Exporting from Melbourne Australia seeking to buy the goods being offered.'

Defines with whom you are going to be dealing by doing some simple research on the internet.

Terminology

The main terms you will need to be familiar with when trading are detailed overleaf. At this stage you just need an idea of these terms so do not be concerned about committing them to memory yet. The terms are divided into three general sections:

1.   Parties to the trade;

2.   Payments;

3.   Delivery.

PARTIES TO A TRANSACTION

Buyer/seller

As far as an intermediary is concerned, there is no such entity as a sole 'buyer' or 'seller'. In a string deal all intermediaries are either a 'buyer/seller' (of which there can only be one in each trade) or a 'sourcing intermediary'. The buyer/seller is arguably the most important person in the whole trade.

Many international trade publications refer only to the general term 'seller' or 'buyer'. Incoterms 2000 also uses the term seller or buyer. UCP600 DLC rules make no mention of either buyer or seller but instead makes heavy use of the terms 'applicant' and 'beneficiary'. These terms have been the bane of the industry for as long as anyone can remember. It is only in the localized code of practice, as used with the UCC 2007 of the United States that has finally expanded upon the definition of buyer and seller by using terms such as 'immediate buyer' or 'merchant'. A 'buyer' could mean the 'end buyer' or an intermediary who is attempting to buy goods in order to resell them to the 'end buyer'. This could also be the case with the term 'seller'.

Within this book a buyer or seller is defined as an intermediary and not a supplier or an end buyer. An intermediary must ascertain quickly if they are dealing with intermediaries rather than principals, as most suppliers and end buyers do indeed also call themselves 'sellers' or 'buyers' respectively. As a rule assume in the first instance that when trading on the internet the terms 'seller' and 'buyer' do not mean 'supplier' or 'end buyer' in the majority of cases, if not in all cases.

End buyer

The end buyer pays for the goods and takes ultimate title and possession of the goods being purchased.

Intermediary

Any person whether agent, mandate, buyer/seller or similar who is looking to make financial gains from a transaction by selling goods on one side at a higher price to another side so as to earn commission or other monetary gain.

Mandateship

A mandate is an entity (company, individual or other legal entity) that has a contractual agreement with an end buyer or supplier to the effect that they are authorized to act on behalf of that buyer or supplier in the selling or purchasing of commodities. They are not a sourcing intermediary and are usually paid directly by their principal, whether that's the end buyer or supplier. Anyone claiming to be a 'mandate' shall be treated as a 'sourcing intermediary' unless documents are provided which verifies their position as a mandate. The documentation must disclose the principal of the mandate holder (that is, the end buyer or supplier of goods). If the claim of mandate-ship proves to be genuine then the mandate holder's position in a string contract is not dissimilar to a supplier or end buyer. A genuine mandate holder should *never* ask for a transferable letter of credit and must be able to secure their commission from the principal they represent and not from the intermediaries' share. Their mandate-ship papers must be provided to any SI (sourcing intermediary) who asks them to disclose their principal supplier or end buyer before the commencement of the deal.

Owner

As far as the intermediary is concerned, the supplier is the ultimate entity that owns and is able to provide a quotation for the sale of those goods to intermediaries. The owner also accepts the non-transferable credit for the payment of the goods as transferred by the intermediary. The terms seller, exporter, shipper and so on may not always mean 'supplier' so the 'buyer/seller' must always be sure that they are reselling goods from a supplier and therefore the owner of the goods, and *nobody else.*

PIA

Principal Intermediary Agent, or 'Buyer/Seller' Controlling Intermediary. The supplier, the buyer/seller and the end buyer together form a union in trinity, or three-party trade. The presence of only these three parties within a deal is the ideal trading scenario.

Principal

The principal has control of the deal and must be prepared to instil their will at all times. The principal will always direct a situation to favour themselves and bears all the legal consequences of a deal as well as protecting the commissions and interests of others who assist them in the deal. The principal is the intermediary who is the 'buyer/seller' or 'head' of an agency. The supplier who owns the goods being offered, and the end buyer who takes actual possession of the goods being purchased are also 'principals'. These are the three main entities or 'the principals' in an international commodity deal.

Seller

The end buyer shall ultimately reach a situation in which he is dealing with the seller, that is the 'buyer/seller' of the whole trading group. Similarly the supplier shall ultimately only deal with the buyer, that is the buyer/seller of the whole trading group.

Seller's side

A potentially ambiguous term in a 'string contract' where there are sourcing intermediaries between the buyer/seller and the supplier. This situation should be avoided at all times as it is of fundamental importance for the buyer/seller to have personally verified that the supplier's goods are in fact genuine before offering them for sale. It is permissible for an intermediary to find and secure an end buyer, but a buyer/seller principal intermediary must not use the services of other intermediaries who are offering to sell goods, but only test the information being provided by them to assess viability. To offer goods for sale without knowing whether or not they exist is fraudulent in most jurisdictions.

Sourcing Intermediary (SI)

A person who assists with a deal by helping to find a supplier or an end buyer of goods and who is one party within the formation of the 'string contract'. This intermediary is not a principal controlling intermediary but must attach themselves to a principal buyer/seller in a string contract. Otherwise, no deal is possible. When intermediaries first start to trade they gain practice and experience by trading as a sourcing intermediary. Once comfortable with this position, an intermediary can become a buyer/seller in their own right.

Step back

Intermediaries in a chain contract step back to the middle controlling 'buyer/seller'. This is because the 'buyer/seller' has guaranteed to protect the interests of all sourcing intermediaries, on the condition that they 'step back' to expose the principal entity of the particular group they represent (whether end buyer or supplier). Therefore only a very proficient trader should hold the position of 'buyer/seller' because the level of skill required in undertaking the transaction means that a buyer/seller must have excellent knowledge of correct trading procedures, banking rules and other rules of trade.

String contract

A transaction involving the end buyer, the supplier, any number of sourcing intermediaries with one predominant intermediary (the 'buyer/seller') who is controlling and directing the group as principal. This trading formation is known, among other things, as an 'intermediary chain' or 'trading group'. As has already been seen the 'union in trinity' (end buyer, buyer/seller, supplier) provides the ideal trading scenario. Often however you will require the assistance of other intermediaries to secure an end buyer or supplier. In this case, the buyer/seller protects the position of all the SIs to enable them to 'step back' from the deal, leaving only the 'union in trinity' to complete the trade.

The type of scenario that must be avoided at all times (but is so often seen on the internet) is end buyer, buyer, SI, SI, buyer/seller, SI, SI, seller, supplier and variants of this formation. In this type of scenario the 'buyer/seller' simply cannot trade only with the person next to them in the string contract. Everyone up to the principal on both sides of the fence must step back to the buyer/seller early on, or no deal is possible.

Supplier

The owner in actual possession of the goods being offered for sale.

PAYMENTS

Payments

The buyer/seller is the only person who can accept a financial instrument. Similarly the buyer/seller is the only person who can issue a financial instrument for transfer to the supplier (and not to anyone else).

UCP600

Uniform Custom and Practice for documentary credits came into force in July 2007 and superseded UCP500. It concerns the applicable banking rules regarding issuance and usage of UCP600 financial instruments.

Back-to-back trades

Where the end buyer issues a bank-endorsed letter of credit, the middle controlling buyer/seller cannot use the security of the first credit to open another 'bank endorsed' credit to the supplier. However they may be able to issue a corporate financial instrument, but this method is *only* to be used by very experienced intermediaries.

Banking

Assume that banks do not recognize intermediaries. Under UCP600, the use of the term 'bank' is very specific. A 'bank' issued letter of credit is a letter of credit issued by a bank. A reference to a 'letter of credit' without the term 'bank' could also mean a non-bank issued financial instrument. UCP600 now allows an end buyer to offer a 'letter of credit' as issued from their own corporate office and not a bank. A buyer/seller will be obliged to accept this credit if the term 'bank' was not included on the offer or sales contract which would result in a failed transaction and possible legal action against the buyer/seller for breach of conditions. The buyer/seller has the power to decide whether or not to use the term 'bank' in any transaction and in all cases the end buyer shall only provide a 'bank' endorsed financial instrument.

Credit

See 'Financial instrument'.

Financial instrument

A letter of credit that the intermediary must secure from an end buyer of goods as issued from their bank. UCP600 governs the way letters of credits are secured and transacted upon internationally. This means that once the intermediary secures the financial instrument, marked with the term UCP600, from an end buyer then these rules apply to payments for the goods being traded. You will find below typical financial instruments that intermediaries may come across from time to time.

LETTERS OF CREDIT

Anyone can write and produce a letter of credit (L/C) to another person. Intermediaries mostly deal with letters of credit which have been issued by a bank and which are guaranteed by that bank, on behalf of the end buyer, and not the buyer directly.

Pre-Advised Transferable Irrevocable Documentary Letter of Credit (PA TIDLC)

'Pre-advised' means that the credit is issued as operational and irrevocable but not yet formally activated, and is subject to a precondition before activation can occur. Under UCP600 once the precondition has been met the bank must make the credit active. Once the credit becomes active it may be transferred as a non-transferable instrument directly to the supplier. A pre-advised credit is a less expensive option for an end buyer especially when a buyer needs proof that the goods are genuine. The intermediary provides the 'PPI' (an in-house created Policy Proof of Interest Certificate) to the end buyer's bank exactly as per the conditions of the contract. Then the end buyer's issuing bank (although now knowing the identity of the supplier) must make the pre-advised credit active once its precondition has been met. As it is transferable, the 'PA TIDLC' is an ideal instrument for intermediaries to use. Take note, however, that under UCP600 banking rules a PA TIDLC is issued at the discretion of the end buyer's bank and the bank has the right to refuse to issue this instrument if it so wishes. All PA TIDLCs must be issued as confirmed when being sought by an intermediary.

Confirmed Irrevocable Documentary Letter of Credit (CIDLC)

Where a credit is issued as being 'confirmed' this is the safest credit that an intermediary can hold. For example, a small Indian bank issues an IDLC (Irrevocable Documentary Letter of Credit) to the buyer/seller which is confirmed by another world leading bank such as Citicorp USA, or even by your own world ranked bank into which the DLC was advised, then the smaller bank is being guaranteed its payment by another bank. Should the smaller bank fail to honour payment the economically larger bank will do so instead.

Thus only a highly rated smaller bank (limited by financial resources and not because of a bad credit rating amongst its peers) would be able to secure another bank's confirmation of its credit. An economically powerful Top 300 world-class bank would prefer not to issue a confirmed credit as their status does not require it. When any credit is issued as being 'confirmed' by the advising bank of the buyer/seller, for collection to be allowed the delivery documents only need to be presented at the intermediary's bank, and not the issuing bank, for collection. A credit confirmed by another bank on behalf of a smaller bank is a 'corresponding bank' to the advising bank, which means that the confirming bank is able to correspond with the buyer/seller's own advising bank.

> *Example: The issuing bank, Bank of China, Guangzhou may need to issue a credit to a corresponding bank such as the Bank of China, New York, who in turn is able to advise the credit to the buyer/seller's ANZ Bank in Australia, which then transfers the credit to the supplier's bank, the SBER Bank in Russia, or another corresponding bank that may be able to transfer such a credit to the said Russian bank.*

When a credit shows that the deal is an 'in trinity' transaction (that is a transaction involving an intermediary), then the intermediary must be very careful to include in their contract with the end buyer that transfer fees relating to issuance are a matter for the account of the end buyer. In addition, the fees for the transfer of the credit from the corresponding bank to the buyer/seller's bank is made for the account of the corresponding bank at cost for its reimbursement to be made by the issuing bank.

Issuing banks may deceptively 'transfer' the credit to a corresponding bank then insist that it has paid the required transfer fee as required by the contract. Depending on the value of the credit, this leaves the buyer/seller having to pay a very substantial transfer fee to the corresponding bank before it is able to initiate such a transfer. It is also possible as per our example that the advising bank of the intermediary is asked to confirm the issued credit of the Indian bank. In this case the expense of confirming the credit is payable by the intermediary.

Transferable and Irrevocable Documentary Letter of Credit (TIDLC)

Of the utmost concern to an intermediary is accepting a 'transferable' credit. The fact that a TIDLC exists is one reason why intermediaries are allowed to trade in the first place. An experienced intermediary can accept a non-transferable credit and issue in-house DLCs, but this is not recommended for the 'apprentice' trader. Under UCP600 the term 'Transferable' must now appear on the face of the credit itself. By its very nature and function a TIDLC prohibits another buyer/seller from being involved in a string contract. The end buyer issues a TIDLC to the middle controlling buyer/seller – the purchase price of the goods is transferred to the supplier directly as a normal DLC. The remaining sum in the buyer/seller's account represents everyone's commission, which is paid out upon the deal closing. Such a TIDLC can only be transferred once. If the middle buyer/seller transferred the TIDLC to another 'seller' then they would only receive a non-transferable DLC. This 'seller' would not be able to transfer the credit to their supplier and the deal would collapse. This form of credit is also suitable for use by intermediaries but as you will soon learn proof of goods will become an issue that will force the issuance of a PA TIDLC. First time around there is nothing wrong with requesting a TIDLC. Such an instrument must be issued as confirmed.

Irrevocable Documentary Letter of Credit (IDLC)

The basic DLC has many variants depending on the type of deal in question. 'Irrevocable' means that the DLC cannot under any circumstances be cancelled once advised, and accepted by the buyer/seller (except for strong, verifiable matters pertaining to fraud). Once an end buyer issues an irrevocable credit in any form the bank takes over in guaranteeing its payment by applying only UCP rules to the credit, so long as the credit states on its form that 'UCP600 applies to its issuance'. This means that all parties must transact using financial instruments permitted within the rules of UCP600. The credit should be marked as transferable for first time traders. More experienced intermediaries can use a non-transferable credit. Non-transferable credits are discussed later under 'in-house' DLCs).

Letter of Credit (L/C)

The general term 'Letter of Credit.' It can also mean a plain L/C, which carries no other stipulation (so it is not 'irrevocable') which intermediaries should not use for anything other than perhaps commission payments. For example, this DLC issued for the payment of commissions can be revoked should the supporting transaction pertaining to its DLC number fail to close. This kind of DLC is sometimes referred to as a 'Revocable DLC'. Intermediaries must never deal with this type of financial instrument.

Revolving credit

Used for multi-shipment monthly delivery transactions, the issuing bank agrees to honour a revolving status on the credit as a non-cumulative revolving TIDLC. So where, for example, the DLC value of three shipments is advised, so as one shipment value is collected from the top of the three shipment 'stack' as a debit, it leaves two payments. At the same time another payment is applied to the bottom of the pile as a credit, so the stack reverts to the originally issued three-shipment value.

> *Example: The contract value of the goods is 1.2 million dollars. Monthly contract shipment value is 120,000 dollars. The credit is opened for a ten-month period. The letter of credit is opened with an initial opening value of 360,000 dollars. As one monthly value is taken from the top, another value equal to that already collected is added, returning the credits value to three. The credit is opened for the whole contracted value, by way of the DLC guarantee, but the actual funds supporting the value are offered usually at the value of three shipments, regardless of the total contracted value.*

In a crude oil deal, for instance, where a contract may run for years and supply delivered monthly, slightly higher initial values of four or up to six initial payments may be requested. Where for example a confirmed credit is advised, even two initial revolving payments would suffice in a contract for supply over an eight-month period. Intermediaries may use these types of revolving credits except the confirmation is applied to the whole amount of the credit supporting the in-advance monthly payments. Thus, as per our example the whole contract value of 1.2 million dollars is issued as a confirmed credit.

Stand-by Letter of Credit (SLC)

A Stand-by Letter of Credit cannot be used for the payment of goods and is suitable only for the payment of commissions or a performance guarantee (PG). If an SLC is used as per the 1998 rules of the ICC's provisions 'International Stand-By Practices', it is often defined using the acronym 'ISP98 SLC'. A UCP600 SLC can only be transferred once from the buyer/seller to the end buyer as issued from the supplier and must be marked as 'transferable'. Intermediaries may use both types of SLC but the UCP600 type is preferable. An ISP98 SLC, unlike the UCP600 SLC, may be transferred among many intermediaries in a string contract, which is the main difference between the two types of credits.

Unlike a normal DLC used to pay for goods, a SLC is not activated based on conditions such as presentation of delivery documents but rather issued as an unconditional instrument: upon a certain single event occurring a SLC is allowed to be presented for collection.

> *Example 1: Delivery has failed to occur at the time specified on the contract, so the end buyer calls for and collects the SLC unconditionally because the delivery (performance) was late.*

> *Example 2: Intermediaries presenting title delivery documents late will activate the SLC unconditionally and give right to the end buyer to collect it, even though the deal still eventually closes.*

> *Example 3: Commission pay order in the form of an 'in-house' SLC is issued by the buyer/seller which may be collected upon so long as a certain event occurs. This imperative event is that the deal supporting the SLC issuance has successfully closed. Therefore the buyer/seller will never issue a SLC commission pay order unless they have cleared funds in their account that have resulted from the successful closure of the deal. The buyer/seller produces a signed SLC that bears their original signature, and emails or faxes it over to the recipient. The active hard copy is marked as 'Original' and delivered by overnight courier. When it arrives, the original allows the intermediary to deposit the SLC into their account to initiate collection procedures. Thus issuance and collection are both unconditional and not subject to presentation of delivery documents, but there may be a condition related to the way in which the funds can be collected, for example, 'Funds to be collected for depositing into the verified bank account of the named holder and beneficiary.'*

Intermediaries may accept these types of credits, which do not need confirmation, as often they are small amounts compared to the opening of a credit for the purchase of goods. An SLC can also be issued carrying the revolving status.

SUMMARY OF LETTERS OF CREDIT

It is imperative that the intermediary secures supply first, as a matter of contract, but must now also ensure the following when accepting the financial instrument: all first time dealings with a new client require the issuance of a *confirmed credit*. On the second and any subsequent dealings with the same client, this rule can be relaxed. In a three-party deal all credits from the end buyer, regardless of the world ranking of the bank, must be issued as *confirmed*. The only exception to this rule is a bank-issued standby letter of credit.

Corporate instruments

A privately issued financial instrument can be issued from the office of an intermediary so long as UCP600 is applied. This is called a 'corporate' instrument. Intermediaries may, on the other hand, either choose to transfer the bank-endorsed financial instrument to pay for the goods or they may choose to pay for goods using a 'corporate' instrument as created in-house. This is the first time these corporate instruments have been supported by UCP provisions. The use of bank transferable DLCs are recommended until intermediaries become very confident in their trading ability. Until then, intermediaries should avoid trading with a privately issued 'corporate' credit.

A corporate DLC is created where a bank has issued a confirmed non-transferable credit to the buyer/seller and, rather than transferring the bank issued DLC (a transferable DLC), the intermediary uses their own stationery to make a corporate in-house DLC and presents it to the supplier of the goods. The supplier of the goods allows their bank to authenticate the credit to the intermediate bank (authentication fees are payable by the supplier) that has the original credit in its account, thereby giving financial support to the privately issued in-house instrument. This type of privately issued credit is acceptable as long as it carries the following statement: 'This credit is issued as a UCP600 financial instrument.'

Secondary market

Primary markets involve the types of goods that are traded between governments or by agencies such as OPEC, and which are unsuitable for intermediaries. Therefore intermediaries must only deal in secondary market goods.

THE VARIOUS ROLES OF BANKS

As far as banks are concerned the three parties to a three-party intermediary deal (end buyer, intermediate buyer/seller and supplier) are all defined as 'beneficiaries'. The end buyer is the 'applicant' of the credit they are wishing to raise through the bank. Banks do not use the terms 'buyer' and 'seller'. The bank of the end buyer is called the 'issuing bank'. The bank of the buyer/seller is the 'advising bank', and the bank of the supplier is the 'accepting bank'. A bank supporting another bank by 'confirming' a credit on its behalf is defined as a 'confirming bank'.

An issuing bank in one country may seek the support of another branch of the same bank or associated bank in another country in getting the credit to the buyer/seller. This is defined as a 'corresponding bank'. A 'free' bank simply means a bank used by a buyer/seller as being their advising bank even though they hold no account there. A 'Top 300' world-class bank, so defined by a leading banking authority or financial reporting institution such as Dunn and Bradstreet or publications such as *Forbes Fortune 500*, does not need to be confirmed. However, the preferred method of dealing is with a confirmed DLC, particularly in times of financial unrest, but also once the world financial markets are more settled. In any event first-time intermediaries should deal only with confirmed DLCs.

A 'soft confirmation' is where the advising bank may act in part to negotiate upon the merits of the credit but not to the extent as required for a credit issued with a full confirmation. An advising bank is an agent or even an intermediary acting between two other banks. The buyer/seller may often become frustrated with the advising bank, because they do not realize that this bank has very limited powers to act independently. The advising bank earns 'commission' through the transfer fee. If there is no transfer fee the intermediary is stuck and the deal will collapse. So it is important to keep this in the front of your mind when dealing with an advising bank. Just like an intermediary, an advising bank is entitled to earn commission. Therefore it is of paramount importance that the buyer/seller ensures that payment of the transfer fees are settled with the end buyer, and that this is agreed on the contract before the credit is lodged into their account.

DELIVERY

Bill of Lading (BOL)

BOL – a document attested by a carrier specifying that the goods have been received on board the ship for transportation to the end buyer. The bill of lading is considered as the primary title or leading delivery document. In an FOB deal the BOL is called a 'received' BOL. In a CIF type of deal the BOL is defined as 'shipped'.

Delivery

Intermediaries must not deal in physical goods, or imply that they have actual possession of the goods, or even that they have proof of goods. For intermediaries, 'delivery' means 'clean document presentation' or 'title' to the goods. Banks deal in documents and not goods, as opposed to suppliers and end buyers, who deal in both physical goods and 'delivery documents'.

INCOTERMS

International commercial terms are used worldwide to determine whether the responsibility for costs and other duties falls with the buyer or the seller. Incoterms can also be used in countries within continents that border each other i.e.: Europe, Africa. However, Incoterms cannot be readily adapted for use within states of a country, for example, the USA or Australia, as federal or state laws of commerce or codes of practice (as per UCC) often govern interstate dealings.

Policy Proof of Interest (PPI)

Policy Proof of Interest: this proves the intermediary's 'interest' in the goods, which have been secured prior to being offered for sale to anyone. The intermediary seller has secured an 'interest' to purchase the goods from a direct supplier. After the buyer/seller has secured the required funds to make the purchase from the supplier, the buyer/seller will only be required to prove capability in being able to supply the goods (as per the terms of the contract with their end buyer). This may not satisfy the need to meet 'proof of goods' but offers a superior gesture in assuring serious intent to complete the transaction. The buyer/seller is taking personal responsibility to ensure that the supply will be met. This is because the buyer/seller has already ensured that their own supply capabilities are secured from their supplier long before the end buyer's contract is signed. The act of promising to supply happens concurrently with the intention that the buyer/seller is willing to supply. If this doesn't happen, in that the buyer/seller offers goods without having secured the interests in the goods being offered, then they may find themselves facing charges of fraud. If the interests in the goods are apparent but the goods are not secured after the DLC from the end buyer is accepted by the buyer/seller then the buyer/seller could be circumvented, or cut out of the deal.

The 'PPI' certificate is incorporated into the body of the contract but the details are left blank. The buyer/seller fills in the blanks to disclose the supplier of the goods, and their proof of interest in them, but only after they have accepted the letter of credit to buy the goods that has been provided by the end buyer. Thus, once the PPI information is supplied, the end buyer cannot make excuses in respect of its suitability as the blank document once filled in is copied and returned to the end buyer – as per the conditions of the contract.

The contract is signed. The end buyer deposits the required DLC to the buyer/seller who in turn accepts it and returns a copy of the PPI document filled with the word 'original' on its header or page margin with the required disclosure information. As the L/C is irrevocable it cannot be cancelled simply because the end buyer has obtained the details of the supplier.

The Policy Proof of Interest Certificate appears near the end of the draft contract. This section informs the end buyer as to the exact information that is going to be provided well in advance of the end buyer depositing the purchase L/C. Thus the intermediary must clearly define the information that is going to be disclosed, the manner in which such disclosure is going to occur and the format the disclosure will take. So long as the information is correct and verifiable, there is no recourse for the end buyer. This is the case whether the end buyer decides to verify the information or not. The act of simply producing the information fulfils the intermediary's obligation to provide PPI.

Waybill

An ocean waybill provides evidence that the goods are on board ship. It is not a title document but merely an official receipt stating that the goods are on board the ship. In a 'Free on Board' (FOB) deal the intermediary is not required to produce a bill of lading but is required to assist the end buyer in securing it, in accordance with Incoterms 2000 delivery rules. Therefore, regardless of whether the bill of lading is produced the intermediary must still provide a 'leading' delivery document that provides evidence that the goods are indeed 'on board' the end buyer's ordered ship.

The non-negotiable waybill may satisfy the provisions of Incoterms 2000 in proving that the goods are indeed on board the ship. Difficulties may arise with issues of negotiability when a ship subject to a charterparty is used (that is, hired by the end buyer from a shipowner). The only other acceptable FOB receipt which provides the requisite evidence, is an original stamped 'ship's mate's receipt'. The use of a 'delivery order' or forwarder's receipt of the shipowners or ship's master should only be used as a last resort. In an FOB deal, intermediaries should offer in the first instance the leading delivery document, the 'ship's mate's receipt'. In a CFR (Cost and Freight) or CIF (Cost Insurance and Freight) bulk deal, the leading delivery document is the marine bill of lading. A deal cannot close unless one of these leading or title documents is presented. The delivery mode for a transaction also identifies the primary presentation document.

In a CIF/CNF/CIP deal the BOL is a primary leading document and other documents such as the seller's invoice and certificate of origin are considered as important secondary documents. However, in an EXW deal the export permit or the seller's invoice may be nominated to become the primary leading document (such nomination becomes a term of the contract). In all cases presentation of documents must comply with the terms and conditions of the credit. In this respect, it does not matter what is specified in the contract of sale: a bank does not care about the terms of a contract and will only perform on sight acceptance of the presentation documents. Whether or not collection upon the credit occurs is based solely on the terms and conditions on the credit.

Shipping

This is another aspect of the role of the intermediary that traders often fail to understand. The intermediary plays no part in arranging matters that are to do with shipping. Again, if a contract seeks to address matters relating to shipping as part of the deal then the intermediary must avoid signing it at all costs. It is very unwise and indeed dangerous to sign up to obligations that are not under your immediate control. Shipping is an automated process over which the intermediary has no control, because the intermediary only deals in documents pertaining to delivery. Once the goods cross over the ship's rail in the port of loading, the intermediary has completed their part of the deal. This is defined as 'delivery' as far as FOB/CIF deals are concerned. The ship slips its moorings and heads towards the end buyer's destination port. Any shipping issues are the responsibility of the shipowner or charterer.

An intermediary who sees anything on the contract that relates to all but the simplest matters regarding shipping must delete them before signing the contract. We have seen contracts, with many clauses devoted to complex shipping formulations, which are totally unacceptable for intermediary use.

Commission

It is the buyer/seller's obligation to protect and pay out commission to other intermediaries involved within a particular string contract. The commission is the difference between the price the end buyer pays for the goods and the price that the PIA pays when purchasing them from the supplier. However, the PIA takes all the legal risk of the trade on both sides, and is contractually bound to both end buyer and supplier separately. In the event that there are minor defects with the goods, depending on the circumstances the PIA may be required to compensate the end buyer and use part of their commission to do so. The PIA therefore secures a larger portion of commission for themselves than for sourcing intermediaries. The primary intermediaries (PI) next to the PIA are also recognized for their additional assistance in the trade, and although they earn less than the PIA, will earn more than sourcing intermediaries. It is unrealistic for sourcing intermediaries to claim that they are entitled for example to 5 dollars per MT (metric ton) commission for doing very little in a deal in which the buyer/seller is taking all the legal responsibilities between two other contracting parties.

The Transaction: No Documents, No Payment

Once the buyer/seller receives the required financial instrument from the end buyer, the buyer/seller has to produce the required delivery documents as per the terms of the contract. When the documents are produced, this is called 'presentation' which enables collection upon the financial instrument issued by the buyer's bank. The implied guarantee that the bank issues to pay for the goods is defined as being an 'Irrevocable Documentary Letter of Credit' or IDLC. The big difference between an IDLC as issued between end buyer and supplier, and a transaction in which a buyer/seller is involved, is that the issued IDLC carries the further stipulation that such an instrument is allowed to be made 'transferable', *once only*, and only to the supplier and not to another intermediary 'seller'.

4

Dispelling the Myths: LOI, POP, ASWP and More

When an email lands in your inbox demanding an LOI (Letter of Intent) and BCL (Bank Comfort Letter), why should you dismiss it immediately? Why don't terms like POP (Proof of Product) and ASWP (Any Safe World Port) work? This chapter explains the most widely used acronyms, which are both unsafe and impractical, along with the reasons why they are not suitable for intermediary use. Those who have already entered the intermediary sphere prior to reading this book will be familiar with some of these acronyms. Such traders will also be well aware that they have not been able to close a deal using these terms. However, many will not admit that these procedures are flawed and make excuses for why past trades have failed. Each new intermediary copies another's flawed methods, and the number of intermediaries using this terminology continues to grow.

ASWP – 'Any Safe World Port' is a term often used by misguided intermediaries when giving costs of goods with freight cost applied. Stop for a moment to think about the practicalities of this. Is delivery to a 'safe world port' that happens to be only 500 nautical miles away from the supplier really going to cost the same as delivery to a 'safe world port' 6,000 miles away? Any deal making reference to ASWP is to be treated as though it is entirely without merit and discarded immediately.

BCL – 'Bank Comfort/Conformity Letter': Why should an end buyer disclose banking details to a third-party intermediary for distribution to other faceless intermediaries in all parts of the world, especially in modern times where identity fraud, internet banking fraud and other scams are rife? Even if a principal does disclose this information to an intermediary, what use is this information to them? They cannot personally conduct a 'soft probe' so what business does an intermediary have asking another intermediary for this type of third-party information?

BOE – Bill of Exchange: A financial instrument for use between a supplier and end buyer, which can be used with or without the issuance of a DLC. Laws pertaining to BOE issuance vary from country to country and therefore simply cannot be addressed in any great depth. A supplier draws against a confirmed credit a BOE for the value of the goods and presents it to the end buyer's bank, which is in turn reimbursed by the issuing bank (the guarantor of the BOE). If the DLC is not confirmed, the BOE is presented to the issuing bank, which in turn checks the delivery documents and pays the supplier's bank (or advising bank) before the exporter gets paid. The intermediary should not be overly concerned about the BOE and should simply seek advice about these matters from their bank only at collection time. The BOE instrument is a very simple instrument that bears very little information and is similar to a cheque in design. In terms of earning commission, the seller's invoice and DLC are the two most important documents. The intermediary should not tempted to deal with a BOE if one is offered, without a DLC being in place first, even if the BOE is guaranteed by the issuer's bank.

ICPO – Irrevocable Corporate Purchase Offer: The much-maligned ICPO is arguably the most frequently misused document used by intermediaries on the internet today. Let's start at the beginning. Are you a corporation? A corporation with valuable assets? Let's assume not. If you were, an ICPO could be used in very limited circumstances.

By using ICPO documents intermediaries are really confusing the internal business of corporate giants with their own nature of trade. Are you prepared to adhere to an 'irrevocable' commitment if the supplier accepts your ICPO?

An ICPO is an instrument of considerable stature and is often used in local or interstate trade, particularly in the USA. Many misguided intermediaries interpret UCC rules to be transferable in the international arena: this is not so – for intermediaries, anyway. An ICPO has a similar implicit value to a bank-endorsed guarantee. A busy supplier often needs to commence servicing an end buyer's order immediately, within days of accepting the end buyer's offer. As such, both parties deal with the issue of payment later on (understandable, if the deal is between two principals both in the same country).

Timing and scheduling are both very important considerations to the busy trader, who will not spend money, time and effort servicing the requests of an end buyer unless there is some kind of irrevocable commitment in place. Often, when a documentary letter of credit is not used to pay for the goods, the end buyer may have the option to get the ball rolling by allowing the supplier to draw a bill of exchange from the end buyer's bank guaranteeing the financial instrument. The supplier has to attach the title delivery document to the bill of exchange (sometimes also called a *draft*), before payment will be made as per its terms and conditions. This commitment, just like the ICPO, must be backed by assets: if an end buyer issues an ICPO and then attempts to cancel the obligations a few weeks later, the supplier could claim for breach of contract if he has already got the goods ready for interstate export. In these circumstances the supplier then takes legal action against the end buyer, targeting their assets. The supplier will only ever accept an ICPO from another readily identifiable corporation with assets. It follows, therefore, that the intermediary cannot and must not entertain any request for an ICPO as in doing so they are playing with fire. ICPOs are only really used in international trade scenarios between large corporations and where one corporation has a subsidiary office in another country outside the USA.

LOI – Today international trade intermediaries are confused; many are using a critically flawed and unworkable doctrine in the intermediary trading process called an 'LOI' or letter of intent. What actual purpose can this document have? Such a letter could be written by anyone, and carries no legal weight. In international trade 'LOI' actually stands for 'letter of indemnity' and isn't relevant for intermediaries.

MOU – Memorandum of Understanding: Similar to the LOI acronym, the MOU stands on weak ground. It is often used in international investment or construction contracts and is not suitable for intermediaries. A memorandum of understanding is generally used in situations of clarification in which the parties do not wish to, or cannot, create a legally enforceable agreement.

NDNC – Non-Disclosure and Non-Circumvention Agreement: This is intended to be a contractual agreement that provides the intermediary with a form of protection from circumvention. Any breach of this document is unenforceable in both practical and legal terms. The reasons why this document is worthless will be explained later. NCND documents (Non-Circumvention Non-Disclosure Agreements), that are so often seen on the internet, are unworkable. Firstly no one can prove that circumvention has in fact taken place and, secondly, even if they were able to prove that a deal that they were involved in did close successfully, the party claiming circumvention wouldn't be able to prove that they were owed commissions which at the time of the signature of the NCND were not even quantifiable. It would be virtually impossible to claim the loss of payment of unpaid commissions because of the inability to prove any financial loss.

In the commercial world, contracts usually contain clauses relating to disclosure and confidentiality. When intermediaries become involved in commercial transactions they often attempt to use confidentiality clauses in conjunction with a 'circumvention' notice. Further, in an attempt to secure and protect any commission payments that may become due, they request a master pay agreement or 'MPA'. The eventuating NCND Agreement is often used by intermediaries in the belief that this document offers protection of commission payments, when in fact the opposite may be true.

FTN Exporting has seen some great NCND Agreements over the years, some of which could be used effectively, albeit in a very limited manner, where the intermediary and supplier or end buyer are both resident in the same country or state transacting upon an 'interstate type' of intermediary deal. As far as intermediaries are concerned an NCND agreement, whether attached or not to a master payment agreement, is at best ineffective and should not be regarded as a document of any substantial value. It cannot be used, or relied upon, to defend against a trader who breaches their obligations to pay commission to those they are supposed to be protecting. There may be a handful of intermediaries who profess to have earned a fortune by virtue of these documents whereas there are countless others who earn nothing from them and claim to be victims of circumvention.

Pro Forma Invoice – Pro forma invoices are raised by a supplier so that a buyer can see all the charges and costs of the products being offered and pay for them. Payment is collected before the goods are shipped. The supplier then delivers the goods, usually by post, to the address of the buyer. This is ideal for use in small parcel orders and deliveries. In international bulk shipments, payment can only be made when the delivery documents are produced as 'clean', which can only occur once the goods have been shipped.

POP – On the internet you will often see 'Proof of Product' or POP. The correct terminology is in fact PPI or 'Policy Proof of Interest', which is discussed in detail later on. In the real trading world, 'Proof of Product' cannot be given without disclosing the physical owner of the goods being offered by a seller. Even if an end buyer is dealing directly with a supplier, proof that the product exists can at best only be treated as a trivial matter of little or no importance, unless the end buyer physically inspects the goods at loading port. For example, an end buyer in one country contacts a supplier in another country for the purpose of purchasing goods. Would they demand 'proof' that the product exists? Even if they did, what could the supplier provide at that early stage in terms of proof of the actual goods the end buyer will receive? Would the end buyer be satisfied with photographs, or a sworn affidavit? Even witnessing the goods being loaded onto the ship does not guarantee that those same goods will arrive at the destination port, which is why third-party internationally recognized experts such as pre-shipment inspectors are important. Furthermore FTN Exporting has given so called 'POP', in the past on numerous occasions, which when FTN lost control of the deal and the hard-sourced supplier has resulted in no deal. There will be a high risk of circumvention if proof is given prior to the buyer/seller securing the required financial instrument from the end buyer.

There are undoubtedly huge sums involved in an international commodity deal. It is unrealistic to expect strangers in foreign countries to 'act honourably' and pay large sums of money to you in commissions when you have provided them with the name of the supplier. If you tell them the name of the supplier at this stage, they will take your hard-sourced business contact and cut you out of the deal. It stands to reason, therefore, that your chance to secure and earn commission from the funds of the end buyer will be lost. It would be very difficult, not to mention costly, for you to take legal action to try to recover any 'losses'.

RF – 'Rubbish Fodder': Any offer of a deal which uses any of the acronyms listed above is not even worth considering and should be discarded immediately. These types of deals are often presented by misguided intermediaries who simply don't know how to trade and are blindly following the example of others (who are equally misguided).

SLC – Stand-by Letter of Credit: An SLC must NEVER be used or offer to be used for the payment of goods. If you come across anyone asking for payment via an SLC, MT 799, SWIFT, PBG and the likes, you have no deal and the enquiry should be discarded immediately. Either the person requesting this type of payment has no idea what they are doing, or it may be some kind of letter of credit scam, of which there are many.

5

Starting to Trade

Due Diligence

Some internet traders use elaborate methods to give credence to the positions they hold in business, especially through their websites. These websites are full of pictures of the products they are touting, with carefully chosen phrases like 'We have been supplying the industry with ...' and so on and can be deceiving. Often there may only be a brief line somewhere within the pages that reveals the true nature of the business. 'We have always ensured to serve our buyers and suppliers well' and other statements are usually difficult to find but are often the only key to the true nature of their business. It is therefore imperative that the intermediary is meticulous in reading the content of other intermediaries' websites while conducting due diligence.

Let's evaluate an enquiry received by a PIA to assess whether it is worth further consideration or whether it should be discarded as Rubbish Fodder (RF).

> Dear PIA,
>
> Thank you for your enquiry. We are able to offer you 100,000 MT of Mesa Crude Oil API 36 grade, per month, for 12 months CIF ASWP for 50 dollar per bbl. Origin is PDVSA South America. Our website defines the offer further on www.idiottrader.com.
>
> We await your reply with a supporting LOI and BCL.
>
> Thank You
>
> Mr Numb Skull
> Oil Fields Trader LLC

The PIA already suspects that the deal is RF, but will spend a few minutes on the internet to conduct due diligence using the information provided. Studying the PDVSA website reveals that the company does not allow intermediaries to trade in their products, so the offer is treated immediately as RF and no more work is undertaken on it. Further research reveals that Mesa crude oil does not come with a 36 API rating. CIF ASWP (Any Safe World Port) delivery is just not acceptable.

Oil Fields Traders LLC is found using a search engine and reveals an intermediary who has been offering all sorts of things as a seller, and applying flawed trading methods. The Oil Fields Trader website also mirrors this information. The PIA did not even offer to reply to the ambiguous offer and simply discarded it. In essence an intermediary has no reason to enter a transaction that collapses later because they have failed to conduct some simple research on the internet. The more information provided, the more effective the due diligence will be. If the person making the enquiry gives the impression that they are a high profile trader, then that information will always be available on the internet.

Another way to test credibility is in the detail of the offer (whether it is an offer to sell or to buy). If you receive an enquiry asking for a particular commodity but the specifications are wrong (for example, the claimed origin of the goods is incompatible with the specifications, or you know that the country of origin does not export the commodity in question) this is a good sign that the person who has sent the offer does not know what they are doing, or has not been sufficiently diligent to check the accuracy of their own documentation.

Fraud

Let's look at another example.

> Dear PIA,
>
> My name is Bill. I am a CEO of IAMBILL LLC. We have been producing bulk wine for over twenty years, and have a quantity of wine available for exporting.

The PIA researches 'IAMBILL LLC' online. In a matter of minutes the PIA quickly ascertains that the wine producer is real. Let's assume the PIA has a real supplier. The PIA needs to now secure the wine, so the next step is just to ask for a quotation with all the applicable terms. If the PIA receives a reply in the form of a good quotation or offer that declares the price of the goods, minimum quantities, and specifications then they can start looking for an end buyer; either of their own volition, through their existing affiliates or by using sourcing intermediaries as found on the internet.

A direct reply from the wine maker with prices attached gives the PIA the explicit right to be able to offer the goods for sale on the global market as a seller. It does not matter that negotiations continue for weeks with the wine maker. The PIA starts searching for end buyers as soon as 'ostensible authority' has been directly obtained. As long as they agree to step back at the right time the PIA guarantees all commission to the sourcing intermediaries who find the end buyer. Using the information on the wine maker's quotation or offer the PIA formulates their own offers to others as seller. To the intermediary group the PIA is the controlling buyer/seller, to the end buyer the PIA is a seller, and to the wine maker the PIA is a buyer. Information from one side will never cross over to the other side because of the position held by the PIA. As a result, no matter what happens, the deal will not fail because of circumvention.

'Ostensible authority' means, 'authority as it is apparent to others'. The fact that the PIA is acting as a buyer and seller of somebody else's goods is not the issue; the issue is only one of performance. The PIA has an implied authority to sell the goods to an end buyer, because they have first secured the implied authority in being able to buy these goods from the supplier.

Since the supplier is willing to sell the wine by providing a quotation to the PIA, the PIA has the right to sell the wine. Technically, the PIA is 'flipping' a contract in which the wine is delivered to an end buyer directly from the supplier as instructed by the PIA. In real terms the PIA is selling the proprietary rights to the goods. The act of obtaining physical possession of the goods will not occur until much later and only by the end buyer. By securing the ostensible authority to sell the goods the PIA cannot be charged with fraud if the deal collapses later. If for unforeseen reasons the goods later became unavailable the PIA can prove that they acted with good intent by providing documentary evidence which shows that they were offering goods from a direct supplier as opposed to another intermediary.

Conversely if a PIA were to accept an offer from an intermediate seller by offering to resell unverified goods this could indeed put the PIA in prison awaiting trial for fraud if it later transpired that no goods were ever available. Furthermore the PIA would also face litigation for breach of contract with the end buyer for accepting payment for goods that never existed in the first place. Receiving the funds for a deal which then collapses and loses the PIA a considerable amount of commission is at the very least disheartening. It may take months for the PIA to recover emotionally, especially if it is their first potential deal.

If a PIA fails to observe the rules pertaining to securing actual supply there is a considerable risk that the deal will collapse. The PIA cannot simply blame another seller offering non-existent goods from a long line of other intermediaries. Apart from anything else, it is not a defence to fraud. It was the PIA, and not any other intermediary, who accepted the letter of credit. The PIA was the one who traded in goods that were not verified as genuine in the first place. This means the PIA has legal responsibilities and the obligation to perform within the trade. If something goes wrong there could be severe consequences for the PIA, which is why a PIA must never trade in goods that they have not personally verified as being genuine.

Over the years FTN Exporting has received pleas of assistance from intermediaries who have accepted a transferable instrument for goods before finding out that they were falsely offered. Often these intermediaries are forced to retreat in fear not just of the authorities but also because of threats being made by the end buyer. Even if FTN Exporting had been in a position to assist these desperate sellers by finding a genuine supply of goods, it would be very unwise to do so. In the vast majority of cases there are flaws with not only the goods but also the terms of the contract and the issuance of the documentary letter of credit. The PIA must start the deal with the intent of finishing it. Under no circumstances can a PIA attempt to enter into a deal where documents such as offers and contracts have already been accepted and signed by other parties. To do so is highly dangerous.

First Days of Trading

There are only a few items you need in order to start trading: a small work area, a computer with a large storage capacity and an internet connection. You will also need somewhere to file your paperwork, a facsimile, email address and a telephone. Perhaps you have decided to work over weekends and after work on a casual basis, or if you are not in full-time employment perhaps you have set aside certain hours of the day to trade. The more time you spend trading the better, as confidence grows with practice. The sooner you build up your confidence the more time you will have available to spend on real deals. So how much time should you spend trading each week? Seven hours per week is not enough, 28 hours is very good, 35 hours per seven-day week is plenty.

What are you going to call yourself? If you can afford to register a company or business name, this makes you look more professional. However, if you do not use a registered business name, or form a company, this does not necessarily mean that you are at a disadvantage. Create a name, obtain an email address and then you are globally identifiable by that name. There are many free website offers on the internet – create a web page identifying your business and business name. In time you can register a business name or form a company or other legal entity, whichever is applicable in your country.

The Golden Rules of Trading

Before you begin to trade make sure you have grasped these seven golden rules of trade:

1. You will always source and/or verify the owner of goods as being a supplier and not another seller.

2. You will not accept telephone calls or instigate international phone calls, fax messages, or the like until you reach contracting stage. Such phone calls result in large and frightening phone bills. Use the internet and email as your main communication tool. If you are put on the spot and asked to give specific information relating to a deal (which is later proven to be incorrect) this could be held to be legally binding. The intermediary must spend time thinking about the response and provide all answers in writing. It would be wise not to include your telephone number on your letterhead especially when you are just beginning to trade.

3. The nature of business is strictly confidential. Nobody is to find out the identity of your suppliers or end buyers. If you are looking for a supplier introduce yourself as a 'buyer'. If you are looking among intermediaries to sell goods introduce yourself as a 'seller'. Even when you close a deal never disclose the source of your supplier as in doing so you may lose a hard-sourced principal. The supplier will find out who the end buyer is eventually – this cannot be avoided – so let that happen naturally as part of the transaction without any

input from you. You are protecting commission: trying to protect the disclosure of the principals once the deal closes is a futile exercise. Don't think for one moment that a supplier or end buyer once secured is your permanent client. Your only concern is earning commissions on any deal at any given time. The principals may use you again or they may not – that's not the issue. Once you secure the DLC of the end buyer, the fact that it is irrevocable protects you from circumvention. It does not matter if the end buyer finds out who the supplier is after the DLC has been secured.

4.   'PPI' or Policy Proof of Interest is never given prior to the DLC deposit being accepted from the end buyer. You must therefore never offer proof of goods or your interests therein until such time as this has occurred.

5.   The terms 'UCP600', 'Bank', 'Transferable' and 'Irrevocable' must be applied at all times to the type of financial instrument you request from an end buyer. When asking for a pre-advised type of credit, this credit must be advised as confirmed. First time traders must ask for all credits to be issued as confirmed.

6.   All fees relating to the transfer of the credit must be incorporated into the costs of the goods for the account of the end buyer and all contracts, or even offers, should state this from the beginning.

7.   A performance guarantee is never offered to an end buyer first – neither an active or inactive one. A DLC is always the first instrument that must be presented from the end buyer to the seller once contracts have been sealed.

More Practice Makes Best Practice

You will learn and become more confident as you trade correctly. It is important to memorize the important aspects of trading as explained here, and in particular to identify 'RF' deals as soon as you receive them. This will all come with practice. You start by researching 'buyers' and 'sellers' on the internet. In all your dealings make sure you have everything confirmed in writing, but ensure you don't promise anything that cannot be delivered. If you are wary or uncertain of a proposal, don't reply at that point: answer only when you know what to say. At the beginning, it is of fundamental importance that you remind yourself that by responding to 'RF' deals you understand that you are only practising methods of reply. You should not imply anywhere in this correspondence that you are moving forward on a deal, but that you are merely considering their offer. Once the deal proves unworkable or unacceptable, reject the enquiry and provide a simple reason for the rejection, such as 'Regrettably we are unable to work to your procedures'. Drafting and sending these types of responses will reinforce the right maxims in your mind, and you will commit them to memory more quickly.

There are Trades to be Done

Before you become overwhelmed in the process that is international trade, remember – if you are not in it for the long haul you're wasting your time. What does 'long haul' mean? In reality it means three years or more. It's extremely difficult to close a bulk export deal, not because of the overall process but because it is difficult to get all the parameters set up in such a way to create a viable transaction. When you do finally secure supply you cannot find an end buyer, and when you have an end buyer a supplier that you had previously secured becomes unavailable.

At the time of writing two intermediaries who have read and understood the rules detailed in this book contacted FTN Exporting to state that they have closed deals within 14 months of practising and studying the rules. Although it would not be impossible to expect to close these deals earlier it would be considered very rare. Like many areas of in-depth study, an apprentice in any field of endeavour would usually take four to five years of training before being classed as a proficient and skilful master of their trade. Trading as an import/export intermediary to become a viable buyer/seller takes time and practice. Contrary to the views of most misguided intermediaries on the internet, the skills required in order to become a successful intermediary are like undertaking a form of higher education.

To obtain all the right trading parameters is difficult even at the best of times so when a viable deal does come your way, you are in a much better position if you know what needs to be done well in advance and are ready to act. You need to minimize the risk of letting one genuine opportunity slip by you for lack of procedural knowledge. Invest your time in learning the business.

Don't try and learn the business when that deal you've been chasing for so long finally falls into your lap.

The idea is to practice, learn and find faults while you trade and slowly but surely eliminate the faults as you perfect your skill level. The way you'll trade in the beginning will be totally different in three months time. The way you trade in three months' time will be totally different in three years' time. You will automatically learn to consider or disregard offers and requests at the blink of an eye as your confidence builds, and reach the stage where you are easily rejecting ambiguous enquiries without much effort at all so that most of your time can be spent replying only to potentially viable enquiries.

Starting the Office

It's Friday night and the weekend is looming. What will your very first approach be? First of all let's take a look at what's out there today. You've opened your internet browser and, for the next few hours, you are going to study the type of deals you will be keeping away from.

BROWSER EXERCISE AND RESEARCH

1.   Go to http://www.alibaba.com Alibaba.com Limited (China) (online). A front page will open which displays numerous products, buyers and sellers.

2.   Click on 'Agriculture'. This will take you to a subheading and second listing. Browse through this area and familiarize yourself with the layout and details provided.

3.   Let's take a look in the 'Agrochemicals and Fertilizers' section. Click on the 'Fertilizer' link.

4.   Have a look at the fertilizers and other goods, in particular those listed under the general term 'Urea' which is a heavily traded global commodity. If a listing for goods has the name of the manufacturer, go to their website. If the company is in fact the manufacturer then you have found a real supplier. Many other listings will also have this information, including any potential end buyer. Remember that the end buyer or supplier will in all likelihood receive many quotes

for a particular product on a daily basis, or indeed be inundated with offers. If you see references to LOI, BCL and other unworkable terms during these searches then you know you are generally dealing with intermediaries and not suppliers.

5.   Now let's go to a real supplier's website. Go to: http://www.pdvsa. com Petróleos de Venezuela SA (Brazil) (online). This is a good example of a genuine supplier's website.

6.   Next, have a look at the front page of this site http://www. ftnexporting.com FTN Exporting (Australia) (online). This is an intermediary site.

7.   Try http://www.gazprom.com OAO Gazprom (Russia) (online) (English language website). This is another supplier's site.

Start a collection of manufacturers' details as you research the market, either by book-marking their websites or making a note of them in another way. Tradeboards are generally a waste of time. If you are serious about succeeding as an international trade intermediary you will need to do business amongst corporate giants in the international arena. You should therefore begin to send enquiries directly to suppliers: if you are able to source a genuine supply of quality goods that are competitively priced, you are in a strong position to secure an end buyer. However, the difficulty lies in securing goods at precisely the time at which an end buyer wants to buy them. However, if you research suppliers now, you'll have this information on hand to seek immediate quotations if you receive a strong or potentially viable sourcing request. To refine your search techniques the websites in the following paragraphs are very useful when you are researching potential deals or conducting due diligence in relation to a specific enquiry. There are many sites like these, and you will benefit greatly by learning how to find them: some of them are not easily found using obvious key words.

A research site is ideal for obtaining up-to-the-minute fuel and other commodity prices; as a guide try http://www.nymex.com New York Mercantile Exchange (USA) (online) or, where specific information is required, take a look at sites such as http://www.sugartech.co.za/factories/index.php Sugar Factories of the World (South Africa) (online).

If you have an offer purporting to sell crude oil from a country you don't know much about, learn how to research it by accessing vital information from a site like http://www.cia.gov/library/publications/the-world-factbook/index. html Central Intelligence Agency (USA) (online).

If you need to find real specifications for exportable sugar products try the following site: http://www.copersucar.com.br Cooperativa de Productores de Cana-de-açúcar, Açúcar e Álcool do Estado de São Paulo (Brazil) (online).

The more extensive your preliminary research is the better placed you will be when a viable deal comes along.

So if you receive an enquiry that is giving you all sorts of strange advice about sugar then go to a site such as http://www.almac.co.uk/personal/roberts/ icumsa.html Cane Sugar Trust Limited (UK) (online) to get to the truth of the matter.

Don't forget to study your own market. Find local suppliers in your own country or state using the Yellow Pages directory or similar. You will need access to many of the same type of suppliers so that when you do receive a potentially viable enquiry, you will be able to send out multiple sourcing letters to many suppliers over a short period of time.

Rather than just waiting for an enquiry to buy, use some of your contacts to ask for a quote for one of the most sought-after commodities. If you receive an offer from a supplier you can then proactively initiate your own offer to sell. Researching and identifying numerous suppliers on the internet is a good start but getting them to confirm your purchase is another matter altogether which we will look at in detail later. Develop your search engine skills, as they are sure to serve you well later on.

Ambiguous Offers

As well as sourcing potential suppliers, you also need to familiarize yourself with the types of offers that you will be sent via the internet that should be avoided at all costs.

Here is a typical example of one 'seller' offering Urea on the Alibaba site that was found within seconds of browsing the website. Details have been altered to protect privacy and to avoid any embarrassment. Try to spot what is wrong with this offer:

> *We are real sellers of Urea, Cement, Sugar, used rails and all other kinds of scrap steel at ASWP CIF prices. Please contact us with a ready LOI and BCL. Please note NC/ND and MPA agreement must be in place first.*

Whenever you see terms such as ASWP, LOI, BCL, POP, NCND agreements, FFDLC, ICPO, RWA and MPA, just to name a few, you can be assured that most of these offers are not genuine, or cannot close as far as an intermediary is concerned. Even if the source using such terms turns out to be genuine, an intermediary would be unable to initiate the procedures as requested to close such a deal. Any offers which make reference to terminology such as 'seller's side' and 'buyer's side' should be avoided at all times. Similarly you should not approach these individuals or companies for quotations. Terms such as 'US$2.00 commission on seller's side' (and/or buyer's side) are also to be avoided.

If, at the beginning of your trading career, you decide to answer these requests do so only for a short time to get a feel for the trading platform and to test yourself as to your awareness of how NOT to trade. For example, let us assume you have read a request on a trade site asking for a quotation for sugar. The language used is dubious and there are several references to strange trading terms. You might decide to respond in any event, which you would word like this (make sure you use a good letterhead in all formal replies):

PIA Import/Export
Box 123 Camino Drive
Hollywood
Los Angeles
USA 920910

Buyers and Sellers of Exportable Commodities

PIA Applies UCP600 and INCOTERMS 2000 Rules of Trade.

Facsimile: 801 881 08888 Phone: 801 881 09999

Transaction Code/Ref: PIASUG001

Validity: Not valid if a reply is not given within 5 days of issuance.

Seller: PIA Import/Export

Date: (for facsimile transmissions)

Dear Sir,

We write with reference to your recent request for a quotation for sugar. Please find below our provisional quotation for your consideration.

ICUMSA 45 grade sugar is currently available at US$310 F.O.B per MT but before we furnish you with a firm offer please note. We do not accept transactions that request 'LOI/BCL etc'. We apply ICC Incoterms 2000 rules of trade and UCP600 rules for the issuance of financial instruments.

Our procedures are as follows.

(1) Quotation (2) Offer (3) Contract (4) Payment is deposited by buyer first (5) P.G. is provided by seller if offered (6) Delivery is instigated as per contact.

If you feel you are able to adhere to these procedures for the purpose of the transaction please advise us and we will issue a full formal offer. If however you are not able to perform as per these requirements we will not be able to service your enquiry. We are able to protect commission at a reasonable rate if necessary.

Should you have any queries please do not hesitate to contact us.

Yours faithfully

PIA
PIA Import/Export

It's good to challenge ambiguous requests during the learning process. Later on, once you are able to identify flawed offers and enquiries, you won't want to waste time replying to them and will delete them from your inbox once you have identified them as flawed. Some traders/brokers may try to challenge you. Again, you might want to reply to test your knowledge. If by any small and unlikely chance at this early stage it transpires that you are trading with a real end buyer requesting a formal offer for goods you have sourced, reply a few days later stating words to this effect:

PIA Import/Export
Box 123 Camino Drive
Hollywood
Los Angeles
USA 920910

Buyers and Sellers of Exportable Commodities

PIA Applies UCP600 and INCOTERMS 2000 Rules of Trade.

Facsimile: 801 881 08888 Phone: 801 881 09999

Transaction Code/Ref: PIASUG001

Validity: Not Valid if a reply is not given within 5 days of issuance.

Seller: PIA Import/Export

Dear Sir,

It is with regret that we must inform you that on this occasion the goods for which you have been provisionally quoted, and bearing the above transaction code, are no longer available at this time. We may be able to offer sugar some time in the future. Please confirm whether you would like to be informed of any availability on a first come first served basis.

Yours faithfully

PIA

There is no point attempting to trade at this stage – especially when you don't have access to supply and in any event it's too early to be thrown into the deep end, so don't be tempted!

Here is an example of the type of reply you might receive from a 'seller' in response to your request for a quotation:

Dear PIA,

Thank you for your enquiry. Please find below a quotation for your consideration.

Quote: ICUMSA 45 Sugar 50,000 MT FOB US$320 per MT Payable 100% on presentation of clean bill of lading. We apply Incoterms 2000 Delivery Rules.

Our procedures are: buyer issue to seller signed LOI with BCL as well as NCND agreement. Buyer opens FFDLC transferable credit. Seller issues 2 percent Performance Bond.

Please reply if acceptable. Please issue LOI with BCL.

Signed

Idiotic Sugar Company

The PIA has realized the whole transaction is suspect because many flawed terms are used. It is also apparent that this 'seller' is simply another ill-informed and misguided intermediary who really does not know how to trade correctly. Apart from LOI and BCL, what's the biggest giveaway that this seller is an intermediary? They have requested a transferable credit. This immediately identifies them to the PIA as an intermediary and not a supplier because (as we shall see later on) a 'transferable credit' can only be transferred once. If the PIA did eventually issue a transferable credit to this seller, the seller could not actually transfer the credit to the supplier for the goods and the deal would collapse.

Since UCP600 banking rules apply in this situation, it is obvious that the seller has no regard for or knowledge of the rules regarding the transfer of the credit. UCP600 notwithstanding, the fact that the credit can only be transferred once is still a prohibitive factor. There are indeed a few banks that do not use UCP600 credits, but they usually have their own in-house rules regarding credits that are not dissimilar from the provisions of UCP regulations. The credit, which must be transferable, can only be transferred once which means that either the PIA or the other intermediary buyer/seller could accept the financial instrument, but not both of them.

In years gone by, 'back to back' transactions were possible. Today's environment does not lend itself to these types of deals. A bank will not accept as security one credit so that another can be opened. Therefore if the PIA accepted a credit that was not transferable, they would have to use their own money to open another credit of a lesser value in favour of their supplier or another intermediary who would do the same. This is called a 'back to back' transaction, which was a method used in the past by wealthy merchants but which cannot be used by intermediaries now, unless they use their own funds. However this type of expense is prohibitive to most intermediaries. In spite of this fact you will still come across these types of procedures on the internet today. So to recap, a seller is not always the supplier and the buyer is not always the end buyer.

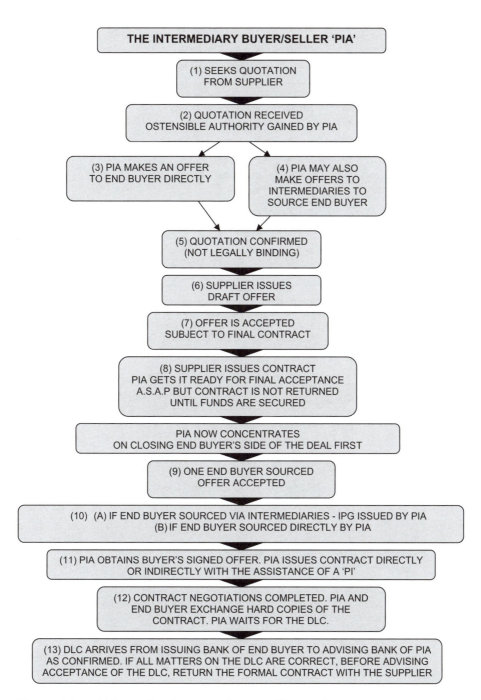

Figure 5.1   Schematic of intermediary trading path

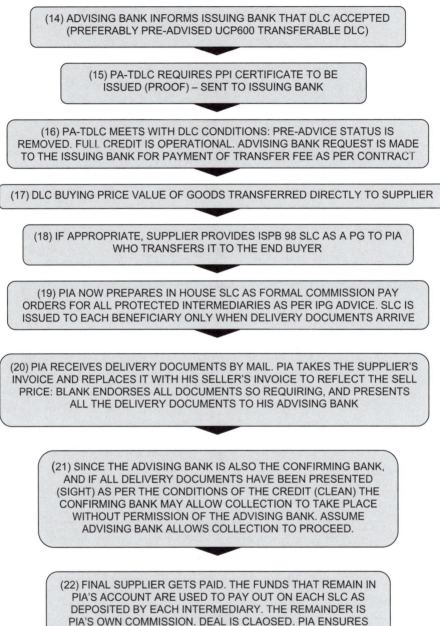

(14) ADVISING BANK INFORMS ISSUING BANK THAT DLC ACCEPTED (PREFERABLY PRE-ADVISED UCP600 TRANSFERABLE DLC)

(15) PA-TDLC REQUIRES PPI CERTIFICATE TO BE ISSUED (PROOF) – SENT TO ISSUING BANK

(16) PA-TDLC MEETS WITH DLC CONDITIONS: PRE-ADVICE STATUS IS REMOVED. FULL CREDIT IS OPERATIONAL. ADVISING BANK REQUEST IS MADE TO THE ISSUING BANK FOR PAYMENT OF TRANSFER FEE AS PER CONTRACT

(17) DLC BUYING PRICE VALUE OF GOODS TRANSFERRED DIRECTLY TO SUPPLIER

(18) IF APPROPRIATE, SUPPLIER PROVIDES ISPB 98 SLC AS A PG TO PIA WHO TRANSFERS IT TO THE END BUYER

(19) PIA NOW PREPARES IN HOUSE SLC AS FORMAL COMMISSION PAY ORDERS FOR ALL PROTECTED INTERMEDIARIES AS PER IPG ADVICE. SLC IS ISSUED TO EACH BENEFICIARY ONLY WHEN DELIVERY DOCUMENTS ARRIVE

(20) PIA RECEIVES DELIVERY DOCUMENTS BY MAIL. PIA TAKES THE SUPPLIER'S INVOICE AND REPLACES IT WITH HIS SELLER'S INVOICE TO REFLECT THE SELL PRICE: BLANK ENDORSES ALL DOCUMENTS SO REQUIRING, AND PRESENTS ALL THE DELIVERY DOCUMENTS TO HIS ADVISING BANK

(21) SINCE THE ADVISING BANK IS ALSO THE CONFIRMING BANK, AND IF ALL DELIVERY DOCUMENTS HAVE BEEN PRESENTED (SIGHT) AS PER THE CONDITIONS OF THE CREDIT (CLEAN) THE CONFIRMING BANK MAY ALLOW COLLECTION TO TAKE PLACE WITHOUT PERMISSION OF THE ADVISING BANK. ASSUME ADVISING BANK ALLOWS COLLECTION TO PROCEED.

(22) FINAL SUPPLIER GETS PAID. THE FUNDS THAT REMAIN IN PIA'S ACCOUNT ARE USED TO PAY OUT ON EACH SLC AS DEPOSITED BY EACH INTERMEDIARY. THE REMAINDER IS PIA'S OWN COMMISSION. DEAL IS CLAOSED. PIA ENSURES THAT PHYSICAL DELIVERY IS MET.

Figure 5.2   Schematic of intermediary trading path

6

The String Contract

In theory there can be many people involved in a string contract. For example, from the PIA to the end buyer, there could be eight people involved before the end buyer is reached as indicated below:

Implicit 'Buyer's Side'

End buyer

Intermediary next to the end buyer (PI – or primary intermediary)

Sourcing intermediary

Sourcing intermediary

Sourcing intermediary

Sourcing intermediary

Sourcing intermediary

Sourcing intermediary

Sourcing intermediary next to the PIA (PI)

The PIA (The buyer/seller)

Implicit 'Seller's Side'

Similarly from the PIA to the supplier there could be, for example, three intermediaries:

The PIA (the buyer/seller)

Sourcing intermediary next to the PIA (PI)

Sourcing intermediary

Sourcing intermediary next to the supplier (PI)

Supplier

As with the 'buyer's side' this 'seller's side' group reports to the PIA. (Don't confuse these sides with 'buyer's side' and 'seller's side' commissions, which you will often see with RF internet deals.) The PIA provides one contract to a buying principal and a separate contract to the selling principal. Both sides remain totally independent of each other and are connected only by virtue of the PIA.

Therefore the PIA has two sets of commissions to secure and protect, two different contracts and in fact two entirely separate transactions. It is perhaps evident from the above example to understand why intermediaries are so often confused about the correct way to trade. When the two separate 'sides' are drawn together the whole transaction would look like this:

a)   End buyer.

b)   Intermediary next to the end buyer. Often this intermediary is confused and call themselves a mandate holder of the end buyer – without documentary proof they are simply an intermediary.

c)   Sourcing intermediary.

d)   Sourcing intermediary.

e)   Sourcing intermediary.

f)   Sourcing intermediary.

g)   Sourcing intermediary.

h)   Sourcing intermediary.

i)   Sourcing intermediary next to the PIA.

j)   The PIA (the buyer/seller).

k)   Sourcing intermediary next to the PIA.

l)   Sourcing intermediary.

m)   Sourcing intermediary next to the supplier.

n)   Supplier.

Again, intermediaries next to the 'supplier' often refer to themselves as a 'seller' or 'mandate holder' of the supplier but will not produce their paperwork to verify this position. This is the intermediary who most often causes problems in a string contract, because they do not understand that if a PIA transfers a credit to them, then the PIA is unable to transfer the credit a second time to the supplier. Therefore the deal simply falls apart at this stage. In any event this type of 'seller' is often found offering goods not from a supplier but from another, even more confused, sourcing intermediary.

A total of 14 people are involved in this deal. Three of them are principals, and 11 are intermediaries looking to collect commission for assisting or simply passing information on from the PIA, who in effect has to protect the interests of both sides.

It is not uncommon to encounter these types of string contracts. The longer the 'string' the more difficult the deal becomes for the PIA to manage. Understandably the PIA puts a lot of effort into this type of deal, so before even considering this they need to instruct their PI on both sides to ensure that the sourcing intermediaries understand that they must 'step back' at the required time to expose the principals. The PIA will look at the information as supplied by their PI before making the commitment to become the 'buyer/seller'. A better string contract would involve fewer sourcing intermediaries especially on the all-important 'seller's side'. While training in the first month or so it is all right to get involved in string deals, even only with the status of a sourcing intermediary who is promised commission by another person. You will soon be persuaded that being an intermediary in these types of deals is simply unworkable. These deals do not have a PIA or 'buyer/seller' and therefore the probability that you will be circumvented is high. As you gain experience you will be able to spot these deals and avoid them.

The PI

The PIA will be relying on receiving information from the two primary (sourcing) intermediaries (abbreviated to PI) to control and keep informed the other intermediaries, especially when it is time to 'step back'. So what do the two primary intermediaries do? Initially they acquire the required personal details and information of the other intermediaries involved in the deal and pass this information on to the PIA. Then they ensure that all the intermediaries on their side step back so as to allow the PIA to have a clear pathway to the principals – the end buyer and the supplier. Throughout the lifespan of the deal they keep the other intermediaries on their 'side' updated as to the progress of the deal. This prevents the PIA from being bombarded by intermediaries while they are trying to close the deal.

Primary intermediaries are usually trusted traders who have a prior association with the PIA, either through an ongoing relationship that has grown online or a trader with whom the PIA has no prior relationship but invites them to assist as their special PI agent. If you only intend to trade as a sourcing intermediary the buyer/seller or the PIA is a very good person to know. The biggest obstacle that intermediaries have to overcome is the issue of trust in relation to the payment of commissions. Once sourcing intermediaries realize that they can trust the PIA to secure and pay out commissions owed to them, they take their positions in the string contract and assist by supervising the other sourcing intermediaries on their respective sides. This 'trust and assist' doctrine baffles many intermediaries because most of them have not built up any relationship with a buyer/seller such as a PIA.

Consider the following scenario: An end buyer wants to buy goods from a supplier, but they do not want to pay for anything until they are able to handle and physically see the goods first, because the end buyer simply does not *trust* the supplier, who is many thousands of miles away, to fulfil the contract.

Similarly, the supplier does not want to sell goods to an end buyer without receiving payment first, because the supplier does not *trust* the end buyer. Both parties need an intermediary who they can *trust* to look after their interests; both parties to a deal seek the assistance of their bank to mediate in the deal. These financial intermediaries are requested to provide their services because they can be trusted to do so, and earn commission for these services in the process. The import/export intermediary also trusts their bank to look after their interests.

The advising bank deals with the issuing bank and the supplier's bank. Each bank has to abide by rules relating to the way in which they trade with one another. If a sourcing intermediary cannot close a deal as a buyer/seller then they need to trust another intermediary to act on their behalf otherwise commission will never be secured. Intermediaries must trade in the same way as everyone else in the international trade arena.

In the 14-party example given above the deal usually collapses at the 'stepping back' stage because the primary intermediary next to the principal end buyer or supplier mistakenly thinks that their position is in some way superior to that of the other sourcing intermediaries. Being the intermediary next to the principal does not entitle the intermediary to refer to themselves as a 'mandate' of that principal, unless the mandateship is disclosed in writing. A PI next to an end principal may even attempt to force the PIA to step back to expose the other side's principal, which is something that cannot happen if the PIA wants to retain control of the deal. If the PIA did step back they would also lose not only their commission but also the commission of all the other intermediaries. There is no guarantee that these would be paid by the other PI because of the lack of a relationship of trust.

When an intermediary purports to hold a mandateship but cannot produce paperwork to prove their position, FTN Exporting advises their PI to tell the trader that their disclosed agency principal is prepared to protect and secure the trader's commission. If the trader still does not step back FTN Exporting drops the entire deal immediately, treating it as RF.

No PIA to Attach To

If a sourcing intermediary cannot find a trustworthy PIA, then the intermediary must learn as quickly as possible to become the buyer/seller themselves. There is no other option in their business. Only the buyer/seller can guarantee that the payment of commission will occur. It is with this insight that the aim of an intermediary should be to become a buyer/seller and not become complacent with the idea that they can remain a sourcing intermediary forever. Being a sourcing intermediary is the step you take in order to learn how to become a PIA. Using the advice provided by this book a PIA would expect to become an entity who was fully trustworthy, but that is not to say that all entities holding the position of buyer/seller applying the edicts in this book are all trustworthy. The intermediary learns whom they can and cannot trust. In any event the intermediary becomes dependent on themselves alone. Therefore for this reason the sourcing intermediary MUST eventually attain the position of buyer/seller if they want a 100 per cent guarantee of being able to secure commission.

Intermediaries in a string contract have to understand that, unless they work together on a transaction, they should refrain from trying to trade using methods that cannot work – after all, the whole purpose of the business is to make a profit! The primary intermediaries closest to the PIA on both sides clear the path to the final PIs closest to the buyer and supplier on either side of the deal. Therefore both PIs next to the PIA are the most influential intermediaries in the string contract after the PIA. As such the PIA treats them as an asset to their business at all times. In order to proceed with a string contract, no matter how many or how few parties there are within it, the following outcome must be achieved:

a)   The PI next to the PIA clears the pathway on behalf of the PIA.

b)   If the PI encounters resistance with the PI next to the supplier or end buyer they negotiate with them.

c)   This leads both the end buyer and the supplier exposed to the PIA. One side is stopped from transacting with the other by the PIA, who in effect, eliminates circumvention from occurring.

Remember, the ideal trading scenario is a PIA trading on their own without the attachment of other intermediaries. It is others who are in need of the PIA's ability to close a deal, not the other way round. Thus the PIA does not need to tolerate the nonsense that often prevails within a string contract. In any case the PIA would have secured the supplier, so in offering goods to an intermediary buying string the PIA has little tolerance of time wasters.

Trying to get a supplier's PI and end buyer's PI to step back in the same deal is very difficult and on many occasions it will not happen. It is for this reason that the PIA should primarily attempt to secure the supplier themselves, or through a trusted PI with whom they already have a working relationship. If a supplier can be secured in this way, it allows the PIA to concentrate their efforts on persuading only one PI to step back. The final course initiated by the PI allows the PIA to close contracts directly with the end buyer and supplier.

The transaction commences when a quotation is first issued. The whole group bears witness to this event, as the offer is passed through the string to the end buyer. After the quotation is provided and the offer is accepted, the PI on any given side makes all the other intermediaries step back. This leaves only the parties to the respective contracts to remain active in the transaction, which makes sense, given that the other individuals are not concerned with the terms and conditions of the contract. The intermediaries remain in the background until either success or failure of the deal is recorded. The PIA may continue to use the closest PI on the appropriate side of the deal at contract stage to update the rest of the intermediaries on the deal as required. It is very important to maintain transparency throughout, and not to exclude or be deemed to exclude any of the parties in the string deal. Shutting out an entity is likely to cause serious harm to the trust built up in the group and the deal as a result has a higher chance of collapsing. Thanks to the PIA's virtue and good intent, the transaction remains transparent and open until either failure or success eventuates.

Of course the best trading scenario is one that does not include any intermediaries at all and consists only of the PIA, the supplier and the end buyer. This is the most difficult situation to achieve, as usually intermediaries appear on one side or the other. Sometimes these can be relatives of principals who appear from nowhere claiming to be mandate holders.

As we have already seen in any transaction the PIA is handling two contracts which are entirely independent of each other. It is not a simple task! However getting the contracts agreed on both sides of the deal will be made considerably easier with the presence of good and trusted intermediaries with a relatively small string contract. Like the PIA, FTN Exporting often prefers to secure suppliers direct and to use only one or a few trusted intermediaries on the buyer's side in any given deal, who in turn often give the offer to other sourcing intermediaries (from which the string deal grows). The PIA, as a buyer/seller, guides and mentors intermediaries under their protection to source potential end buyers. In turn the intermediaries look for buyers for the PIA and, once a suitable buyer has been found, ensure that the end buyer can be exposed to the PIA for contract negotiation and signature. Once a deal has been successfully closed the PIA secures the commission and pays each trusted intermediary who assisted in finding the end buyer. It is advisable not to trust intermediaries on the seller's side except those who are close to the actual supplier and who know exactly how to verify goods. The PIA is therefore assured that the goods are real and that the act of stepping back will indeed expose the actual supplier. Anyone trying to close a deal as a private import/export intermediary must use the above method.

Many people involved in the import/export industry who are acting on behalf of a disclosed or undisclosed principal are using similar rules of trade without realizing it: ship masters, shipping agents, forwarders, mercantile agents, stock brokers, couriers, transport personnel amongst others are often acting in a position defined by rules of agency as per the agency rules or laws of their own country.

Why NCND Agreements Don't Secure Commission

The sourcing intermediary who does not take the position of a buyer/seller in any string contract must seek the protection of and be attached to an informed, honourable buyer/seller if they are to have any chance of claiming commission in a successful deal. The use of a NCND (Non-Circumvention Non-Disclosure Agreements) agreement, the type often seen touted by uninformed sourcing intermediaries, is about non-disclosure of relevant details of the deal they are attempting to close, and confidentially relating to the deal. When intermediaries are involved in a deal it is often an intermediary seller who issues the NCND and/or MPA (Master Pay Agreement).

The purpose of the NCND agreement is one of confidentiality as it pertains to each intermediary involved in the deal, with each another as well as with the seller. This does not bind the end buyer or supplier: these matters are only of concern to the middle controlling 'buyer/seller'. Accordingly, it defeats the very nature of an NCND agreement that a protective mechanism is in force within the intermediaries' collective realm, when each one is listed on the same document and disclosed to everyone else. This is especially the case if a MPA is attached.

Some intermediaries get a greater share of commission than others in the same side of any deal. The amount of commission depends on the level of involvement in the deal. If intermediaries are privy to each other's commission payments it can and often does create friction within the deal. Sometimes it can cause the deal to collapse, not because of any irregularities, but purely because of greed. An NCND agreement does nothing to appease the situation. If an intermediary who at first agreed to step back to expose their principal later becomes stubborn and obstructive it is not considered circumvention to bypass this person if it is in the interests of the deal to do so. Why must the deal collapse because of one person?

The NCND and MPA documents are often produced in a deal that is very far from being closed. Intermediaries are often asked to reveal sensitive information such as banking details, which are also viewed by all, involved in the deal. Although in a Utopian world it would be nice to know that we can all trust each other this is not the case in the real world. Business is business – friendship must not be relied on as a prerequisite to a successful trade. Intermediaries have been known to act dishonourably on many fronts including using the type of information found on MPA documents and NCND agreements. The business between an intermediary and an intermediate buyer/seller must be conducted on a personal and private level, and should not be subject to manipulation by other intermediaries. When something goes wrong the buyer/ seller is held accountable and advises each intermediary individually as to what went wrong. The process is made much more difficult when intermediaries are all blaming each other for the collapse of a deal especially if there is an NCND agreement and MPA document. Using a NCND agreement to claim circumvention amongst a group of intermediaries will make no difference to the outcome.

A breach of an NCND agreement does not constitute either a loss of profit or loss of potential gains. Even if the breach is pinpointed at the very end of a successful deal, there aren't many intermediaries who can afford the millions of dollars it would cost to prove that a breach of an NCND agreement has in fact led to a loss of gains. One cannot take action to recoup only 'potential gains' without first proving that such gains have been realized. The NCND agreement cannot bridge the matter of confidentiality all the way to proving the loss of any gains.

When claiming circumvention in any particular trade, you first have to prove that the deal has closed. Given the very nature of circumvention, which is to prove that you have been cut out of the deal, it is very difficult if not impossible to prove because you are not a party to the final contract of sale. The NCND agreement or MPA does not provide sufficient evidence to link that relationship to the contract between supplier and end buyer. If you are unable to prove that the deal has closed, how can you then prove that you have suffered loss in relation to that deal?

Let us suppose that you can prove that the deal has closed. You then need to show entitlement to commission by producing the MPA. The MPA must show a direct correlation to the deal that has closed. Even if all these elements are in place to prove the loss, the intermediary is very unlikely to be able to fund the cost of international commercial litigation. If the 'buyer/seller' has kept all the commission in the transaction, they will be in funds to be able to defend themselves against claims of circumvention by an intermediary.

Remember that the whole purpose of an MPA is to allow the disclosure of one principal to another. Often all intermediaries agree to step back once matters of the MPA are settled, leaving the end buyer to close the deal directly with the supplier or indirectly with the buyer/seller. What is to stop the two principals letting this deal collapse on the understanding that they enter into a new agreement, weeks later, with a different transaction code? This is why an intermediary holding the position of buyer/seller as defined under URPIB rules of trade would never allow any part of an intermediary chain on one side of the deal to contact the other. This ensures at the very least that should a deal fail, the supplier is unable to connect with the end buyer.

The MPA agreement is a separate document given privately to each intermediary involved in a deal with the buyer/seller. Those intermediaries may indeed have a business relationship with the seller. The seller issues a pay order, the information on which must remain confidential. If the deal closes and commission becomes payable and one intermediary has disclosed their payment to others, this intermediary could lose their share because they have breached confidentiality with the seller. Therefore the true relationship of any NCND or MPA with the intermediary is that which is issued by the buyer/seller. It has nothing to do with the business between the buyer/seller and their principals, or the contract that the buyer/seller enters into with the end buyer or supplier.

The contract between the principal parties will address issues pertaining to confidentiality and disclosure. It will likely be in breach of contract for a principal to disclose any contractual matters to intermediaries involved in any associated chain. This matter is of utmost importance; the supplier may be able to sell goods to a middle buyer as long as the buyer does not imply that the goods are heading to a country in which the supplier already has an agent. In such a situation the supplier would need to know that details of the transaction are going to be held in the strictest confidence.

The supplier could indeed breach their contract with the middle buyer/seller if a group of misguided intermediaries later contacted the supplier directly to find out if the deal is closing. This would give the supplier the right to cancel the middle buyer's order for 'breach of confidentiality'. Therefore the seller cannot disclose specific matters relating to the transaction to intermediaries, even if those intermediaries themselves are all holding NCND agreements with the buyer/seller. The whole idea that the activities of an occasional intermediary are dependent upon the merits of a NCND/MPA to be able to collect commissions is simply not viable: especially if all that is done is that one side is disclosed to the other. In practice, it creates a very precarious situation and must be avoided at all costs.

The MPA is supplied in two parts: the first part is a personal guarantee given only to the named intermediary being protected, the beneficiary. If the beneficiary rightfully earns money in relation to a deal and, for instance, dies before collecting the gains the payment becomes part of the estate. The person entitled to receive the payment then becomes a matter for the executors to determine under the terms of the will. Imagine if this document had seven other beneficiaries named on the same MPA: if this was allowed to occur, not only would it create legal difficulties but some of the other intermediaries may try to take advantage of the situation by making further claims on the commission amount. These seven others are also in a precarious position, because the full commission amount is held by the middle controlling intermediate buyer/seller protecting the deal. There is only one person who can be assured that commission will be earned if a deal closes – the buyer/seller themselves. In fact sourcing intermediaries are at the mercy of the buyer/seller at all times, no matter what type of document they hold giving assurance of commission payments. As sourcing intermediaries must step back in order to allow the deal to close, they do not control the deal. However, if no one 'stepped back' there would be no deal. They could resort to litigation, but for a private individual or novice trader the costs of international litigation could be prohibitive. In reality, if one does not hold the position of buyer/seller, then in fact the chances of securing commission are greatly diminished. For such reasons the buyer/seller places no value whatsoever in any NCND/MPA documents. The nature of business as it relates to the closing of the deal is associated not with the intermediaries involved in bringing both parties together, but with the principal parties to the contract of purchase and sale.

For in-house use, FTN Exporting has renamed the MPA an IPG (Intermediary Protection Guarantee). By virtue of this document the seller personally guarantees unconditionally that, should a deal close as per the conditions on the IPG, then the seller owes the guaranteed sum to the beneficiary. An IPG is issued at the start of the transaction and only after an offer is ready for acceptance by the end buyer. The second part which consists of the actual financial instrument is provided by the buyer/seller to each intermediary at the time the goods are paid for, or just before the funds enter into the account of the buyer/seller (and therefore just about to be accepted).

The personal guarantee is the first part of the IPG that acts as a prerequisite to the second part, which is the issuance of the SLC as backed by its guarantee. You cannot use the guarantee on its own to make a claim for payment – it must be supported by an instrument that can be presented and collected. If the in-house SLC fails, and funds cannot be collected, the guarantee becomes important. Failure to perform as per the terms of your personal guarantee is enforceable in the courts. It is therefore evident that the personal guarantee is more reliable for the intermediary than NCND and MPA documents.

The buyer/seller issues a UCP600 in-house DLC (defined by UCP600 as of July 2007). This kind of SLC is issued as backed by the funds already in the account of the buyer/seller when they have accepted the DLC for payment of the goods. The single specific instruction on the SLC tells each intermediary when they should deposit the SLC into their bank and apply for collection of their commission payment from the intermediate buyer/seller's account (the same account used to accept the end buyer's DLC for payment of the goods). The virtue of this procedure speaks for itself: if an intermediary were to deposit the SLC for collection from their own bank, from which a dishonourable seller/buyer has already taken the entire commission amount for themselves leaving their own account bare of any funds, then each beneficiary could indeed face fraud charges for attempting to defraud a bank by falsely representing that the credit was worth something, when in fact it was not.

In this case, any criminal investigation would reveal that each intermediary acted in good faith – because they would be able to produce their IPG in evidence. Investigators would chase after the dishonourable buyer/seller and, at the very least, verify the details on the IPG. Any denials by the buyer/seller will lead them further into trouble, to the extent that their accounts could be frozen and documents seized, which would reveal a wealth of information concerning the buyer's/seller's activities. What if the deal never closed? If the buyer/seller never earned any commission, they should have at least mitigated their own position after issuing the SLC by informing all intermediaries not to deposit the SLC into their respective accounts. In any case the intermediaries would still be cleared of any wrongdoing but the buyer/seller could still be charged with fraud.

However, if the intermediaries deposit their SLCs into their account expecting to be paid and the buyer/seller has fled to another country with all the commission, then the intermediaries may not be able to avoid fraud charges so easily. All the intermediaries affected would need to unite in an attempt to convince the authorities that it was the buyer/seller who had committed the dishonourable act. They would have to achieve this based purely on the strength of the documentary evidence they have.

Having said this, if it becomes evident that the buyer/seller is avoiding paying commissions and has not fled, then any subsequent investigation would reveal the buyer/seller's dishonourable act in their attempt to keep all the commission for themselves. This provides a good opportunity for the injured parties (the intermediaries) to claim their entitlement to commission through the courts. The intermediaries do not need to prove the most difficult aspect of the deal – that it actually closed. They only need to prove to the court that the buyer/seller 'personally guaranteed' to pay the commission once they had collected it. The action is against the failure to honour the guarantee and not the actual effort of needing to prove that the deal closed.

In effect the IPG is the only method by which intermediaries can be assured that they will receive their commission payments (from a bona fide buyer/seller). In order to guarantee that they receive commission payments, the intermediary must take up the position of acting as a 'buyer/seller'. As a sourcing intermediary, the only other way to ensure that you receive your commission is by becoming attached to a buyer/seller who is acting in good faith and, in time, to become their primary intermediary.

7

Securing the Goods

FTN Exporting examines hundreds of offers every week. Most have been simply passed down a long chain of intermediaries, all of whom believe that the goods are real and available for purchase. None of them have actually verified their existence and yet traders continue to offer these goods, each adding a further commission amount to the previous price.

As we have already seen the fundamental, and perhaps most obvious, rule of conducting business as an international trade intermediary is never to offer goods that don't exist. For a start, you will never achieve a sale! You cannot accept an offer for goods from another intermediary especially one who claims to be a seller. Therefore the PIA must ensure that the goods being offered actually exist and are ostensibly available for sale. The only safe way of doing this is personally to secure goods directly from the supplier or owner of the goods.

The PIA must therefore ensure that they source goods that are in demand, so that once the goods have been ostensibly secured there is a good chance that the PIA will be able to sell them to an end buyer. Other intermediaries source potential end buyers for the PIA. Therefore a network is created whereby the PIA sources the goods from a real supplier and offers them to end buyers or to intermediaries who have sourced end buyers and who have requested a quotation from the PIA. These intermediaries know to step back, exposing their principal in return for the PIA's pledge to secure and protect commissions. This method of trading means that the PIA buys products that have a fixed and reasonable rate of commission applied to them and that all transactions commence in a safe and workable way. The PIA can only offer goods as sourced from a supplier with a firm value or price attached to those goods. Once the offer has been made to the PIA, the offer can then be made to others for sale. If the supplier did not want to sell the goods, they should not have offered to sell them to the PIA.

In essence the PIA is approaching a supplier as a 'buyer', and must act accordingly, that is, as a 'buyer'. So how does the PIA go about achieving an offer to sell goods from a supplier? A simple letter of enquiry will *not* suffice:

> Dear Sir or Madam,
>
> We have a client who wants to buy your goods, could you please provide us with a quotation for these goods, a firm price and specifications. We will provide an LOI and BCI, after the quote is advised.

This approach is a complete waste of time and will not give you the requisite 'ostensible authority' to be able to offer the goods for sale elsewhere.

The PIA is the buyer, and must approach the deal in a manner consistent with that capacity. Therefore the PIA does not mention end buyers; simply that the PIA is looking to buy the goods from a supplier.

The Different Meanings of 'Delivery'

Intermediaries deal only in documents, so to an intermediary the term 'delivery' actually means 'documentary delivery'. To a banker, documentary delivery is called 'presentation'. The PIA has to obtain the relevant delivery documents and present them to the end buyer's issuing bank. To a carrier, the term 'delivery' means delivery of the physical goods, because the carrier takes physical 'possession' of the goods on board ship. The carrier's position, unlike the intermediary's, is very clear in, for example, a CIF (Cost, Insurance and Freight) deal. The carrier will deliver the goods to a destination port in consideration of freight (the charge for delivering the goods). The carrier is not entitled to the freight until the goods are delivered. Should the end buyer fail to arrive at the destination port or pay freight when the goods arrive, the carrier might decide to resell the goods in order to secure the required freight payment.

However, as is so often the case, the supplier is forced to pay the freight and the goods are offered to potential buyers as a 'spot' deal at the destination port, on a first come, first served basis. Spot deals are unsuitable for intermediaries, because of the constraints of the way in which intermediaries must conduct business. The intermediary has to secure both the end buyer and the supplier, secure payment quickly and then manage two contracts of sale effectively. Negotiating overnight deals is simply not plausible for intermediaries working in this way, which is why the period from offer to first delivery should be at least 60 days, or preferably 90 days. Given that the intermediary only deals in the delivery or title documents, the business of the carrier has very little to do with the PIA.

8

The Enquiry Letter

Let us assume the PIA has an enquiry from an intermediary wanting to buy Portland cement. The PIA attempted to make contact with global suppliers by writing 15 letters of enquiry to potential suppliers on the internet. This resulted in one positive response from a company in China.

The PIA's letter was as follows:

(PIA Letterhead/Contact details)

Transaction code: PIA-USA-010

Date of Enquiry: 1st July 2007

Validity: 5 days from the above enquiry date

Re: Supply of Portland Cement

Buyer: PIA

Dear Sir or Madam,

PIA Import/Export has a general interest in purchasing Portland grey cement of various ASTM grades. Quantities usually required, and which may need to be secured in the near future, often exceed bulk carrier shipments of 10,000 MT per month and require multiple monthly allotments.

We would therefore be grateful if you could kindly send us your specification list, minimum quantities and a general indication of FOB price for our consideration. We understand that any quoted price may not be applicable in the future due to market fluctuation and will always request an updated price before submitting any purchase offer. Please also confirm port of loading.

Please Note: PIA Import/Export adheres to UCP600 banking rules and applies 'Incoterms 2000' rules of delivery as a minimum standard of trade practice.

We await your response, and hope that we will henceforth be able to establish a sound and profitable business relationship with your company in the near future.

Yours faithfully

PIA
http://www.itsi.itgo.com

This letter was sent by email and although brief, stated exactly what was required.

The PIA received a reply from a supplier that contained all the necessary information to enable the PIA to make their own resale offer. This information would include the specifications of the goods, the amount, a price or price index, the applicable Incoterms delivery method, payment instrument, certificates, packaging options and so on. Clarification of these details at this early stage ensures that the goods are suitable and of the requisite quality. For an example of a typical offer, see Chapter 19.

In sourcing the goods and receiving this offer the PIA has the required ostensible authority to resell the goods, simply by getting a positive reply from a supplier. The PIA is therefore allowed to provide an offer for cement to a potential end buyer. Also the PIA can provide an offer in response to a request from another intermediary that will lead to an end buyer. Further, even without receiving a buyer's enquiry directly the PIA can seek potential end buyers using intermediaries to sell the goods. Now that the ostensible authority has been obtained the PIA is allowed to offer goods and will be offering to sell the goods as a 'seller' on behalf of an undisclosed principal.

By approaching a supplier with an informed letter to 'buy' the PIA has completed the first step in creating the required trading path to close a potential deal. There is no obligation to expose the seller when reselling and neither is it wise to do so. All legal responsibilities of the deal remain up to a certain point with the PIA by virtue of the performance of documentary delivery.

This is a globally recognized effective commercial method of trading. The first and most important rule of agency, which applies in many countries, is that the intermediary has decided not to disclose the end buyer, supplier or even buyer/seller and is acting on behalf of an undisclosed principal. Thus the buyer/seller is working from a position at all times without ever disclosing the identity of the supplier. Similarly, sourcing intermediaries may in the first instance use their discretion as to whether or not to disclose the identity of their newly found buyer/seller.

9

The Undisclosed Principal

Acting on behalf of a 'Disclosed Principal' is not an issue for most intermediaries, as most of us will never obtain a mandateship or be employed by a supplier as their official agent. In any event neither of these positions are ideal for the independent trader because of their restrictive nature. The independent 'buyer/ seller' works from the position as 'Acting on behalf of an undisclosed principal'. In this position the supplier, up to documentary delivery, is specifically obligated to the PIA. In relation to possession of the goods the supplier is indirectly obligated to the end buyer.

These respective obligations become important where disputes arise in relation to warranty and claims of defective goods being delivered to the end buyer. It does not matter who pays for the goods, they must arrive in the condition in which they were purchased. Otherwise the supplier has to provide a remedy by which to rectify any defects as per the provisions of the contract of sale.

The supplier will already know or have assumed that the PIA is acting on behalf of an undisclosed principal. This fact will be apparent by the time the PIA and the supplier finalize the terms of their contract, or may even become evident beforehand when the PIA requests a quotation for the sale of goods by issuing a 'Procurement Offer'. Further, the fact that the PIA lives in one country and is attempting to ship goods to someone in another country gives a clear inference that the PIA is not the intended end user of the goods. Other matters at contracting stage will also identify the PIA as having very limited scope to negotiate on terms and conditions. This is because although the PIA actually controls the deal as buyer/seller when reselling the goods, the PIA is also bound by the terms and conditions imposed by the supplier. The PIA can only accept the supplier's terms and conditions as they prevail, and cannot accommodate the personal needs of the supplier. Because a PIA is in such a restrictive position they are often prevented from obtaining access to many products offered by suppliers. This is simply because their contract terms are incompatible with the trading terms of the intermediary.

Many internet intermediaries do not understand the importance of being able to enforce changes to a supplier's terms and conditions. This is where the letter to the supplier, as per the example in Chapter 8, plays a crucial role in allowing an intermediary to accept the contracting conditions of a limited number of suppliers. When we say that goods must be secured before they can be offered to anyone else, not only does this mean that the PIA must acquire the goods directly from the supplier but also that the PIA must have the ability to purchase the goods. The fact that the supplier has offered goods to the PIA is irrelevant if the supplier's terms in the contract of sale are prohibitive. There are two independent processes. Firstly there is the ability to make an offer to resell. The second is tested later at the offer and contract negotiating stage with the supplier.

In FTN's experience only about 2 per cent of suppliers' offers or quotations have procedures that are required for the PIA to be able to purchase goods from them. Surprisingly even some of the ambiguous offers on the internet may involve a real supplier. However, these offers inevitably fail to become effective trades because of the imposition of harsh, unfair or even improper trading terms and conditions at contract stage.

The situation is both precarious and tricky. The PIA has the required 'ostensible authority' to resell the goods (as dictated by their own trading terms and conditions to their end buyer). Because there are two distinct contracts in any one deal, the PIA must be able to mirror the same trading terms and conditions with the supplier who has dictated their own contracting terms to the PIA. The PIA cannot and must never sign the contract with a supplier unless and until two things occur: the funds from the end buyer are in their account and the important aspects of the end buyer's terms are compatible with the terms of trade held between the PIA and their supplier. If for instance the end buyer is asking the PIA for a performance guarantee (PG) of 2 per cent, but the supplier in their deal with the PIA had offered no performance guarantee, then the two deals are not mirrored. The PIA should never have reached contract stage in this deal. FTN Exporting has seen a vast number of misguided intermediary dealings develop from being a simple quotation stage to the contract stage of a deal which is doomed to collapse from the outset. The importance of the steps to take from a good quotation to an offer cannot be over-emphasized, and will save a lot of time later on.

The letter to the supplier (as per the example in Chapter 8) stated that 'Incoterms' and UCP600 apply. Assume that the supplier gave the PIA a basic quotation and both parties have accepted the rules. In effect this gives the PIA an excellent reason to negotiate any of the supplier's terms and conditions that do not meet UCP600 or 'Incoterms' rules. The original letter to the supplier becomes a useful tool in reminding the supplier about the applicable trading rules.

This act alone will give an intermediary leverage to alter the terms and conditions of an offer carrying the supplier's unworkable terms and conditions. The PIA is only required to ensure that a universally safe and acceptable trading regime prevails. If the PIA has the ability to close a contract with the supplier at the right time, then the PIA has the ability to close the whole deal.

Therefore the PIA must know which rules of trade apply. The PIA may get an opportunity to amend a supplier's trading terms and conditions for their own benefit simply because the PIA has decided to use the very same safe trading methods that over 80 per cent of world exporters use. The PIA, an intermediary, is conducting business using only the safe and widely accepted rules of trade as used by corporate trading giants and banks. With this trading knowledge the PIA could attempt to persuade the supplier to change or omit terms and conditions within their contract that seem harsh or unworkable, by making reference to those that pertain to UCP600 and Incoterms 2000 (which have already been agreed upon by both parties as per the additional letter of enquiry). There is no reason why, when offered by a buyer/seller issuing a quotation or offer, a genuine supplier would not consider such trading terms.

When the PIA makes an offer to sell goods to the end buyer, they also make an offer to the supplier to procure the same goods. This is defined as a 'procurement offer'. In essence after the PIA has obtained a quotation from a supplier and the deal with the end buyer is moving along, then it is the PIA who makes the first move by issuing a procurement offer to the supplier. This allows the supplier to examine the offer before giving them a chance to issue their own document. This is preferable to waiting for the supplier to issue their offer to the PIA and thereby applying their own trading terms and conditions. This is the mechanism that gives an intermediary a better chance of securing goods from a supplier while simultaneously pre-empting their own process. At the same time it also prevents the PIA from having to argue the merits or otherwise of a supplier's offer or contract.

The Procurement Offer

The PIA has to handle each aspect of the deal, one step at a time. An offer is sent out to a potential end buyer that the end buyer eventually has to sign and accept. In the meantime the PIA provides a procurement offer to the supplier to 'buy' the goods as previously offered to them.

The procurement offer is a very strong document. It outlines everything the PIA is willing to offer in purchasing the goods. The supplier can only either consider the offer and negotiate its terms or simply reject the offer outright. Getting the supplier to accept the procurement offer means that the PIA is going to have fewer problems in due course with finalizing the contract of sale.

When the supplier and the PIA are at the stage pending acceptance of the procurement offer, the end buyer's contract with the PIA should be nearing final acceptance too. Timing now becomes a critical issue. For this reason all quotations and offers must carry a validity date. Working from this validity date, the PIA can work out a time schedule for the trade in question.

There will be a stage in the transaction during which the PIA needs to sign the contract with their end buyer, binding both the PIA and the end buyer, while holding the final contract from the supplier that is also awaiting signature from the PIA. The very first document that is signed is the supplier's contract although the very first document that is sent out for formal signatures is the end buyer's contract.

The contract to buy is signed, dated and is time stamped *but not returned* to the supplier. The PIA cannot commit themselves to the supplier without having legal confirmation that the end buyer is also proceeding with the transaction. The end buyer's contract is also signed, dated and time stamped so as to indicate that the end buyer's contract was accepted after the PIA ostensibly had a valid contract with the supplier. Should a dispute arise later, the contract copy from the supplier shows that it was signed at an earlier time than the end buyer's contract.

There is nothing deceptive in this course of action. The PIA could, for example, sign the supplier's contract on Monday morning at 10.00 am, and sign the buyer's contract a few hours hour later at 12.30 pm. After this the contract is returned and a DLC is advised and accepted within three days, as per the terms and conditions. By returning the signed contract to the supplier on Thursday the PIA is not acting in a dishonourable way. The PIA is simply protecting their own position should the validity of the transaction ever be questioned either during arbitration or in a court of law.

The supplier would have stipulated that in order to be valid the contract must be returned by Thursday, which would have allowed enough time for these procedures to be carried out. Thus it would be returned on Thursday, with the date and time as signed on Monday. This technically shows that the PIA had not just an ostensible 'interest' in the goods being sold but also a formal interest in the goods, before the contract of sale was signed and returned by the end buyer.

If for some reason one party has tried to circumvent the PIA from either side, the PIA would have a case to claim a loss of profit (commission) because, using these documents, they can show that they had an interest in the goods and the right to sell them. One cannot claim a loss of profit on goods not yet formally purchased for resale. In order to claim a provable loss of a sale and the resultant loss of profit the PIA needs to show a clear link with the buyer's breach of contract. It may be difficult to prove any loss if the end buyer's contract carries a date which is before the date on the purchase contract.

The PPI method on the other hand protects the whole commission because the loss is provable as a breach of contract and is not directly relevant to the delivery of goods. When the end buyer deposits the financial instrument into the PIA's account, the PIA can then formally accept the supplier's contract by sending it off. The end buyer's contracting timeframe for lodging the payment is short in comparison to the PIA's obligations to the supplier.

The parameters and trading path of a deal have been explained above. The trader conducts their business slowly, and in a regimented fashion, one step at a time. Enquiries which state that the 'deal must be closed in 24 hours' or that the goods are required 'ASAP' are clear indications that the viability of the deal is negligible. Such requests should be treated as RF. Trying to transact on four or five offers simultaneously is a waste of time because so much work is needed to close one genuine deal. Similarly trying to transact on many different products simultaneously will lead to serious mistakes being made.

The PIA has spent time sourcing and securing a potential deal and must go to great personal efforts to try to close it. This is not an easy task for even the best traders, so when gains are made they are usually big. Trying to make, for example, 100,000 dollars in personal profit over six or seven weeks also means that you have earned those profits because of the effort, skill and abilities required. You will never make money simply by passing silly offers around and using ill-informed trading procedures. The only way to make large gains is through skill and knowledge of procedures.

Of the many intermediaries attempting to trade using these methods, the vast majority will give up trading within six months. One intermediary will still be around two years later, and would be close to being able to transact on an import/export deal outright as a buyer/seller within the next few years thereafter. It would not be unrealistic to expect an intermediary well versed in these procedures to actually secure a large DLC within four years of trading. At this point it is up to each individual trader's ability and skill to close the deal. Similarly it is up to the individual trader to decide the size of the gains made on any such successful closure. It is doubtful whether an intermediary would be able to secure a deal to DLC stage before this time although it depends on the nature of business and the skills of the particular intermediary.

In effect, regardless of how many deals FTN Exporting has closed we cannot promise that the guidance in this book will result in the successful closure of any deal because the method of trading is only part of the business – personal skills, attributes and abilities of the intermediary contribute considerably to the final outcome of any deal.

10

Contacting the End Buyer

It is time to concentrate on genuine documents and correct procedures. The way you commence a deal is the way it will continue. Remembering this, we will now advertise secured goods to potential end buyers. In this case, the PIA is going to attempt to secure a buyer of ethanol.

> (Header Info)
>
> Date:
>
> Transaction code:
>
> From Seller: PIA
>
> RE: Product offer – Automotive Ethanol
>
> Dear Sir or Madam,
>
> The PIA is currently selling Automotive Ethanol. Should your firm have any interest in purchasing this commodity, please do not hesitate to ask us for a FOB quote or offer. Please specify delivery, grade, quantity and final port of destination. The PIA uses only safe trading rules and practices as defined under Incoterms 2000 and UCP600 Banking rules as its minimum trading standards.
>
> Yours faithfully
>
> PIA Import/Export

The above letter clearly defines the matter at hand. It is uncomplicated, neither an offer nor a quotation, it is merely an invitation to others who may be interested in buying goods you have secured. The PIA is unsure if the person being contacted is a real end buyer or not, so there is not a lot of information provided about the product at this stage because a good trader would wait and see what type of response they received. A good reply will provide a great deal about a real end buyer or end user of ethanol. This information will immediately indicate to the PIA whether a deal may be possible or whether the information received is simply RF.

Even corporate giants who know very little about ethanol may attempt to buy these goods from a PIA in the hope that they could flip the contract over quickly. This is a situation that must be avoided, as the PIA would not be selling to an end buyer but another buyer/seller and as the letter of credit can only be transferred once the deal would collapse. As we have already seen the PIA must only sell to an end buyer who takes actual possession of the goods. It is best not to give too much information away when endeavouring to secure an end buyer. Use an informal approach and wait for them to respond.

A real ethanol buyer knows what they want. When the PIA receives a reply, they use the information in it to conduct further due diligence to test the buyer's veracity. Once a deal begins to prove viable then the PIA should concentrate on it until its conclusion, whether failure or success. The PIA creates a separate transaction code for each enquiry, quotation or offer to each end buyer or intermediary chain. The transaction code should not be changed. This enables the PIA to track the offers relating to each string contract until such time as a potential deal begins to look viable.

Email is the main communication device for enquiries, quotations and offers. Other means such as a facsimile may also be used but hardcopy mail-out is still believed to be the superior medium, albeit a slower one. Experience shows that mailed letters sent directly to a named CEO of a company increases the chance of receiving the principal's attention than a facsimile or email. This is true in approaches both to the end buyer and the supplier and can be particularly effective if written in their native language.

There can be no doubt when you've contacted a company like Sinopec or Mitsui because some simple research would lead you to the company's website. You would use information from those websites to write enquiry letters. You will also have researched websites like Forbes and others to establish who the buyers or sellers of these commodities are. Approaching trade board websites is generally a waste of time, as you are unlikely to find many legitimate buyers or sellers on these websites. If you are serious about wanting to trade in commodities, then you'll eventually have to start trading personally with the corporate giants of the world (unless you wish to remain a sourcing intermediary). A good sourcing intermediary is a rare being and a diligent buyer/seller will notice these abilities and treat them as an asset to their business.

A Good Quotation

By now you will want to begin the process of finding and closing an import/ export transaction. You have practised researching the markets, have the ability to spot the RF deals among the very few potentially viable deals and have practised sending letters of enquiries. With experience you start to have a general feel about the way a trade must start and complete as per Incoterms 2000 and UCP600.

The whole process starts with the issue of a good quotation, which will be issued as the result of an enquiry. This process is the same whether it is an end buyer or an intermediary who has supplied some basic information in their request to you. Later when you gain experience and confidence you will attempt to trade directly with an end buyer. For now you'll mainly be mixing with other intermediaries. Some will eventually see that you offer a more logical and sound trading environment and will seek attachment to you, as you begin to form your own trading group and teach those around you. Some intermediaries will also form a strong relationship with the PIA based on trust.

It is not worth dealing in single container loads but in bulk carrier deals. The effort needed to close a single container deal worth only 10,000 dollars is no different to closing a 10 million dollar bulk contract. If you are going to apply this level of skill then it may as well be for deals that will earn you significant commissions. Don't ever think that smaller deals are easier to close, because they are not. Closing one bulk FOB carrier deal will give you enough insight to tackle all types of deals, whereas closing contracts on only small container loads will not.

A good quotation will dictate whether you can commence and continue with a trade or whether it is going to collapse early on. It is always far better to push for a good quotation at the commencement of a deal as doing so will tell you very quickly if you are to proceed or cease trading in this particular deal. The PIA needs to know if they have a potentially serious end buyer or could finally reach such a buyer with the issue of a good quotation. Although you can commence a deal by issuing an offer, it is not desirable. Under no circumstances should you start a deal at the contract stage. You should always start a deal by asking for, or by receiving, a good quotation. It will also enable you to decide quickly whether a trade is potentially viable or not in that you are able to see whether, as the PIA, you are able to work to a supplier's procedures or not. It is better to begin to trade in a thousand deals that collapse within days of the quotation than to waste energy on one single deal for weeks or months that finally collapses despite all your efforts. You may have to dismiss 999 deals as RF before being able to attempt to secure that one potentially viable deal. While going through this process you will be gaining excellent experience and will become increasingly conversant in correct procedures as opposed to RF deals.

In the event of a serious contractual dispute the offer could prove, in certain circumstances, to be a more important document than even the contract itself as far as the intermediary is concerned. A good quotation will lead to the issuance or acceptance of a good offer. The likelihood that you will close on such a deal increases dramatically once these two stages have been successfully completed. In FTN's experience, even though there is still a long way to go, getting the quotation and offer accepted gives a trader a better than 60 per cent chance of closing the deal. Whether you have the goods and are studying requests for a quotation, or whether you have secured the goods and want to make quotations to intermediaries and potential end buyers, a basic premise prevails. When sending a quotation to intermediaries include some information regarding procedures and commissions, not in the quotation itself but in the accompanying email. The quotation for an end buyer does not make any mention of commissions.

A Sample Quotation

In the next example we will use the increasingly popular global commodity 'automotive ethanol' again. Assume in this instance that supply is not a concern but that you have two buying enquiries from intermediaries requesting ethanol. You are also researching the internet and have found a potential end buyer and user of this type of product for whom you are also preparing a quotation.

a)   The first intermediary is asking for ethanol and has mentioned things in their email to you like an 'LOI' with a 'BCL' will be issued and 'Urgent request, will close in 24 hours using SWIFT', as well as other ambiguous terms. Understanding that such procedures are critically flawed you immediately dismiss the email enquiry and don't even respond.

b)   The second intermediary, let's call him Hassan, making a request for ethanol has taken a different approach. The email states that they may have a potential end buyer for ethanol, asking whether the PIA would be prepared to secure and protect their commission and that of two others in the matter if the information provided leads to the closing of a deal. Hassan is not a confident dealer and is looking to find attachment to a trustworthy buyer/seller.

The PIA considers the request from the second intermediary as being reasonable and proceeds to prepare a PDF quotation to send to Hassan attached to an email. Ideally such documents are made in advance as a template so you can simply make changes as required.

(Letterhead, Date, Validity)

Dear Sir,

Please find enclosed a quotation for automotive ethanol for your client, and please note the following.

1)   The PIA as seller, will secure, protect and pay your commission and those serving you on the completion of a successful transaction.

2)   You shall remain contactable and within the ambit of the deal in order to assist the PIA until either failure or success of the transaction has been recorded.

3)   You are to remain as a trusted Primary Intermediary of the PIA in this transaction advising all others in your group as to the progress of the deal.

4)   You are not allowed to change any part of the quotation, but are allowed initially to sanitize our contact details if you so choose, so long as the quotation remains intact when reaching the end buyer.

5)   Upon the end buyer signing and accepting the quotation, you are to collect the required personal details of the intermediaries involved who are claiming commission protection, including yours, as well as all relevant bank details. The PIA will then issue a guaranteed commission pay order for forwarding to your intermediaries. The information, once issued, cannot be altered so please ensure names, addresses, and contact details are recorded entirely accurately. You are then to collect the signed quotation and return it to us disclosing the end buyer's details. The PIA will then issue a formal offer to you which you forward directly to the end buyer. Once accepted and returned the PIA will issue you a draft contract in the same manner for the end buyer's further and final consideration, which will define the continuing stages of the transaction from there on in.

6) The preset non-negotiable commission rate secured for this transaction for protected intermediaries of the PIA will follow accordingly: US$3.00 dollars per MT to the PI assisting and US$1.20 per MT to each other intermediary being protected by us.

Commission Pre-advice offered by the PIA in accordance with URPIB

In the unlikely event that a verifiable mandate is next to the end buyer then, if genuine, they must collect commission from their own principal and not claim a share of the allotted commissions.

The PIA does not tolerate circumvention and the end buyer may not make contact with the PIA unless permission is given by you to do so whether now or in the future for any other transaction.

Should you have any questions please feel free to ask before offering the goods on the PDF document to the end buyer. If you leave our heading and letterhead on the quotation to the end buyer, this will promote trust and shows that you have confidence in your seller. Please be assured that your interests and that of your group in this matter will be protected at all times.

If you cannot work to our terms and conditions please disregard this quotation immediately.

Kind regards

Yours sincerely

PIA

PS: Attachment PDF Quotation issued.

Please also note: If you decided to forward the quotation as it is without sanitizing it, please use the PDF attached. If our letterhead is to be covered please retype the body of the quotation on your document.

The PIA attaches the following quotation to Hassan:

(Heading/logo/contact)

QUOTATION: PDF

Issue Date: 1/1/2008 AEST 12.00 Noon

Transaction Code: 118-PIA-ETH-001

Seller: PIA Import/Export

Attention: Protected Primary Agent acting on behalf of the Seller:

Mr. Hassan Ayatollah and all involved with such.

Email of Agent: 'mailto:hassanawdallah@yahoo.com'

Quotation must be returned to the agent above and not the seller if disclosed. It is hereby agreed that internet acceptance is allowed until after the offer has been accepted.

Validity Date: 5 days from above issue date.

The Quotation:

Product: Automotive Ethanol; EB121 Density 791.5

Specifications fully defined on offer.

Origin: Santos Port, Brazil.

Price: US$550 per MT

Quantity: One shipment per month for 3 months at 15,000 MT each

Contracted Quantity: 45,000 MT +/– 10%

Performance Guarantee: 1.25% per each delivery;

Delivery: FOB Name port of shipment as per Incoterms 2000

Payment: Pre-advised, irrevocable transferable and Confirmed Documentary Letter of Credit applying UCP600 banking rules and issued as Non-cumulative and revolving.

First delivery: As per contract – 1/3/2008 or earlier.

Procedures:

1) Quotation is issued then returned filled in as accepted (non-legally binding).

2) Offer is issued, end buyer returns as accepted (legally binding).

3) Draft contract issued/negotiated agreed and returned.

4) End buyer issued PA-DLC as per offer/contract.

5) Proof of Seller's interests/verifications of goods advised as per contract.

6) PA-DLC reverts to a fully active DLC.

7) Performance guarantee issued as per UCP600 SLC rules.

8) Delivery initiated by document presentation as per offer/contract.

9) Collection applied per each shipment until final delivery.

Seller's Declaration:

I, the Seller acting on behalf of an undisclosed principal(s) do hereby make this non-legally binding quotation with good and honourable intent, subject to final availability.

Date:
Print Name:
Signed:

Buyer's Declaration:

We the end buyer taking possession of the goods confirm the acceptance of this quotation, and this information contained in this quotation shall be included in the pending offer.

Name of Company/Entity:

Import Manager's/Agent's Name:

Address:

Contact Details:

Port of unloading:

Name of bank used to pay for goods:

Certificate of Origin (Please mark one) Required: (   ) Not required: (   )

Date:
Print Name:
Signed:

Summary

There is no confusion as to what is being offered by the PIA, or how the PIA is to conduct business when using intermediaries. Hassan would probably be very pleased with this document. The quotation seems to be more in line with the presentation of an offer, than a simple quotation. The PIA has also provided guiding instructions to Hassan, in effect outlining the required mechanism needed for the PIA to be able to take control of the deal. The PIA will know within days if the end buyer will accept or not accept the quotation. Non-acceptance means that the end buyer has not provided 'confirmation' of the quotation so it is time to move on to another deal. Acceptance on the other hand means the end buyer has provided 'Confirmation' so the quotation is affirmed. Note that number (2) in the previous extract states that the offer is later to be produced and provided as a legally-binding document. The inexperienced intermediary is to include the phrase 'Not legally binding, subject to contract' in this space.

Remember a quotation is 'confirmed' and an offer is 'accepted'. Therefore you must ensure that the term 'Quotation' appears on the form. Also remember, once Hassan becomes comfortable with the PIA all these first time procedures aren't required in other subsequent dealings as their business relationship strengthens.

The PIA will prepare an offer, which is essentially an extended version of the original quotation. The deal has started on a firm footing, and everyone involved is informed as to its progress. Should most aspects of the quotation be accepted save for example the performance guarantee (PG) value offered then the quotation is said to have become qualified. In this case, negotiation is conducted by email until the matter is addressed to the satisfaction of both parties. Once settled, the PIA includes the new information in a new quotation carrying a new transaction code, which is then returned to the PIA. Thus the second quotation becomes the official start of the deal.

Let us say that the end buyer has indicated that a 2 per cent PG is required and the seller eventually makes an offer of 1.5 per cent, which is acceptable to the buyer. The original quotation is cancelled and corrections are made as per the negotiations (that have taken place via email between the buyer and the seller via the primary intermediary Hassan).

Once you have an official 'start' to a deal the current transaction code remains with the deal until the end. Thus if an offer is issued as the starting document and it needs to be changed six times then there would be six different transaction codes. The last quotation carries the same transaction code as the one on the contract and will remain until the completion of the deal, whether successful or otherwise. Adopt the same method when providing a quotation. The viable deal must be commenced cleanly, so that all previous documents become invalid. This is to ensure that the intermediary does not confuse past documents with the current transaction.

The previous example offers a performance guarantee. However it is good practice in the first instance, when making an offer or quotation, *not to offer a*

PG. Let the end buyer or the seller request a PG: refrain from offering one until you have had an opportunity to consider the alternatives. It may be that you apply a further discount to the price of the goods that will reduce your own commission or you may decide to add a higher price to the goods (higher than the value of the PG). The fewer formalities applied to the deal the better, as the easier it is to transact. A performance guarantee is not a vital component in a transaction, so it is better to attempt to trade without the extra burden of a PG. Misguided internet traders often ask for a 2 per cent performance guarantee as a matter of course, as though it were standard international protocol – which it is not.

Returning to the instant example, Hassan has now advised the PIA by email that the end buyer has accepted the quotation. The primary intermediary next to the end buyer has been in communication with Hassan, along with all other intermediaries involved. Hassan has provided the PIA with details of all the other intermediary parties to whom commission pay orders are to be issued unless an alternative agreement has been reached. The PIA issues all the pay orders and once they are all returned, correctly completed, the process of 'stepping back' begins.

The issue of a quotation has more weight than first perceived, especially in terms of scheduling the various stages of the trade. It is appropriate to assume that from the date of the issue of a quotation that there will be no less than 90 days before delivery of the first shipment, and 30 days thereafter for all others if it is a multi-shipment deal. (So much for all those 'deal must be signed in 48 hours' demands!)

Timescales

Allow a period of 90 days in total from the quotation to first delivery. From the very start of a trade allow up to five days for the reply to, and acceptance of, a quotation. Allow ten days for a reply to, and acceptance of, an offer and up to 15 days for acceptance of the contract. After the contract with the end buyer is signed and sealed allow seven days thereafter for the issuance of a DLC and three days for the issuance of a PG (if one is needed). Therefore the trading timeframe is 40 days in total. From signature of contracts allow another 50 days for delivery, unless your supplier has stated otherwise. Therefore the minimum trading timeframe is 90 days. Estimating any less time than this will more often than not get you into trouble.

The PIA begins to take control of the deal from the earliest stages of the transaction. If the supplier later indicates that they can deliver 30 days after the initial contracting period this will be consistent with the timeframe the PIA has already provided to the end buyer. The PIA now understands that the period from the quotation stage to signature of contracts with both the end buyer and supplier is confined to a 40-day window. Unless otherwise agreed delivery of the first shipment will be set to occur 50 days afterwards. If it is a multi-shipment deal this is followed by another delivery every 30 days thereafter. It will take time for the supplier to organize the transaction at their end. The more notice they have the better it is for the sake of the deal.

The intermediary uses the 50-day delivery window as a benchmark to establish a viable transacting and delivery timeframe. Usually, when an FOB end buyer decides to buy the goods from the seller, they initiate the process of chartering a ship. Sometimes the end buyer is able do this quickly but at other times there may be long delays. For example an end buyer in the USA who is buying bulk goods from a supplier in Bahrain has to get a ship to the Bahraini port of loading by the delivery date. Securing the ship from a contractor within 50 or 60 days may be difficult. Other issues may also hinder the carrier from berthing within the conditions in the offer and final contracts. The seller (meaning the supplier) has to reserve berthing at the Bahrain port as well, so they are able to bring the goods alongside the ship within the required timeframe. The seller will immediately seek reservation at the loading port the very moment they feel that they have an active deal in hand and may initiate this process before the DLC is even advised. This is the reason why a period of 90 days, from the issue of the quotation to first delivery, is the minimum acceptable timeframe.

So the procedure, which should not be deviated from, is as follows:

1.   Quote.

2.   Offer.

3.   Contract.

4.   Seller receives payment first.

5.   Forty days is allowed up to this stage, even though the delivery process may start as early as (2).

6.   The PPI Certificate issued.

7.   Seller issues PG if appropriate.

8.   Delivery is initiated.

9.   Collection made on financial instrument.

The main sticking point in the past has been one of proving that the product being offered is real and genuine. Most misguided intermediaries will ask first for a quotation which is immediately returned as not being accepted and that 'Proof of Product' is needed first. This is never going to happen. It is ironic to think that an intermediary demanding 'proof of product' today is the same intermediary who tomorrow will issue an offer without 'proof of product', and yet such traders continue to do this day in, day out.

If you put on the quotation that a pre-advised DLC is being requested this will help to allay these fears. The PIA is trying to accommodate the request for verifiable proof, that both satisfies the end buyer and that protects the PIA and the intermediaries from circumvention. Someone who truly understands what they are doing will be aware that proof of goods is simply not an option until the funds have been secured in one form or another. If the PIA does not have the funds and discloses the supplier's or end buyer's details, they could easily deal directly with one another and the PIA would lose the deal. If a genuine end buyer will not accommodate the issuance of the least expensive of all credits, the pre-advised credit, then there is no deal and the PIA simply treats the transaction as 'RF'.

The PIA, when issuing a quote to PI, is also trying to reassure the sourcing intermediaries that doing business with the PIA means that their interests will be protected at all times. Showing honourable intent is very important, especially since the traders involved may have never met the PIA before and have no knowledge or experience of them.

Giving reassurance from the start will assist with establishing a bond with the intermediary group. This is especially so where the PIA has not just assured the protection of commission but has also allowed the closest intermediary to remain within the deal to ensure transparency is maintained. This method is something that very few other buyers/sellers provide, often insisting that they need to conduct business with the end buyer or supplier only. Such requests often alienate the sourcing intermediaries who for lack of knowledge disclose vital information to the buyer/seller, as a desperate measure. This often leads to a situation in which the buyer/seller is conducting private business with principals and because of the lack of transparency intermediaries have no idea whether the deal has closed or not.

Whereas others in a string contract may not accept the PIA's intent they may accept the good intent of PI who is dealing with the PIA. A trusted buyer/seller has nothing to hide and can trade openly while protecting the interests of the group who sourced the end buyer and simultaneously preventing circumvention. The intermediaries may have important information regarding a real end buyer and have approached the PIA because they lack the required skill to close the deal. Hence the only real and moral consideration is to make sure that such intermediaries are fully protected within a deal.

So you now understand the importance of the issuance of a good quotation. If no intermediaries were involved, the email part of the letter would not apply. Remember in the first instance that you should offer nothing by way of a PG. You could avoid asking for the issue of a pre-advised credit, and request the issuance of a normal active irrevocable credit. Most end buyers and indeed suppliers do not offer or expect the issuance of a PG as being of major concern. The point here is that once an intermediary has become confident, firmer trading methods become a matter of course. Intermediaries can start to format their own letters and quotations/offers/contracts so long as the basic trader's parameters as stated above are upheld. End buyers will often trade at a much slower pace and if they see procedures on subsequent documents that don't make sense they will simply not take up the final offer. It is only when dealing with other misguided intermediaries that issues concerning the PG and the like reoccur.

11

Offers to Buy and Sell

The end buyer, via the intermediaries and the PI, has accepted the quotation and the subsequent supporting offer. Commission pay orders from intermediaries will be addressed in detail later on. The PIA receives the signed quotation from a potential end buyer in the form of a scanned PDF document. In the meantime you have asked for a quotation from a supplier, and the supplier has replied. You as the 'buyer' are not formally 'accepting' the quotation, but merely give 'confirmation' that the quotation is acceptable. Ideally the basic quotation is not legally binding or 'subject to contract' but when a formal offer is required then make sure the following wording is present on the document: 'Acceptance of this offer is legally binding.' On the supplier's side of the deal you stress that the contract is the legally-binding document and *not* the offer. If you are sure that you have a supplier under your control, then you should adopt a more forceful approach in respect of your end buyer in order to achieve a quick legally-binding status on that side of the deal.

US contract law dictates that once an offer is accepted it can still be avoided without repercussions. This is not the case in English law. Because of its long colonial past, England's legal influence is spread far and wide in Europe, Africa, India, Hong Kong and all the way down under to remote Australia, to name just a few. Even China, as the emerging leading economy, is still finding its own form of legal precedents. The Chinese often use a combination of civil and English common law principles in their trading environment. English common law principles combined with English maritime shipping laws affirm the importantance of the past and present role that England has played in the realm that is international trade.

If you have a real supplier the last thing you want to do is to become legally obligated to them before getting the buyer's DLC into your account. If your end buyer pulls out of the deal (which they would be entitled to do, as at this stage they are not legally bound to you), you would find yourself in breach of contract with the supplier. This could have severe financial consequences unless you could find a replacement end buyer extremely quickly. Finding another end buyer is not something that you can rely upon given the number of elements that must be compatible with one another in any single trade. With the end buyer's deal the opposite is true, you want to enforce a legally-binding situation as soon as possible and secure the DLC as quickly as you can. If you have supply capability then you have nothing to lose in forcing an end buyer to become legally bound to you. However, you must at all costs avoid a situation in which you seal a contract with a supplier at a time when you have not secured the end buyer.

In English law an offer once fully disclosed, considered and accepted by a potential buyer acts as confirmation that the end buyer wants to become legally bound to the PIA, and vice versa. The PIA becomes obligated to the end buyer to perform once the offer is formally 'accepted'. The PIA has to be very sure by offer acceptance time that the supplier has the goods they are claiming to sell and also has the capacity to sell them (that is, that the supplier is not simply another buyer/seller). Once the quotation is confirmed no part of it is allowed to change and the information in it is duplicated onto the offer. The offer provides much more information than the quotation. The offer in turn is incorporated into the sales contract that provides the rights and obligations of both parties in full.

We have seen that an offer needs to be accepted by the end buyer before it can be made legally binding. A quotation on the other hand is simply a confirmation informing the seller that the end buyer is interested in the goods being offered. The confirmation is secure when the quotation is signed and returned as accepted. If you assure the end buyer on the quotation that it is not a legally-binding document it allows the deal to progress to the next stage with the issuance of an offer.

If the PIA issues a draft contract and the buyer does not notice that the draft contract does not cover some of the terms that were on the offer, the buyer can still enforce a legally-binding status to the transaction and may ask to have the missing conditions added to the contract forthwith (without altering anything else). The effects of providing or accepting a sound offer in the first place cannot be overemphasized. This is because the contract will be the one document that defines everything that the end buyer and supplier must do in the transaction. Not including all the rights and obligations in the contract could lead to significant problems later on.

If the PIA refuses to make these amendments they are still legally bound to perform as per the offer. In a real trading situation, if the PIA refused to make the required changes, they could end up in court. In reality though there would not be many end buyers prepared to spend the time and resources to take the PIA through the international court system for 'breach of conditions'. If the buyer is a corporate giant then the PIA could find their name published on internet scam forums and websites as a fraudster. The trader's reputation could indeed suffer which again is something that the PIA must avoid at all costs. Search for '419 scams' on the internet for countless examples of these frauds.

Supply Capability

As we have already seen the PIA must be sure that they have supply capability before they make any offers to sell. The very foundation of any deal is to ensure you have supply capability. Once you are sure of this then chase the funds needed to close the deal. Although in legal terms the formal contract is the most important document, the instigation of the trade itself – and the means by which the trade reaches contract stage – commences with the offer.

It is acceptable to use the internet as a communication tool up to offer acceptance stage. PIAs can trade all they want with quotations and offers transmitted via facsimile and/or email. To reinforce this a simple statement on the body of the offer should be included, which states 'the end buyer and seller agree upon the use of electronic documents as received and issued via the use of internet, intranet or other telecommunications devices'. Such a statement will in most cases actually override any relevant internal laws if matters concerning performance become a major legal issue later on. However, this statement will not be effective when dealing with countries where the government has full or partial control over this media, for example North Korea, Iran, Cuba or in a country which is ruled by a military regime, for example Burma.

In the USA trades conducted within a single state or across state borders will be subject to federal and state laws as applicable. These trades will be governed by UCC (Uniform Commercial Code) rather than international trade laws.

For example, if Giovanni who lives in Italy entered into a contract to buy goods from a local manufacturer when in fact the supplier is prevented from selling the goods to Giovanni by virtue of local laws, the supplier cannot then rely on the local law to void its obligations to Giovanni. Although the supplier will not get into trouble for not selling the goods, they are still obliged to perform as per the contract with Giovanni. The contract does not simply become null and void because of the local laws preventing the supplier from selling the goods.

In another instance a UAE buyer signed a contract to purchase goods but later found out that the bank would not open the required pre-advised credit as defined under UCP500 uniform banking rules (note that UCP600 is in force now). The buyer claimed that because internal laws prevented the bank from issuing this type of credit, the underlying contract was not enforceable. In fact the buyer was still required to perform as per the sales contract as they should have conducted due diligence on the matter of the credit prior to committing themselves to the contract.

If, for example, an end buyer failed to secure an import permit for the goods creating a situation that meant that the goods could not be legally imported into the buyer's country, then the seller will still collect upon the credit as defined on the sales contract. This is because the buyer is at fault for not conducting due diligence prior to entering into a contract. Consequently electronically transmitted documents can have legally-binding consequences, regardless of the fact that the internal laws in the buyer's country state otherwise.

The end buyer has accepted your offer. The PIA prepares the draft sales contract to the end buyer but before sending it the PIA first issues their own procurement offer to their supplier for acceptance. Remember that the supplier will dictate terms and conditions to the PIA (as the PIA has to the end buyer). The ability of the PIA to be able to perform is strictly based on the demands they make of the supplier, or the demands the supplier is willing to accept.

The quotation from the supplier to the PIA provides the PIA with the legal ability to make the resale offer to the end buyer. The PIA has little scope to negotiate matters of delivery and performance and can only issue an offer to the end buyer within the confines of which the PIA is personally able to perform. The risk here is that the deal might reach stalemate as the PIA is unable to perform within these confines.

This is the most crucial part of any deal. It is also arguably the most difficult: get past this stage, and you've considerably improved your chance of closing the deal. The PIA has the quotation from the supplier, and the PIA was conscientious enough to ask for a quotation to which Incoterms 2000 and UCP600 apply. By using these very strong trading rules the PIA is well protected. It is likely that these rules provide more protection than the terms and conditions drafted by the supplier's own lawyers.

The PIA must apply a mechanism, one of many at this stage of the deal, to ensure that they remain in full control of the deal. The PIA cannot simply write to the supplier to say, for example: 'Thank you for your quotation, could you please send me a full offer for further consideration.' Doing this is very risky. The PIA could end up with an offer with a totally inappropriate or unworkable set of conditions, which come nowhere near to the conditions offered to the end buyer. The PIA should make a full procurement offer to the supplier in which the terms and conditions mirror the offer the PIA has made to the end buyer. The supplier's terms and conditions may or may not be acceptable to the PIA. However the PIA is only seeking to secure the best, most safe and effective trading method from the buyer to safeguard their own position from the start.

Applying the timeframe for the deal gives the PIA the chance to ensure that at the very least a good viable offer is secured with the supplier before the PIA accepts the offer issued to the end buyer. The PIA takes control of the deal with a 'procurement offer'. In essence the PIA is saying to the supplier: 'Dear Sir, thank you for your quotation. Please find herewith a procurement offer, which determines our safe and strict, minimum risk procedures that you will find are also of great benefit to you. If you want to make a sale, these are our methods of trading.' (In other words, take it or leave it!) The PIA is limited in terms of the way in which they can trade, so there is no point chasing trades that they will not be able to close for procedural reasons. Therefore the PIA informs the supplier as to the safest trading requirements that suit their own needs, rather than letting the supplier dictate their requirements.

The supplier now has one of two options: (1) To reject the offer and negotiate further upon some of the terms or (2) to accept the offer. The acceptance of the offer means that your terms and conditions are close to that which the supplier was prepared to accept in any event. In this case an offer is likely to be signed and returned to you very quickly. The rejection of the offer means that the supplier did not like some aspects of the deal and is likely to state that the offer has become 'qualified'. This means that any proposed changes to the requirements in the procurement offer are suggested by way of a 'counter offer'. If the PIA and the supplier cannot come to an agreement as to the new demands in the counter offer, the deal collapses. The PIA will not issue the offer to the end buyer because the PIA cannot accept the terms and conditions of the supplier's counter offer.

The communication to the end buyer is usually to this effect:

Dear Sir,

Unfortunately it has come to our attention that goods as offered on the quotation are no longer available, as a result of which no formal offer can be provided.

This is not a lie. It's a statement of fact. The PIA had the 'ostensible' rights to sell the goods but unfortunately was not in a position to 'buy' the goods for reselling. Therefore the goods are indeed 'no longer available' to the PIA. There is no need to explain why the goods are no longer available. The PIA needs only to explain that an unforeseen situation has arisen and as a result they are unable to supply on this occasion.

Assuming the counter offer issues are resolved to the satisfaction of both the PIA and the supplier, the required changes are included in a new procurement offer that carries a new transaction code. In effect a counter offer cancels the old offer, and the new procurement offer becomes the active one. The PIA is still able to adhere to the end buyer's offered terms and conditions.

The PIA has negotiated the terms and conditions of the counter offer and is preparing the documents to send to the supplier for acceptance. It is at this stage that the PIA issues the offer to their end buyer for formal acceptance. This is the very reason why, when dealing with a supplier, an offer must be provided before anything else. The acceptance of the offer will typically carry a three-day period of validity when offered to the end buyer. The offer you are preparing for the supplier may also carry a similar timeframe. Such a timeframe may stipulate that the offer is open for (or the timeframe within which to accept is) ten days.

You will want to receive the accepted supplier's offer first which will in turn mean that you are ready to be legally bound with the end buyer. Unlike the end buyer's deal the procurement offer you have issued means that you are signing an agreement with the supplier that will only become legally binding upon final contracts being signed. This is an acceptable means of securing the supplier's intent without becoming legally bound at the offer stage.

In other words by not signing the contract the PIA still has a 'get out clause' from their obligation with the supplier. If the end buyer changes their mind at the last minute and decides not to make the purchase after all, the PIA is not yet legally bound to the supplier. Trivial mistakes will not cause the deal to collapse at this stage as long as the later critical issue of the performance guarantee has been properly dealt with. (This matter is discussed in more detail later on.) Although the contract stage of the transaction is now looming, there should not be any problems as both offers have already defined the most important part of the deal, again reiterating once more how important the offer documents are in relation to intermediary business.

The Offer to Sell

Let's consider an example of an offer to the end buyer. As you will notice the offer is simply an extension of the quotation. If you are not using an intermediary to source an end buyer then all mention of intermediaries is omitted. We'll assume the quotation was accepted within the five-day validity period. Let's introduce the end buyer as 'Mr. Pink.'

Offer Example:

(PIA full heading/logo/contact)

Issue Date: 6/1/2008 AEST 12.00 Noon

Transaction Code: 118 – PIA – ETH – 001

Seller: PIA Import/Export

Attention: Protected Agent acting on behalf of the Seller:

Mr. Hassan Awadallah

Email of Agent: hassanawdallah@yahoo.com

Quotation must be returned to the above agent and not the Seller if disclosed. Internet trading up to offer acceptance agreed.

Validity Date: 7 days from above issue date.

Offer issued to the end buyer: Mr. Pink of Smallville LLC USA

THE OFFER:

Product: Automotive Ethanol; EB121 Density 791.5

Specification: Fuel Anhydrate Ethanol for Automotive Use. Origin Brazil: Technical Regulation: Appearance: Clear and free of suspended matter: Total Acids Mg/Litre-30 P.P.M Max.(ASTM D – 1613) Electrical Conductivity: u S/m-500 Max.(ASTM D – 1125) Specific 'Point of Production' gravity at 20 C Kg/M3 791.5 max. (ASTM D – 4052) Ethanol at point of production – 99.3 min Copper as Cu – 0.07% P.P.M Nil of: Fe, Na, Cl, SO4.

Origin: Santos Port Brazil.

Price: US$550 per MT

Quantity: One shipment per month for 3 months 15,000 MT

Contracted Quantity: 45,000 MT +/– 10%

Performance Guarantee: Late deliver discount (LDD) US$4.50 per MT discount applied on the seller's invoice as a credit to favour the buyer for each and every shipment which fails delivery.

Delivery: FOB Name port of shipment as per Incoterms 2000

Payment: A bank issued pre-advised, irrevocable transferable and confirmed documentary letter of credit, applying UCP600 banking rules issued as non-cumulative revolving. Collection shall be facilitated with the presentation of a 'shipper's on board certificate, ships mate's receipt or forwarder's receipt' and other standard presentation documents as defined on the contract in accordance with delivery application as per Incoterms 2000. In accordance with UCP600 the price quoted for the goods do not include bank issuance and transferring and pre-advising fees. The end buyer has agreed with the seller to pay these fees on behalf of the seller, at the time the credit is issued for the payment of the goods.

First delivery: As per contract 1/4/2008 or earlier.

Procedures:

1) Quotation is issued then returned completed as accepted (not legally binding).

2) Offer is issued – end buyer returns it as accepted (legally binding).

3) Draft contract issued/negotiated and returned as accepted.

4) End buyer issues PA-TCDLC as per offer/contract.

5) Proof of seller's interests/verification of goods provided as per contract terms (PPI)

6) PA-TCDLC reverts to a fully active DLC.

7) Performance guarantee issued as per ISP98 SLC rules if applicable.

8) Delivery initiated by document presentation as per offer/contract.

9) Collection applied per each shipment until final delivery.

Offer is legally binding once accepted.

Seller's Declaration:

I the aforesaid seller acting on behalf of an undisclosed principal(s) do hereby make this legally-binding offer with good and honourable intent (subject to availability*).

* Goods may not be available if the offer has been rejected or is accepted after the expiry of the validity period.

Date:
Print Name:
Signed:

Buyer's Declaration:

I/We the end buyer taking possession of the goods hereby accept this offer, and acknowledge that the information contained herein shall be included in the contract.

Name of company/entity:

Import manager's/agent's name:

Address:

Contact details both business and personal:

Name of bank used to pay for goods:

Account Name:

Account Address:

Account Number:

SWIFT Code:

Bank, Phone, Facsimile:

Port of discharge:

Certificate of Origin required: Yes (   ) No (   ) (Cost for buyer's account)

Date:
Print Name
Signed:

The offer to the end buyer is nothing more than a detailed quotation. So how does this offer differ to that which the PIA will eventually need to issue to the supplier? The PIA has offered the end buyer terms and conditions that they can adhere to, as an intermediary. Thus the PIA has to ensure that these terms will mirror their own when seeking formally to procure the goods from the supplier. Let us assume on this side of the deal that the PIA has managed to secure the goods from a supplier directly without using other intermediaries to assist them. Below you will see an example of the procurement offer and the 'mirror' effect of the two separate sides of the trade.

The Procurement Offer

(PIA full heading/logo/contact)

Issue Date: 12/1/2008 AEST 12.00 Noon

Transaction code: 118-PIA-ETH-001

BUYER: PIA Import/Export

Validity Date: 5 days from issue date.

The Purchase offer

Product: Automotive Ethanol; EB121 Density 791.5

Specification: Fuel Anhydrate Ethanol for Automotive Use. Origin Brazil: Technical Regulation: Appearance – Clear and free of suspended matter: Total Acids Mg/Litre-30 P.P.M Max.(ASTM D – 1613) Electrical Conductivity: u S/m-500 Max.(ASTM D – 1125) Specific 'point of production' gravity at 20 C Kg/M3 791.5 max. (ASTM D – 4052) Ethanol at point of production – 99.3 min Copper as Cu – 0.07% P.P.M. Nil of: Fe, Na, Cl, SO4.

Origin: Santos Port, Brazil.

Price: US$539 per MT +/– 5%

Quantity: One shipment per month for 3 months 15,000 MT

Contracted Quantity: 45,000 MT +/– 10%

Performance guarantee: The buyer will require a PG 1.5% per each delivery as defined on contract issued as a UCP600 SLC or similar. Issued as non-cumulative revolving letter of credit.

Delivery: FOB named port of shipment as per Incoterms 2000

Payment: Irrevocable restricted documentary letter of credit issued applying UCP 600 banking rules issued as non-cumulative revolving and advised by a top 100 world ranked banking institution. Collection shall occur with the presentation of a clean on board 'ship's mate's receipt' and other standard presentation documents as defined on contract in accordance with delivery under Incoterms 2000. Should the seller be required to assist in securing a clean on board marine bill of lading, this shall accrue a further cost for the account of the buyer in accordance with delivery rules as applied under FOB and/ or 'FOB with added services' variant as per Incoterms 2000 delivery rules. All fees relating to collection and authenticating the credit are for cost of the Seller. The rules applied for collection shall define the use of URC 522.

First delivery: As per contract – 01/4/2008 or earlier.

Procedures:

1) Quotation is issued then returned as accepted (not legally binding).

2) Offer is issued from buyer for seller's consideration, upon which seller returns as accepted or negotiated upon until accepted (acceptance is legally binding).

3) Draft contract negotiated upon and returned accepted by the buyer, as issued by the seller, unless seller will consider buyer's contract (an email advising this shall be issued). Upon acceptance of the contact, one copy shall be sent via email; one copy marked 'Original' shall be sent via facsimile; and the hardcopy shall be sent by overnight courier. Hardcopy shall be deemed as the ruling document, in case the facsimile copy fails to arrive or vice versa whereas the email copy is sent for clarity.

4) Buyer issues DLC as per offer/contract.

5) Seller issues PG as per contract if applicable.

6) Delivery initiated by document presentation as per offer/contract.

7) Collection occurs as per each shipment until final delivery.

8) Offer is issued as being legally binding once accepted.

Seller's Declaration:

I the aforesaid seller agree to offer the goods as herein defined to the buyer and do hereby accept this offer made by the buyer with good and honourable intent.

Contract to be issued by: Buyer (   ) Seller (   )

Date:
Print Name:
Signed:

Buyer's Declaration:

I/we the buyer(s) acting ostensibly on behalf of an undisclosed principal issue this offer to purchase the goods as herein defined.

The following information shall be included in the body of the contract:

Name of company/entity/buyer:

Address:

Contact details both business and personal:

Name of bank used to pay for goods:

Account Name:

Account Address:

Account Number:

SWIFT Code:

Bank, Phone, Facsimile:

Port of Loading:

Certificate of Origin required: Yes (   ) No (   ) (Cost for the buyer's account)

Date:
Print Name:
Signed:

Offer Comparison

The PIA is ensuring that the terms and conditions of each principal's agreement are 'mirrored'. The PIA has the capability to resell because of the 'ostensible authority' to do so, and the PIA can prove this through their email correspondence with the supplier. The contract with the buyer states as follows:

Upon the pre-advised credit being advised to the seller (the seller on this side of the deal is the PIA) the seller shall disclose a document, correctly filled in, as described on the sales contract in blank form under the heading 'Policy Proof of Interest' certificate (PPI). This document shall state the name of the supplier, all contact details, a transaction code for the allocated goods, and permission for the buyer to make contact with the owner in possession of the goods one time only to verify that the goods being offered by the PIA are genuine and real. This shall immediately cause the pre-advised credit to lose its status as 'pre-advised' and to become a fully active documentary letter of credit.

The PIA obtains the pre-advised letter of credit from the buyer, but provides a fully operational letter of credit to the supplier. Note the obvious difference here: the PIA has no concerns about disclosing genuine details that identify the supplier. Whether or not the end buyer verifies this information has no bearing on the deal at hand. The very act of surrendering this information means that the pre-advised credit must be converted to a fully operational and active documentary letter of credit as per UCP600 Rules.

The letter of credit is restricted to the PIA, meaning it cannot be transferred any further. The PIA conversely has obtained an unrestricted letter of credit from the buyer, which means that the buyer has issued a transferable credit to the PIA. However, the PIA will issue a non-transferable credit to the supplier in accordance with the UCP rules of trade, but only after the PPI has been given to their end buyer.

The following is an ongoing serious problem and it is appropriate to highlight it at this stage as it has resulted in the loss of otherwise viable deals. An intermediary cannot and must not attempt to transfer the whole pre-advised DLC as obtained from the end buyer: the advising bank will not allow it. Instead the intermediary offers a condition (such as the production of a specific document or documents) so that once this condition(s) has been met the pre-advised status on the credit is removed. Once removed the credit can be advised as a non-transferable instrument. The supplier does not get a 'transferable instrument' regardless of whether the buyer/seller has asked for one from the end buyer. The transfer is from the end buyer to the buyer/seller, after which the financial instrument has the buy price portion of the credit issued to the supplier as a non-transferable instrument.

Furthermore the PIA has let it be known that the price of goods does not include the transfer fee and pre-advising fee relating to the letter of credit. The PIA has told the end buyer to pay it as well – and why not? Intermediaries are in a precarious position and although UCP600 implies that such costs are for the beneficiary of the credit it is a very ambiguous provision indeed and shows that UCP600 has not addressed the matter as it applies to intermediaries. If the deal did not include the PIA and an end buyer was issuing the credit to the supplier directly then upon advising the credit to the supplier, the cost associated with doing so is applied for the account of the end buyer as a 'bank charge'. Yet as soon as an intermediary is involved this charge becomes known as a 'transfer fee'. Similarly with a pre-advised DLC, if an end buyer were to buy directly from the supplier they would not usually accept a pre-advised DLC. Rather, they would expect the much more expensive confirmed DLC. In any event, the supplier has nothing to lose by disclosing 'proof of product'.

In terms of the 'transfer fee', there is light at the end of the tunnel. There is a rule under UCP600 that in effect states: 'Unless agreed upon, such transfer fees are for the account of the beneficiary'. 'Unless agreed upon' has a very specific interpretation aimed squarely at the intermediary. Incredibly, most intermediaries are not aware of this. As the offer already indicates the end buyer is to pay for the transfer fee, so that upon acceptance of the offer 'the end buyer has agreed with the seller to pay the transfer fee'. The issuing bank may take issue with this but as the contract is bound with the end buyer then it is for the end buyer to tell their bankers to issue the transfer fee as a cost added to their account. Most internet traders currently have no idea about this transfer fee and the extent of the costs involved which can stretch to tens of thousands of dollars depending on the value of the DLC.

Once verification has been provided which proves the seller's interests in the goods being sold to the end buyer, the credit converts into a normal DLC and can then be transferred. There will also be other expenses before the end buyer actually receives the goods, so the cost of the goods is 'gross' as opposed to 'net and clear'. The addition of the transfer fee as a business expense is both morally and legally acceptable. If these fees become a sore point with the end buyer, the PIA has two options to mitigate the expense. Firstly, the PIA could drop the price of the goods as an incentive for the buyer to follow through with the deal at hand. However, the PIA is really reducing their own secured commission and giving the difference to the end buyer as a further price drop. (This is not a good idea if it is a large bulk deal, but perhaps acceptable if it is a small deal such as a full container load.) In the alternative the PIA could return the transfer fee as a full refund on the seller's invoice as a credit to favour the end buyer, which is the better option.

The PIA should *never* pay these fees from their own pocket, but rather uses the end buyer's funds to pay them. He will deal with many end buyers; it is not beyond the realms of possibility that many deals could reach this stage and still fall apart. Even though getting to this stage in a deal dramatically increases the chances of closing it, it does not guarantee that the deal will close. If the PIA were to pay these fees personally on every single deal they were trading upon at any one time in a one-year period it could potentially cost them millions of dollars. As a new trader, you must be particularly careful in this regard. After you have closed your first deal then you would have the required experience (and the funds) to decide if and when you would pay the transfer fees.

The issuance of a PA DLC may be avoided altogether if you ask for an operational irrevocable transferable DLC directly. This may occur particularly when dealing with buyers with whom you have previously closed a deal. If the end buyer insists that you pay the transfer fee, then at the very least (if you feel that the parameters of the deal are intact) you must obtain a normal DLC which is also confirmed with your advising bank. However, first time around you must avoid paying the transfer fee at all costs, no matter how tempting the deal may seem. The only exception to this would be if the fee were so small that one would encounter similar fees if they were selling a single container load of goods.

As an intermediary you should trade as per the directions in this book until you gain sufficient experience. This is a critical factor of survival in the industry, which enables you to obtain the requisite experience before you close your first deal. The credit from the end buyer is to come from a top 300 bank. Just in case this does not happen, you may if you wish offer the supplier 'safe' credit without the need to add a number to the banking world financial ranking. As a matter of fact it is good to avoid the use of the term 'bank' when dealing with the supplier. Conversely the term 'bank' should always be used when dealing with the end buyer for very good reasons as provided in the newly formed UCP600.

If the term 'bank issued' is not used, UCP600 allows a person to issue a DLC from their own desk as a 'Corporate DLC' to the PIA. This is a letter of credit that has not been issued by a bank, but rather issued from within a company. The intermediary could end up with a fake or otherwise useless DLC simply because they failed to include the words 'bank issued DLC only'. As a result the intermediary would be compelled either to accept it or face a breach of contract. With sufficient confidence and experience, however, a buyer/seller could indeed accept a 'non-transferable' bank issued financial instrument, and then issue a corporate DLC from their own desk to the supplier, which is backed by the real DLC in their account. This is similar to a person writing a cheque. A cheque is honoured as long as there are sufficient funds in the account.

The performance guarantee requested from the supplier is different to that which is offered to the end buyer. You could indeed offer no PG to the end buyer and still insist on one from the supplier for your own peace of mind. In any case the PG from the supplier must always be higher in value to that which the PIA is offering to the end buyer.

The PG being sought from the supplier in our example could be issued as a 'UCP600 SLC' or 'ISP98 SLC' but ideally, since there is nobody between you and the supplier, then a normal UCP600 transferable SLC is the preferred instrument. The banking rules define that UCP600 SLC issued for use as a PG can only be transferred once, whereas the ISP98 SLC can be used and transferred several times between traders. You are allowed to ask that the transfer fee is for the account of the supplier, but generally a SLC transfer fee is small and often affordable to an intermediary (often involving hundreds, rather than thousands or tens of thousands of dollars). It is better for an intermediary not to ask for the payment of the SLC transfer fee, unless the SLC value is at a value of at least 100,000 dollars per each delivery.

If required, the PIA would ideally offer a PG or, even better, FTN's own instrument, the Late Delivery Discount (LDD), to the end buyer as per the example offer above. Further the PIA would omit the term 'bank issued' in favour of the term 'bank advised', if the credit is being transferred from the account of the intermediary. If an intermediary is actually transferring the SLC as obtained from the supplier to a lesser amount favouring the end buyer, then the phrase 'bank issued' SLC should be used.

In these circumstances FTN Exporting prefers a bank issued SLC for the PIA's account. The PIA then issues a private 'corporate' SLC to the end buyer, which in turn is backed by the active SLC in their account. This would in fact make for a much easier transaction and, although this practice is not recommended for a first deal, it can be used when the trader has sufficient experience. The best method first time around for the intermediary is simply to secure a UCP600 SLC as a PG that is made transferable.

If you compare the procedures in place with the end buyer to those required of the supplier, you'll see that the supplier must only adhere to minimum essential elements in order to facilitate the deal. The end buyer, however, is being made to comply with more stringent requirements in their agreement with the PIA. If the supplier is eager to make a sale they will try to accommodate the PIA: after all that is the whole essence of being a manufacturer and exporter.

Luckily, the same rationale is applied to the end buyer. An end buyer who has invested millions in, for example, being able to supply ethanol, is doing so to make profits. The ability to buy goods at slightly better than mainstream price allows this potential end buyer to make better gains in their home market. The PIA is in the middle and must work twice as hard as the end buyer and supplier, as they have double the amount of work to do.

The PIA has an independent deal with the end buyer and the end buyer's bank and is using an advising bank to transact with the other banks. The advising bank and all other banks make profits from their involvement in such deals. Therefore the PIA must act in such a way with banks that enables them to conduct their part in the transaction in accordance with UCP600. It is important to remember that banks have to be cautious in giving advice and often refrain from doing so, so it is best not to expect or depend on advice or assistance from them. When dealing with banks the PIA must act in a way that ensures the banks are able to conduct their business under UCP600. Similarly banks may not always know the relatively new UCP600 rules very well – there were problems with banks complying with the rules under UCP500. It is therefore the PIA's responsibility to ensure that the bank acts properly and to inform them in writing if they make any mistakes.

The quotation, the subsequent offer and then the contract are all matters the PIA must handle with the two principals. The PIA, however, must also handle commissions and pay orders in their dealings with the intermediaries. Once the contracts have been agreed the PIA begins the financial instrument transactions between themselves and each bank. It is important to remember that the financial instruments are independent of the sales contract and the goods that are the subject of the trade. The bank is not a signatory party to the contract between buyer and seller in either side of the transaction. Contrary to the views of many ill-informed intermediaries, banks are not allowed to interfere in matters regarding the contract of sale as defined under Article 4 UCP600 paragraph (a) and (b).

The issuing bank issues a credit to the PIA, which means that the bank and not the end buyer is guaranteeing payment based on performance. The bank issues the credit as per the buyer's instructions, adding any conditions the buyer wishes to attach which pertain to their contracting conditions with the seller. The PIA is only required to perform as per the rules of the credit and the rules of its issuance under UCP600. If there is a dispute as to the contract once the credit is advised, bad luck: under UCP rules of issuance the end buyer cannot cancel credit because it has been issued as 'irrevocable'. As long as the terms and conditions of the credit are met by the PIA the issuing bank will allow payment to be collected in accordance with rules of collection: Uniform Rules for Collection publication 522 (URC 522).

If a dispute arises over a delivery matter within the sales contract after completion of the deal there are two options: either to settle it amicably or through arbitration. The arbitration process decides who is at fault and the remedies required (if any). If these matters are present on the offer this will reinforce these conditions at an early stage and in turn make the offer a more authoritative document. Further, if the contracting party has notice of the likely terms and conditions at offer stage there will be less to negotiate once the contract is issued. Both parties will already be familiar with the likely terms and conditions, which provides for a more swift and seamless transaction. This again reiterates the important role the offer plays in the overall scheme of things.

It is important to remember that matters of dispute in relation to the credit are settled between the bank and the intermediate buyer/seller. They have nothing to do with matters of breaches implied in the offer and the subsequent sales contract. In other words the PIA could successfully close a deal and collect the commission but could still face legal action for breach of contract.

In such circumstances the bank has performed so the dispute is between the end buyer and the PIA. In turn the PIA looks to the supplier for support, as it is most likely that the breach occurred because of the supplier and not due to any fault of the PIA. Likewise, the buyer may have collected the performance guarantee and the deal still closes without any further action. In another scenario a deal could close with the PIA and the end buyer but the PIA could still be answerable to the supplier for a breach of contracting conditions. It will be useful at this stage to study the difference between the two offers (set out above) to see where the differences are. Ask yourself what these changes are and why they are made. The answers are given throughout this chapter.

12

The Contract of Sale

The contract formalizes the information contained in the offer (which is why the contents of the offer are so important). The contract can be more extensive than the model contract set out later in this chapter, or it can be simplified. In short, however, the simpler the better – although it is important not to make it so brief that it omits important and necessary details. The supplier may dictate terms and conditions to the PIA, but the PIA dictates terms and conditions to their own end buyer. In essence the PIA may be dealing with two very different contract models simultaneously. As long as the main elements are apparent in both, the PIA would still be able to close the deal effectively.

There are 'association' type contracts available on the internet, for instance on Nymex.com or Nybot.com. It may be instructive to study what they require from their clients and see whether there are any terms that could be applicable to your business.

As an example take a look at the contract basics for crude oil on http://www.nymex.com/lsco_fut_cso.aspx New York Mercantile Exchange (USA) (online).

If you were selling the same type of crude oil then information as found on the site would be incorporated onto your on contract as appropriate. Although new traders would not be expected to reach contract stage in a deal it is good practice to become familiar with these procedures in advance. If a new trader were to find a viable deal, attachment with a good buyer/seller like the PIA would enable that person to learn how to use contracts over time. Drafting contracts takes time to master but arguably, no matter who has drafted it, all contracts can be subject to interpretation.

This brings us back to the matter of 'intent'. It is only when problems associated with failed deliveries and defects arise that issues of contract interpretation become problematic. By ensuring that you issue a clear offer, which is further supported by an unambiguous contract, you will go a long way to dealing with any problems that may arise. This is especially because the offer and contract are founded on strong, safe trading procedures that are reflected in the elements embodied in the formation of a contract.

Often where a supplier is eager to make a sale, they will consider the terms and conditions of the intermediary's contract. One approach in this instance is to wait until the supplier furnishes their draft contract. If it is found to be unworkable to the PIA, the offered draft contract is cancelled with an email stating that: 'The draft contract offered has been rejected.' The intermediary then offers the supplier a draft copy of their own 'created' contract. There is nothing wrong with this procedure; indeed it is an acceptable part of negotiation prior to doing business. This is also the period in which both parties try to settle any matters requiring clarification or exploration. Thus the rejection of a contract should only be used as a final resort, if the supplier's contract model is completely unworkable. This is a situation that is often encountered where the terms and conditions on the offer were not repeated on the contract.

However, continually providing counter offers instead of negotiating the terms and conditions of a draft contract could result in a precarious trading situation to the intermediary. Too many forms, offers and draft contracts could lead to confusion and more seriously, any later delays in the deal could end up generating all sorts of invalid documents. This may especially be the case if the end buyer is seemingly trying to avoid their obligations in the deal, increasing the risk of 'induced frustration'.

It would be difficult to convince a judge or arbitrator that you have a breach of contract where for example ten different contracts are produced by the supplier or end buyer. Therefore it is important that the intermediary is the one who creates 'back doors' in order to disentangle themselves from becoming legally tied to a deal that they did not want to enter. So how is this done? The best means of doing this is for the intermediary to self-impose a strict policy, so that if they feel that they need to get out of a deal they have previously entered into, they would be best placed to do this by knowing the rules of trade very well. A sound knowledge of the rules enables the intermediary to identify mistakes that the end buyer or supplier has made.

In adopting this approach the intermediary needs to be very strict with their methods in omitting to tell the transacting parties when they have failed to observe the rules to the letter. After all, it's the 'intent' that matters, right? Why inform either one of the principals about their mistakes if you are always able to stand on firm ground, and be able to close a good deal where goods are delivered and money is paid upon effective delivery? If your intent is indeed good, then your only concern is to get the goods to the buyer as ordered. End buyers and suppliers will not hesitate to take action against you if you are the one who has destroyed a deal by making serious mistakes. Therefore you as an honourable trader will not use obvious mistakes against a principal, unless there comes a time where you need to stand firm in protecting yourself against a potentially damaging claim.

For example, having accepted the end buyer's funds on, say, Monday, you are getting ready to return the contract to the supplier the same day, having signed it on the previous Friday. However, you receive an email from the supplier, which arrives half an hour before you were going to send the contract by facsimile, email and courier. This email states that they were unable to hold the price of the goods, and that they require at least another 10 dollars per MT. You are already aware that the supplier's contract is offering 2.75 per cent performance guarantee when in fact it should have read 1.75 per cent.

The first course of action is to 'avoid' responding to the email and proceed with issuing the contract. It is obvious at such a late stage of the deal that the intermediary is prepared to perform whereas the supplier is arguably heading for a breach of conditions. The contract is therefore sent away first. Some time later you respond to the email and advise that the contract is on its way via courier, that the contract has also been provided by fax and email, and the irrevocable letter of credit is in the process of being transferred. You also remind the supplier that you will be awaiting the arrival of the performance guarantee and finally state that no change of price is possible, however you state that you are prepared to accept a 1.75 per cent performance guarantee. The deal could be saved from litigation simply because you kept in reserve a mistake that favoured you and not the supplier. An even better situation would have been if you had offered a LDD (Late Delivery Discount) to the end buyer of a far lesser amount than the PG you were going to get from the supplier. The PG could be lowered even more to act as consolation for the supplier in relation to this added expense. This is not an unusual scenario, especially if the supplier is in possession of much sought-after goods in a market with increasing prices.

To summarize: if you need to find a back door to avoid a deal later on, an earlier mistake made by a principal could serve you well. If it is not affecting the trade, leave it, but only as long as the mistake favours you. The offer stated that a 'Top 300' world class bank is to be used to pay for the goods on the offer. It is mentioned again in the contract. But what if you have a LC being advised by a small, unsupported Third World bank? The credit is as a result not accepted so you advise that an amendment is required. The credit now needs to be confirmed as well. Naturally there is going to be a considerable dispute. There may be days or weeks of arguments and contract scheduling may also become compromised. You could also lose your performance guarantee for being late with delivery. In turn you don't accept any credit, even if it is confirmed, until another amendment is issued that cancels the effectiveness of the performance guarantee as a condition of the credit. The buyer is at fault and is facing breach of contract conditions. Therefore 'don't accept the credit' does not mean that you remain silent: on the contrary, under UCP600 'silence' now implies acceptance. The protocol for notifying 'non acceptance of a credit' is by writing to the issuing bank to advise of your instructions to the advising bank. You provide a reason as to why the credit is not accepted and the amendment required in order for you to be able to accept the credit.

This is another situation in which a mistake in procedures may indeed favour you. The buyer cancels the performance guarantee before you accept the confirmed credit, or the buyer faces a breach of contract for issuing the original credit on different terms to those specified on the contract. Finally, you accept the confirmed credit and the deal closes. The end buyer may become forceful and insist for instance that they have confirmed the credit as requested, and refuse to alter the credit's terms and conditions as to the performance guarantee requirement. At this stage, suggest to the end buyer in the first instance they are already in breach of contract and provide the nature of the breaches accordingly. This is also the time to also advise the end buyer that their breach is serious. Further, you can insist that the matter of the performance guarantee should be corrected, within the next three days or so, in order to 'continue' with the deal at hand or 'face the consequences of your actions'. Reserving your threat for a genuine mistake is also the best course of action because, once such a threat is issued, the 'amicable' status of the deal is lost and the situation could become litigious.

If the PIA can see in advance that an end buyer is attempting to take advantage of the situation, in that they know that the deal will go through but they will gain the performance guarantee, then the buyer is acting dishonourably and the PIA may issue a 'threat' of legal action in response. Obviously the PIA is only going to make this type of threat as a last resort, especially in a situation where amicable relations are still possible. If the intermediary has only used strict trading procedures then the transaction often continues to move forwards. When the next major problem arises it is tackled accordingly. By continuing with the deal, the intermediary cannot point to previous problems already addressed and rectified in their defence if the whole deal collapses later on, for whatever reason.

If a potential deal starts badly, then it is usually a sign that the rest of the deal will also progress badly. Knowing when to use 'mistakes' made by others takes time to learn and is dependent upon the intermediary knowing the rules of trade, especially the UCP banking rules and Incoterms 2000. This is another reason why so many intermediaries on the internet today have no idea how to trade in a strict and disciplined environment: they lack the critical understanding as to the trading rules that are designed specifically to favour them. If you know the rules they can be used to your advantage.

Trade associations have their own model contracts, thus those who, for instance, sell sugar might use the Refined Sugar Association (RSA) of London model contract and the terms and conditions therein. There are no standard contract models as far as secondary transactions are concerned. The intermediary cannot run for advice to a trade lawyer every five minutes to have contracts drafted on a deal they are working on because, as you will soon learn, many such deals do not complete and the expense of engaging lawyers on a weekly basis would become prohibitive.

Each contract is drafted to reflect the nature of the particular trade in question. Contract models are produced in the simplest and most effective manner. The basic model offered in this chapter gives the trader a simple yet effective guide for use with a wide range of products, should a trader progress to such a position in a trade.

Once at contract stage use the term 'draft contract' on each contract document until negotiations are completed, at which time a 'final' contract is made. Until the contract is finalized the rules of acceptance regarding the offer change slightly, in that the transaction code as applied from the acceptable offer remains on the draft stage of the contract and does not need to change again when the final contract is created. The contract itself includes all the information included in the quotation and the offer. As we have already seen getting past the offer stage is the most difficult part and in terms of the trading process the offer is arguably the most crucial aspect of the deal. The contract, however, is the document that is relied upon should a dispute arise at delivery or when the goods arrive in possession of the end buyer, or where a dispute has arisen from the supply side of the transaction.

If the contract terms and conditions are unclear or if a dispute has failed to be resolved amicably, the offer is produced in an effort to reinforce or settle the disagreement. It is for this reason that traders must ensure that the documents they produce are comprehensive and unequivocal so as to present clear intent, in case of any future legal challenges. When faced with a serious dispute, being ignorant of the law is not a defence. Equally, if you are attempting to defend yourself against litigation there is no excuse for being ignorant of the facts. A contract is the defining document that sets out the intent, obligations and risks to each party. It is extremely foolish to sign a contract that you either do not understand or have not properly studied.

The PIA issues a draft contract to the end buyer to initiate the final set of procedures and to tie both parties into a legally-binding situation. Remember you are both already in a legally-binding situation once the buyer has accepted the offer (unless you had issued the offer subject to final contract) but the final agreement is dictated by the terms and conditions of the contract. If the terms and conditions of the contract contradict anything that was agreed at offer stage, and the offer was signed as being accepted on the condition that a final contract is sealed, there is no 'breach of contract'.

If the buyer has agreed the offer, but for some reason rejects the contract (although the terms on the offer are the same as those on the contract), and no attempts to resolve the issues by negotiation are successful, then an implied breach of an 'agreement' is said to have occurred. The 'agreement' is evidenced by the fact that the offer still remains effective. Assume the PIA had produced a well-defined offer. If the buyer is refusing to sign a contract and making trivial excuses in an attempt to avoid being formally obligated to perform, they can be sued for 'breach of conditions'. This is especially so where a PIA can show that their obligation to perform has already cost them time, effort and money, and where potential gains on the deal have been lost. So does the 'offer' constitute a contractual agreement? That depends on whether there is among other things, relevant 'consideration'.

Consideration is (usually) the payment for the goods. Without consideration, there can be no contract in the first place. Consideration must be apparent as it effectively validates the impending contract. Misguided intermediaries often issue poorly drafted offers and contracts that fail to contain any valuable consideration.

Here is an example:

Dear Sir,

Please find enclosed an offer for Mazut 100 crude oil and a draft contract. 2 million barrels per month for 12 months is on offer. If you have a buyer please provide an NCND agreement for you and your group so we can close upon this transaction ASAP. When you are ready to return the contract I will advise the price of the goods.

Surprisingly this is a more common scenario than you might assume. Many misguided intermediaries consider this to be an offer worth considering because it has some kind of contract attached to it. However, it's not worth even a minute of effort because, among other things, one essential element is missing – a readily identifiable price or price benchmark for the goods being offered. All contracts have elements of varying importance: some elements are essential, without which the contract is ineffective. There are six elements that the intermediary must look for immediately before taking the time to consider the other terms and conditions:

1. The intention of the parties to create a legally-binding relationship must be apparent on the contract (but this event occurs before the contract is seen or even drafted).

2. The deal starts when a readily identifiable seller of goods declares expressly or implicitly that the goods are being sold to a buyer and that buyer is readily identifiable. This happens upon first contact with one party to the other. Hence whether you are communicating by facsimile, email or telephone – the very first time one party contacts another in relation to the prospective transaction – this establishes the commencement of the deal (and the time when each party becomes aware of their intention to create a legally binding situation). In the example above, 'Dear Sir' is simply not good enough. 'Dear Sir' bearing the letterhead of a supplier and or end buyer is good, but even better is 'Dear Sir' addressed personally to the PIA.

3. The third element is 'Valuable Consideration'. The elements of the contract are evident long before the contract is drafted.

Other essential elements applied as a matter of contract itself include:

4. Legal capacity;

5. Genuine consent; and

6.   Legality of objects.

All of which are of great importance as far as intermediaries are concerned.

Despite these requirements, there are often situations in which an initial introduction by an intermediary 'buyer' or 'seller' is followed swiftly by a contract. These contracts usually have at least one of these vital elements missing. This creates a very dangerous situation in which the intermediary could find themselves relying on the fact that they have created a legally-binding situation when the contract could be null and void.

The contract model below is for an FOB Incoterms 'Named Port of Shipment' deal. It is fairly comprehensive – more so than some real contracts – and is deliberately so for the purposes of study. It does not matter what type of goods are being bought and sold, the contract model stays the same and can be amended to reflect the relevant commodity. The general terms and conditions remain the same regardless of the type of goods.

The model contract is reproduced below (indented and in smaller type) and, where appropriate, commentary follows after each section. This example provides a clear insight into the issues and the reason for the inclusion of a particular paragraph in the body of the contract. As long as the salient terms provided here are also provided in the supplier's contract, regardless of the words used to express those terms, then one contract will 'mirror' the other. The supplier's contract terms, which don't appear to have any reference to the clauses in the model below, should be examined closely and, if they are of concern, the buyer/seller should ask the suppliers to amend or even omit the terms that seem not to favour the buyer/seller. This is especially so in relation to matters regarding the carrier.

The FOB contract model below reflects the simplest type of contract format that the first time intermediary should learn to use as the PIA for the contract between the PIA and the end buyer. Over time and with experience the intermediary will learn to identify variables and adapt the model for their own use.

Contract of Sale UCP600 FOB
Supporting Incoterms 2000 'FOB Named Port of Shipment'
UCP600 DLC Applies
Internet Trading Compliant

Made Between:

PARTIES:
SELLER
FTN Exporting, ABN: F345623
Authorized Representative: Davide Giovanni Papa, CEO
PO BOX 30 Carlton North, 3054
Melbourne, Victoria, Australia.

Full name and business address will need to be provided as well as a mailing address. Avoid using just a post office box address.

BUYER

ABC Corporation, 77 Sunset Drive, Hollywood, Los Angeles 90122 California USA
Authorized Representative: Mr. Pink, CEO

Full name and business address will need to be provided as well as a mailing address. Avoid using just a post office box address.

On this the   day of   in the year 20--

TRANSACTION CODE   XXXXX

This transaction code is the same on the purchase offer with the supplier. Once issued, the transaction code cannot be changed. Words are better than numbers for documenting dates and values although both can be used for the sake of clarity, for example $350 (three hundred and fifty dollars).

WHEREAS: (also known as the 'Preamble')

The seller is a private independent intermediate seller or vendor acting without disclosure of any other principal as per the procedure commonly and legally applied under various rules of agency.

It is of great importance to protect the seller's position, which is why the extra term such as 'vendor' is also provided. The end buyer knows that they are not dealing with the supplier.

The buyer or end buyer is a corporate or individual entity paying for and taking both documentary and physical possession of the goods.

This is clear: you are not selling to another intermediary buyer, but an end buyer who gets both physical possession and documentary title of the goods. An intermediary cannot ever obtain possession of the goods, but only clean documentary title to them.

It is up to the seller if they choose to incorporate a 'Preamble' or 'whereas clauses' by way of an introduction. Nothing legally binding should be included in these clauses as their purpose is to provide the background to the transaction.

NOW, THEREFORE, IT IS AGREED AS FOLLOWS:

1. DEFINITIONS

All acronyms and the most important terms relating to the agreement should be defined at the beginning of the contract. This reduces the length of the contract and makes reading and interpretation much more simple. Parties to the contract are able to refer to the meaning or interpretation of a specific word or term in one section of the contract.

> 1.1 Date of issue: The date of this agreement, and therefore the validity commencement date, shall be the date on which the seller issues this agreement to the buyer.

> 1.2 Buyer: The buyer taking documentary title and physical possession.

> 1.3 Seller: A private independent intermediate seller and vendor of the goods.

> 1.4 Supplier: The manufacturer or other supplier of the goods to the seller.

> 1.5 PPI: The Policy Proof of Interest certificate shall be the instrument by which the letter of credit will cease to have a 'pre-advised' status and become a fully operational transferable documentary letter of credit.

> 1.6 All times and dates quoted are as per Australian Eastern Standard Times (AEST) and are taken from 12.30 PM.

> 1.7 Days shall have their ordinary meaning of 24 hours and there are 7 in every week.

> 1.8 Months shall be defined as a period of 30 consecutive days.

> 1.9 Years shall constitute 365 consecutive days.

By setting out the above information there can be no confusion. Thus if you put 'Banking days' then banking days should be defined. 'Days' is the preferred terminology for contracts. Although UCP600 credit rules define the use of 'Days' as meaning 'banking days' this is not appropriate for use in contracts when intermediaries are involved as it makes clarification of timescales difficult.

Remember that intermediaries always need to allow for more 'days' than will actually be needed.

2. VALIDITY AND CONTRACT ACCEPTANCE

2.1 This contract is not valid until such time as an offer has been accepted in relation to the purchase of the goods.

2.2 This agreement shall be valid for a period of fifteen days from the date of issue. The date of issue is the date on which the seller issues this agreement to the buyer as defined under 'Validity Date'.

The contract is only valid for a limited time. This is because the PIA, having obtained 'ostensible authority' from the supplier, must assume that they are not in a position to offer the goods *ad infinitum*.

2.3 Should this agreement not be signed within the stipulated timescale the contract shall become invalid and not legally binding.

2.4 All times as per (AEST) Australian Eastern Standard Times and Dates quoted are as per Australian Eastern Standard Times (AEST).

2.5 This contract cannot be entered into unless and until the seller has accepted the buyer's signed offer.

2.6 Once signed and dated the buyer must return this contract to the seller via facsimile transmission, and in addition a scanned Portable Document Format (PDF) or other electronic copy of the document must also be transmitted via electronic mail.

2.7 The time and date of transmission and acceptance of the contract by the buyer shall be deemed to be at the time and date when the buyer sent the document.

2.8 The arrival of either the facsimile copy bearing handwritten signatures and/or the PDF format copy bearing the term 'original' shall mean that the intent of the buyer is to proceed, as being legally bound by the terms and conditions of this contract.

2.9 Good and honourable intent shall govern the parties to this contract at all times.

3. PRODUCT TO BE SOLD

3.1 Automotive Ethanol

Anhydrate Ethanol made from sugar biomass, which is fit for use as a gasoline additive or for any machinery made and designed to be operated using Anhydrate ethanol. Unfit for human consumption.

3.2 Origin Brazil, South America

In case of serious delay or unforeseen events (see clause 17 below) the seller has the right to secure goods from another port or country, of equivalent quality to the goods offered in this agreement in accordance with the specification below.

3.3 Specifications, Grade, Packaging

Fuel Anhydrate Ethanol for Automotive Use. Origin Brazil: Technical Regulation: DNC 01/91 'AEAC' Appearance: Clear and free of suspended matter: Total Acids Mg/Litre-30 P.P.M Max. Electrical Conductivity: u S/m-500 Max. Specific 'Point of Production gravity at 20 C Kg/M3 791.5 max. Ethanol at point of production – 99.3 min Copper as Cu – 0.07/ 8 P.P.M Nil of: Fe, Na, Cl, SO4.

A good supplier's quotation or offer includes the specifications of the goods. These are then included in the body of the contract. However, intermediaries are not industrial chemists and do not need to concern themselves with the meaning of the specifications. A buyer should know what they are buying and that the information has come directly from the owner of the goods, the supplier.

3.4 Quantity

3.4.1 Total contracted quantity being sold: 60,000 cubic meters (metres) defined as 'M3'. 'M3' is defined to mean 1,000 (one thousand) liters (litres) plus or minus 10 (ten) per cent.

3.4.2 1,000 liters shall also mean as an average 264.1 USA gallons, but only for the purpose of clarity: the 'M3' is the nominated quantifiable method for the purposes of this transaction.

Intermediaries are now no longer allowed to change the supplier's quantity into another measurement value at the end buyer's request. For example, if a quotation specifies a supply of 1,000 kilogrammes of gold bars at 1 kilo each, then the buyer/seller must not convert this amount to 1 metric ton. When reselling the goods they must be referred to in exactly the same way as they are described on the quotation. The issue here besides accuracy is one of clean presentation of delivery documents.

3.5 Shipment Schedule

The total minimum contracted quantities being purchased shall be defined as:

a)   60,000 cubic meters delivered over a 3-month period.

The total monthly minimum shipment delivery range offered:

b)   20,000 M3 per month plus or minus 10 per cent.

The total minimum shipment per year offered:

c) 3 shipments of: 20,000 M3 per shipment, per month, consecutively for 3 months.

Name of port and country of loading goods:

d) Santos, Brazil.

FOB, as per the delivery provisions in Incoterms 2000, applies so you must name the port of loading.

3.6 Price and Weight Tolerance

As per UCP600: plus or minus 5 per cent on final contract shall be accepted as a tolerance for the purpose of the financial instrument used to pay for the goods. Up to 10 per cent is allowed as a tolerance of the goods weight without affecting presentation of delivery documents.

3.7 Price of Goods

US$400.00 PER MT FOB (Four hundred United States dollars).

Cost of goods per month/shipment: US$8,000,000.00 (Eight million United States dollars).

Total contract value per 60,000 M3: US$24,000,000.00 (Twenty-four million United States dollars).

Total revolving opening credit value: US$24,000,000.00 (Twenty-four million United States dollars).

4. DELIVERY

FREE ON BOARD 'NAMED PORT OF SHIPMENT' (FOB) as per the ICC Paris, France; (International Chamber of Commerce) delivery mode, as applied under rules Incoterms 2000.

5. PERFORMANCE GUARANTEE

5.1 The seller shall provide the buyer with an authenticated copy of the seller's performance guarantee, which declares that the seller is ready willing and able to abide by the performance guarantee as defined therein.

5.2 Should the buyer be at fault in not ensuring that the carrier is at the loading port on or before the time as stipulated in this contract, the performance guarantee will cease unconditionally to be valid for the total contracted value of the goods ordered, from the time such fault is recorded.

5.3 The presentation of the leading document that invalidates the performance guarantee will be delivered in accordance with the conditions scope and terms of this contract as defined under 'Delivery Documents'.

5.4 The performance guarantee value will be in the format of a UCP 600 defined standby letter of credit (SLC), or similar.

5.5 The performance guarantee for the net and clear value of not less than the amount defined below is payable unconditionally on first demand upon the buyer identifying that a genuine breach of delivery performance has occurred, as verified by the issuing bank to the advising bank of the seller.

5.6 Where multi-shipments are involved the issuance of the performance guarantee shall be defined as being 'non cumulative revolving'. The performance guarantee shall be issued within 3 days of the acceptance of the buyer's financial instrument.

5.7 The buyer shall allow a tolerance of plus or minus 1.0 per cent and accept the performance guarantee bearing this tolerance for each and every delivery.

5.8 Performance Guarantee Value

1.2 per cent, plus or minus 1.0 per cent per each shipment contract value of the goods being purchased.

5.9 The buyer agrees to accept the performance guarantee when lodged carrying the above value plus or minus 1.0 per cent. The buyer agrees to accept a performance value equal to more than, but not less than, the defined rate.

The intermediary has to make the deal work to their advantage. More about the PG later: for now this clause provides a clear indication of its value. The PIA in their wisdom has even allowed for a 1 per cent tolerance.

Note: The PIA is attempting to offer a PG as a personal instrument without the term 'bank issued' or 'endorsed' on it. If the end buyer requires changes on the contract to reflect a bank issued SLC, then the seller will add the term accordingly. If the goods were sold without a PG all mention of it is omitted from the contract.

5.10 Option: Late Delivery Discount (LDD)

In the event that the performance guarantee cannot be provided due to circumstances beyond the control of the seller, the seller shall communicate this in writing via email or facsimile immediately to the end buyer and in any event before accepting the financial instrument for payment of the goods. In this situation the seller shall offer a substitute 'Late Delivery Discount' (LDD) for any late or failed delivery. This will show on the seller's invoice as a discount against the price of the goods offered on this contract, favouring the buyer as per the rates shown below:

5.11 LLD Discount Rate: US$8.00 per M3

5.12 If the buyer wishes to accept the LDD rate instead of the performance guarantee they should when issuing the credit use the term 'Performance Guarantee: LDD Certificate Accepted'. The seller's LDD certificate will be provided in place of the performance guarantee SLC instrument, which once issued will remove the pre-advised status of the credit and convert it to a fully operational and active credit.

6. DUTIES OF THE BUYER

6.1 It is of primary importance that the buyer assists the seller in all matters. The buyer must not in any way hinder the seller in ensuring that the goods are delivered within the scope, terms and conditions of this contract.

6.2 The buyer shall be required to open a letter of credit to the seller within 7 days of signature of this agreement. Bank issued payment required: An irrevocable Transferable UCP 600 Confirmed pre-advised operational documentary letter of credit unrestricted, issued as transferable.

6.3 The buyer hereby accepts that signature of this internationally enforceable contract creates a personal legal obligation regardless of the domestic laws of their country.

6.4 The buyer, having paid and obtained the title to the goods shall be entitled to possession of them in accordance with the terms and conditions of this agreement.

7. DUTIES OF THE SELLER

7.1 The seller has purchased or is holding a contract for purchase or has the ability to purchase the interest in the goods offered from an undisclosed source(s) prior to offering the goods to the buyer. The seller is offering clean proprietary title and interest in the goods free of liens at an agreed price. The seller will transfer their interests and title to the goods or required parts thereof to the buyer without obtaining possession of the actual goods.

7.2 The seller has forthwith used a high degree of sourcing ability, skill and expertise in being able to offer a product to the buyer for reasonable gain and the buyer has obtained the lowest fair price for such goods as a direct result of the seller's ability, skill and expertise.

This a simple statement to reinforce to the buyer that the seller is indeed an intermediary, and that once the contract is signed; the buyer cannot 'pretend' not to have been informed of this fact. It is also a statement of fact, supporting the provision in the 'whereas clauses' that the PIA will give assistance to looking after the buyer's interests at all times.

> 7.3 The seller shall ensure that all matters of quality and warranty of the goods follow the goods, for the benefit of the end buyer.

> 7.4 The obligations to ensure quality and warranty shall be the responsibility of the seller.

The warranty related to the goods remains an obligation of the supplier. The seller must ensure, when sealing the contract with the supplier, that the warranty obligations follow the goods.

> 7.5 The seller shall be responsible for all maters up to final delivery. 'Delivery' is as defined by Incoterms 2000.

> SELLER'S WARRANTY OBLIGATIONS

> 7.6 The seller declares with good intent that the goods being sold are as described, fit for purpose and of merchantable quality and that if the producer, manufacturer or supplier of the goods is at fault for delivering goods which are of a defective nature from the point of manufacture the seller is responsible for any such reasonably defined defects in the goods.

> 7.7 The seller will initiate procedures to remedy those defects for the buyer taking final possession of such goods, within a period of 90 days after such goods having come into the possession of the buyer.

> 7.8 All claims of such defects and/or damage must be made within 28 days of the buyer obtaining possession of the goods.

> 7.9 The seller has obtained the implicit and specific right to transfer the warranty obligations, upon resale of the goods once only, and the manufacturer or owner of such goods has agreed to endorse this.

> 8. PROCEDURE IN THE EVENT OF DEFECTIVE GOODS

> 8.1 The procedure for claiming a remedy for the supply of defective goods shall be as follows:

> 8.2 The buyer shall first give notice to the seller of such defects in writing providing detailed information about the claim and proof of the same, sworn under affidavit or other acceptable statutory authority declaring that the goods did arrive in a state other than ordered, and that the goods are defective or damaged in such a way as to indicate that the supplier or manufacturer of the goods is at fault.

> 8.3 Photographic evidence of the damage shall also be provided where appropriate. Should a notice be communicated to the seller by facsimile transmission, JPEG or email the seller shall attempt to rectify the defect

on behalf of the buyer in the first instance to the mutual satisfaction of both once the evidence provided has been authenticated proving that the goods were delivered by the manufacturer or supplier in a sub-standard condition.

8.4 The buyer shall allow any authority representative of the seller visually to inspect the damage to the said goods in the buyer's country and/or premises and report the same to the seller.

8.5 The benefits conferred by the warranty are in addition to all implied warranties and other rights and remedies available to the buyer in respect of the goods being purchased under the Trade Practices Act and/or similar state or territory laws of the country from which the goods are being exported. This is in addition to statutory provisions under the Hague-Visby international shipping rules and in conjunction with the English Sale of Goods Act 1979 (as amended) which provides the law in relation to the carriage of goods, where such matters incorporate damage caused to goods that fall to be remedied by the carrier, as defined by the terms and conditions on the back of the bill of lading form.

8.6 The seller shall be required to remedy the damage or defect on behalf of the supplier once such evidence has been established in determining that the supplier or manufacturer is at fault for selling the damaged or defective goods.

As long as the buyer can prove that the supplier is at fault for the defective goods the seller shall cause the supplier to remedy the fault with the buyer directly. The seller can only interplead on behalf of the buyer and cannot be made to bear personal responsibility for any damaged goods that they have not even seen. Furthermore exporters in nearly every country in the world have to meet basic standards in order to export goods. If a buyer takes issue with an exporter regarding goods that are proven to be damaged goods and remedy is not forthcoming this could result in the supplier's export licence being revoked. Thus once the PIA has obtained the required assurances from the supplier as regards warranty and remedy, the warranty is endorsed over to the end buyer. If the supplier fails to act on the warranty obligation in relation to the goods, which arrive damaged or defective because of the supplier's negligence, then the end buyer can still take the matter up directly with the supplier as per the laws applicable to the supplier's country. Government agencies who issue export licences to suppliers do not look favourably on those who sell defective or damaged goods. The exporter's own representative, the consulate in the buyer's country, is the first port of call in seeking a satisfactory remedy for the supply of defective or damaged goods where the dispute has not been resolved to the end buyer's satisfaction. Failure to resolve the dispute may mean the matter could be decided through arbitration or litigation, depending on the nature of the disagreement and the terms of the contract.

9. PAYMENT

9.1 The buyer will open a bank issued irrevocable transferable UCP 600 confirmed pre-advised operational documentary letter of credit unrestricted, issued as transferable within seven (7) days of signature of this agreement.

If a letter of credit is to be issued as transferable then this term *must* appear on the letter of credit, otherwise the credit cannot be transferred. This is a new edict under UCP600. Ideally, unless you are dealing with a top ranked world bank, all pre-advised credits are to be issued as confirmed. The intermediary offers a non-confirmed credit to the supplier, but stipulates to the end buyer that the credit is to be issued as confirmed. If the buyer objects to having to apply an expensive confirmation on the issue of the credit, and a top 200, 300 or even 400 ranked world bank is being used then the supplier will be appeased. However, if the supplier has asked for a confirmed credit then the intermediary will already have asked the end buyer for one. The credit must not be issued from a Third-World country or a small bank in a First-World country without it being confirmed. The seller has to accept the credit before it can become an 'acceptable credit'. If it is not accepted because the buyer provided the wrong type of instrument, the buyer is in breach of conditions. This is because the seller will advise non-acceptance of the wrongly issued credit, citing the contract clause as the reason for the rejection.

9.2 The credit shall be issued and become payable 100 per cent at sight upon presentation of the required delivery documents as specified under Incoterms 2000.

9.3 At Sight: present the required title/delivery documents for the issuing bank to examine. Five (5) days are allowed for examination of the documents to take place. If after such time all the delivery documents are presented 'clean' the issuing bank will allow collection to proceed with the financial instrument used to pay for the goods.

9.4 The credit shall be opened as operational and seller shall serve a document that provides 'Proof of Interest' in the goods being offered, as per the terms of the contract. Once the proof of interest in the goods is disclosed, the pre-advised credit reverts to being a normal active operational transferable credit, which carries with it the confirmation if applicable. The document bearing the heading 'Policy Proof of Interest Certificate', (the blank version of which is herein provided) shall be the only document which, once such disclosure information has been applied to it as surrendered to the issuing bank of the buyer, shall cause the pre-advised credit to revert into a fully active irrevocable transferable letter of credit. The term 'bank' must now also be apparent.

The buyer opens the pre advised credit as operational. The seller surrenders the PPI, which makes the credit active and able to be transferred so long as the transfer fees have been paid.

> 9.5 The actual contract price shall include the costs of bank charges and fees, including transfer charges, pre-advisement fees and conversion of the pre-advised credit into an operational credit. The buyer, as the applicant of this credit, bears these costs. Costs related to the issuance of the financial instrument used to pay for the goods are paid from the issuing bank to the seller's bank within 3 days of the disclosure of the PPI Certificate, or within 3 days of the request by the advising bank for payment of these charges, whichever is sooner.

> 9.6 The transfer fee only shall be returned as a credit to favour the buyer on the seller's invoice. The buyer hereby agrees with the seller that charges related to the transfer fee shall be additional to the cost provided on the quotation or offer, for which the buyer is required to issue payment on behalf of the seller. This is in accordance with Article 38 of UCP600 Paragraph (c): in that the buyer has 'agreed upon' the seller paying for such fees once the credit becomes transferable and after proof of goods has been disclosed via the issuance of the PPI Certificate.

Once the intermediary gains confidence in trading effectively this is one variable that can be omitted. 'Only the transfer fee shall be returned as a credit to favour the buyer on the seller's invoice.' The first time intermediary has to maximize their gain in the first instance. Although the buyer may not be too happy about having to pay the transfer fee if they want the offered goods, and the goods are well priced, the buyer will agree to the fee. In an effort to at least appease the buyer's apprehension about this fee, you could indeed make the whole idea much more attractive if you agree to return the transfer fee as a credit on the seller's invoice. Remember you have also offered payment by allowing the use of a pre-advised credit, which is the least expensive type of credit to open. You could instead have asked for the expensive confirmed type of credit in the first instance.

Although it is not immediately apparent UCP600 Article (4) provides the option for the buyer to pay the transfer fees. A bank must not get involved in the contract for the sale or purchase of goods. By virtue of mistake perhaps or lack of insight, UCP600 Article 38 contains a clause which states 'Unless agreed at the time of transfer'. This specifically refers to the pre-condition that exists prior to the issuance of the credit. The transfer fees must be paid before transfer of the required credit portion can be initiated by the 'beneficiary', that is unless a pre-condition exists which provides otherwise. Article 38 specifically advises on this matter as it pertains to the applicant opening the credit with the issuing bank. The end buyer must tell the issuing bank to allow the transfer fee or any other fee to be an expense for their account. The issuing bank is to agree to do so, but only after the end buyer accepts the bank's terms and conditions on this extraordinary matter. The end buyer will only initiate this demand if they are compelled to do so, after they have a signed contract that contains the pre-condition to favour the seller and beneficiary of the credit.

The 'unless agreed' clause can indeed only be applied and tested at contract time, as arrangement for the issuance of a credit is based on the terms and conditions of the contract. This provision must therefore be included. If not, the end buyer will not be compelled to make their own bank pay the fees associated with the activation or transfer. Furthermore under Incoterms the intermediary seller is obligated to produce a seller's invoice detailing all the unit costs of goods and associated expenses in the form of debits and credits. Again this clearly infers that the price of goods is the cost of only the goods and nothing more. Article 38 also refers to the 'beneficiary', which is a term not specific to a 'supplier in possession of goods' but to anyone accepting the credit for the sale of goods. The intermediary may insist on this provision based on the fact that it is agreed as part of the contract. If the bank refuses to pay the transfer fee the buyer shall insist that the bank complies with its wishes or else the buyer may face a serious breach of contracting conditions with the seller. There are two reasons for this: firstly, Article 38 does not unequivocally state anything in direct contradiction to the above. Secondly, the contract was agreed long before the issuance of the credit was required.

> 9.7 If the buyer or their bank is unable to issue an irrevocable confirmed pre-advised credit, then a normal active irrevocable confirmed transferable credit shall be provided instead. This will not affect the overall basic terms and conditions of issuance, in accordance with UCP600. If the second credit cannot be opened, the seller will accept the credit as a non-transferable instrument as long as it is opened as confirmed with the seller's advising bank.

The 'top ranking' bank status remains, as does the acceptance of the DLC, and the fees. Instead of issuing a pre-advised credit, the credit is issued as being already active and operational ready for transferring: 'PPI' is still provided within the scheduled timeframe, but the acceptable DLC can be transferred immediately once the pre-advised condition has been lifted. It is at the discretion of the bank to issue a pre-advised credit. The buyer is at fault if they sign the contract and later find out that their bank does not issue pre-advised credits. A normal credit must be issued instead, or the buyer will face a breach of conditions.

> 9.7.1 The credit shall be marked so as not to allow Transshipments, but will allow partial drawing(s) in relation to the expenses and payments for securing delivery documents as required.

> 9.8 When the delivery documents are successfully presented the rules of collection apply as provided by URC 522 (ICC Uniform Rules of Collection Publication 522).

In the same way that rules apply to the issuance of the credit, there are rules that govern collection of the credit.

> 9.9 In the case of multiple shipments, the credit is issued as 'Non-Cumulative Revolving'.

Cumulative revolving credits however are not for the inexperienced intermediary and in any event are rarely used: for example, 10 dollars one shipment first month, 20 dollars two shipments second month, third payment 30 dollars, three shipments in the third month making a total of 60 dollars, over three months.

A 'non-cumulative revolving' credit retains the value of the credit on a continuing basis. For example the total multi-shipment contract value is 60 dollars, the DLC value is 60 dollars, the monthly shipment value is 10 dollars. There are to be six shipments over six months. When 10 dollars is paid from the top of the 'stack' another 10 dollars' value is added to the bottom of the stack. The value of the DLC remains at 30 dollars in advance at all times: when one shipment is delivered 10 dollars is paid from the top of the stack, and another 10 dollars is added to the bottom, and when another shipment is delivered, the same rule applies. When three shipments have been delivered, the stack accordingly reduces in size from three, to two then finally to one standing active payment. The filling of the stack stops once the arrival of the pre-established number of advance payments has been reached. Although the bank actually guarantees the whole contract value by allowing the issuance of a non-cumulative revolving credit, the buyer is actually only financing the value of three payments at any given time. The act of guaranteeing the whole contract is intended to appease the seller. The act of ensuring three payments in advance remain active is to finance the end buyer at a fixed rate of interest. The performance guarantee works on the non-cumulative revolving basis as well. In the USA the term 'cumulative revolving credit' can also mean an 'Evergreen credit'.

Under UCP600 partial payments (whether pre-advised letters of credit or not) are allowed for partial delivery. However, transshipments are not appropriate for intermediaries. Trans shipments are shipments in which bulk goods are loaded onto one ship then transferred to another ship for final delivery. Because an intermediary is dealing with one ship and one bill of lading, one buyer, one shipment, one quantity allotment of goods and one port, they must not deal in goods that are destined for off-loading at more than one port. Conversely, in a container deal, the opposite applies. In a container deal there are many customers each with one or more container loads delivered to the same or different ports.

> 9.10 The non-cumulative revolving value of the financial instrument lodged for payment shall be clearly defined on contract in United States Dollars or Euros. The final debit or credit amount is dictated by the tolerances on each set of delivery documents, presentation of which is defined specifically on the seller's invoice. This includes all credits and debits related to subsidies and the necessary expenses of each party to the contract, as defined under Incoterms 2000.

The rules provided by Incoterms 2000 dictate which party pays for each element of the transaction. Thus debits and credits apply for all such deals. When we see on a contract or an offer an entry like 'certificate of origin' as an expense for the buyer it means that the buyer opens the credit, but the seller will obtain a certain certificate or document on behalf of the buyer. However, the buyer's account will be debited for the expense accordingly (that is the buyer will pay for it). The intermediary simply needs to follow the provisions in Incoterms for a FOB or CIF transaction in order to become aware of who pays for what. In the same way as the supplier arranges the documents for the buyer/seller, the buyer/seller transfers or endorses the documents over to their end buyer.

> 10. DELIVERY DOCUMENTS 'FOB Named Port of Shipment'
>
> 10.1 In accordance with the delivery requirements provided by Incoterms 2000 the seller will serve, in hard copy or electronic format, a minimum of one copy of the following documentations for authentication and presentation. (For documents to be treated as 'original' they must be clearly marked as such, regardless of the method by which they are served.)

The following scenario explains what happens when the trader transfers or endorses the documents over to the end buyer:

You are waiting at home or in an office, a courier arrives and hands over a document that you sign for. You take out the seller's invoice and replace it with your own invoice which details your costs for the goods sold, with the added term 'original' stamped on its face or margin. If, as sometimes might occasionally happen in an FOB deal the supplier asks you to accept the bill of lading in your own name, you take out the bill of lading marked 'original', and on its back in any clear margin available you print a date and name of the end buyer. This has the effect of creating a 'blanket endorsement' (in blank) of the

BOL to the end buyer only. Once you are satisfied the seller has provided you with all the delivery documents as per the terms and conditions of the credit you place all the documents in an envelope. You then send them by overnight courier directly to the end buyer. The end buyer checks the documents and presents them to their bank, which formally checks them against the credit terms and conditions. If the documents are in order, the bank allows collection to occur on the issued credit.

These are the correct procedures, but because you as the intermediary can't afford to trust that the end buyer will deliver the documents to their bank quickly, you should actually deliver the documents to the bank yourself via courier. Then your advising bank, unless otherwise directed, will do exactly the same thing via internal bank to bank procedures using electronically transmitted methods and bank identifying codes.

Once in possession of the delivery documents the seller contacts their bank to instigate the transfer of the documents to the buyer by electronic means after replacing the supplier's invoice with their own. In the alternative the seller may simply replace the supplier's invoice with their own invoice and endorse the hard copy documents over to the buyer's bank without using the advising bank.

Let us assume a first-time trader has encountered a supplier who is stating that their bank will advise the delivery document via eUCP to your advising bank. The advising bank will inform the intermediary of the arrival of the documents. The intermediary then goes to their bank, produces the seller's invoice for replacing with the supplier's invoice and instructs the bank to deliver the document to the buyer's bank electronically if appropriate (or if not by overnight secure courier). Although electronic production of documents (eUCP) is commonplace it is only really practised amongst big traders and banks, where an end buyer is dealing directly with a supplier. However that is not to say that it could not be used when intermediaries are involved. Letters of credit, however, are mostly transmitted in electronic format as long as it is clear on the document that this electronic version is indeed the active credit.

Unless there are sweeping changes to law and custom intermediaries should at first only deal in hardcopy delivery documents from a supplier and hand deliver those documents personally to the advising bank after ensuring they have made the required changes. Hardcopy does not mean 'original', but rather a copy produced from the original which is hand signed by the seller. As long as the copy also bears a stamp or is marked as 'original', then under UCP600 the bank will accept the document as 'original'. One 'original' document is sufficient to meet delivery requirements: there is no need to provide duplicates. The documents, where appropriate, carry the name of the seller and are endorsed over to the buyer taking possession.

For example, if the buyer asks the seller in an FOB deal to secure the bill of lading the end buyer will meet the cost of this. Although the intermediary seller is not required to do this it may sometimes be necessary to assist the end buyer in order to secure the deal. Under UCP500 collecting the bill of lading was only preferable because in the vast majority of deals the end buyer would insist that the seller secured the bill of lading. However, this is something that needs to be taught and for reasons of complexity it is better to revert to strict Incoterms delivery rules. Now, therefore, if the bill of lading is requested this is defined as 'FOB with Extra Services' as a variant of FOB. However, intermediaries are strongly advised not to offer these types of extra services until they are highly conversant with trading methods.

> 10.1.1 Provision of Leading Primary Delivery Document is a condition of financial instrument presentation, which is in the first instance a Clean on Board ship's mate's receipt signed on behalf of the ship's master or ship owner evidencing that the ordered goods are on board the named vessel of the buyer.

The leading or primary delivery document is one of the documents required for presentation in relation to the financial instrument. A clean on board ship mate's receipt, signed on behalf of the ship's master or ship's owner shows that the ordered goods are on board the named vessel of the buyer. However it is not always evident which document will be available first. Therefore it is advisable to add a secondary condition to the contract, which allows for different documents to be used as primary evidence that the goods are indeed on board the named vessel. For example if a ship's mate's receipt is delayed from being issued because of a looming hurricane but the forwarder's receipt is already in hand, it would be more practical to use this receipt as a leading delivery document as an acceptable presentation document. Other documents that could be used are a leading clean on board delivery document such as a non-negotiable waybill or other document such as that produced by an authorized forwarder's agent of the shipowner or master, signed and identified accordingly.

The issued credit will, of course, stipulate that presentation of the primary leading document is required but by providing an allowance for an alternative document on the contract the intermediary could, in the event of a serious delay, ask for an immediate amendment on the credit to allow another document to suffice.

> 10.1.2 The abovementioned documents shall indicate, amongst other things, the quantity of goods on board. Should the secondary document be presented in lieu of the ship's mate's receipt, the buyer shall agree to notify their bankers to accept one of the alternative documents and issue an amendment to the credit at the expense of the buyer within 24 hours of presentation of an alternative delivery document.

(Because banks deal in documents and not contracts the buyer must notify the bank. As we have already seen it is not for the bank to interpret any agreement between the buyer and seller.)

The requirements of Incoterms 2000 are simple: all that must be produced by the intermediary is evidence that the goods are on board ship. The bill of lading is issued and usually given to the end buyer and not the seller, because it is the end buyer's ordered (often chartered) ship that is being used to transport the goods. The seller is required to provide 'evidence of the goods being on board' and the best documentary proof of this is the on board ship's mate's receipt. The bill of lading is the actual title delivery document, whereas a ship's mate's receipt is a document attesting to the fact that the goods are on board ship as issued by a representative of the ship's master. A ship's mate's receipt is evidence, whereas the bill of lading is a title document pertaining both to property and possession. The bill of lading is filled in by the supplier. Then the ship's mate, or an equivalent officer as delegated accordingly under the direct authority of the ship's captain (who represents the shipowner) physically checks the cargo against the supplier's bill of lading to ensure that all is in order. If it is, the bill of lading is 'clean'. If the intermediary in an FOB deal is not required to produce the bill of lading, then in order to complete delivery he may be required to secure a forwarder's receipt or a ships mates receipt.

Additionally there are other documents that are required to be presented:

An Export Permit. Cost for the account of the seller. An export permit is required as a delivery document, the cost of which is included in the price of the goods because the supplier secures it. The cost is ostensibly transferred to become a cost incurred by the seller. The end buyer secures the import permit.

An Original Seller's Invoice. The signed commercial invoice issued by the seller declares the price and actual cost of goods and all debits and credits as applicable under Incoterms 2000. The seller also agrees to refund if applicable, the previously paid 'transfer fee', which shall appear on the seller's invoice as a credit favouring the buyer. As the supplier provides an invoice to the seller, the seller replaces this document with their own seller's invoice. The seller may or may not offer to return the transfer fee as a credit. FTN Exporting often does not offer to return the said transfer fee unless the end buyer protests sufficiently strongly.

A Certificate of Origin. This is an expense for the buyer as debited on the seller's invoice in accordance with Incoterms 2000. A non-preferential or preferential certificate of origin shall be issued unless the buyer specifically communicates that it is not required (in which case no charge is applicable). Similarly, most importers will require a certificate of origin. Unless the buyer has stated that it is not required it should be included in the terms of the contract. The best practice is to include it as a clause in the contract, so if the buyer does not require it let them advise you of this fact. A non-preferential certificate is one that is issued by the exporter's consulate where available, in the buyer's country; a preferential certificate is one that is issued from the consulate or other government agency as applicable in the exporter's country. The supplier secures the required certificate, pays for it, and adds the charge to the supplier's invoice as a debit. The seller does the same to the end buyer.

An 'In Rem' Certificate of Quality. Issued by SGS (Societe Generale De Surveillance), this inspection and internationally recognized analytical agency assess the product in order to determine whether or not the goods are fit for their specific purpose.

An ISO Certificate of Manufacturing. This certificate is endorsed accordingly by a world class issuing agency and is used to show that the manufacturer is offering goods produced in accordance with manufacturing standards. If an '*in rem*' certificate is offered, as per above, this is a certificate issued by an inspection agency from the premises offering the goods at infrequent intervals, usually once a year. This quality 'standard' certificate issuance is a cost incorporated in the goods being offered. The matter of certification is very important and complex. The buyer is entitled to know exactly what they are buying.

An '*in rem*' certificate provides details of both the quality of the goods and the standards of the manufacturer. The quality and ISO certificates can be issued by the same authority. However, if the buyer will not settle for the information on the leading certificate and requires further information such as a tally count, packaging, total weights and visual inspection of the goods, this should be carried out by a different agency to the one issuing the quality certificate. These further certification requirements are expenses to be met by the supplier.

If, for example, the end buyer wants a pre-shipment inspection (PSI) certificate issued by SGS, the ISO '*in rem*' certificate could still be offered to appease the buyer but not the standard SGS quality certificate. The contract would, in these circumstances, state that a PSI certificate is being requested. PSI quality certification is issued when the goods are loaded or on board ship. The supplier secures the services of the agency which provides an independent analytical service to test the quality of the goods and to issue the appropriate dated certificate accordingly. Such a certificate is described as an '*in personam*' certificate, which under Incoterms 2000 is an extra expense for the account of the seller. In a real trading scenario this expense could in fact be a cost made for the account of the end buyer. Even though the theory may seem sound, the practice may be somewhat different. Intermediaries must be careful here, as these are confusing issues and not apparent in the wording of Incoterms 2000. The supplier has often already paid for '*in personam*' inspection services, not at the time of loading but from inspection carried out weeks or months earlier from, for example, a storage warehouse at a nearby port or loading facility. If Incoterms were to be followed to the letter, the supplier has to meet the expense of a second inspection at the time of loading – which isn't going to happen. If it did, you could expect the price of the goods to rise considerably. A simple misunderstanding like this could cause the loss of a viable deal.

Therefore if a buyer demands the issuance of a PSI certificate, the seller secures it but applies the cost to the account of the buyer. The buyer has two options: to accept the standard certificate at no extra cost or to request a further PSI certificate at their own expense.

It is very important, when negotiating with the supplier, to identify exactly the types of certificates that are being issued and to ensure that the end buyer's contract reflects these requirements. The intermediary should ascertain exactly what kind of quality certification is available in each country and ensure that only these options are offered to the end buyer. Where government endorsed agencies issue quality health certificates in relation to the goods, for example in a chicken meat processing plant, then a request for a PSI certificate would be entirely unnecessary. PSI inspections are usually very expensive and, depending on the nature and quantity of the goods to be inspected, can run into tens of thousands of dollars. But if the government in the supplier's country is guaranteeing the quality of the goods, what better guarantee could you need? If the end buyer is not satisfied with this type of certification then they can ask for a PSI certificate, the added expense of which will be included on the seller's invoice for the cost to be met by the end buyer. Many suppliers are also confused about these matters and depend on relying on the '*in rem*' issued quality certificate alone.

In summary there is:

1. A certificate of manufacturing standards issued by the supplier '*in rem*' (supplier's expense);

2. A certificate of standard ISO quality '*in rem*' (supplier's expense);

3. A certificate of specific quality issued prior to or when goods are loaded as requested by the buyer of the supplier '*in personam*' (buyer's expense);

4. A standard certificate of quality as issued prior to the goods being loaded, that is issued by a governmental department due to internal policies and laws of the manufacturer's country (supplier's expense); and

5. A 'certificate of inspection' can also mean a simple certificate which has nothing to do with quality: it concerns visual inspection of the goods prior to loading by way of a report that details the condition of the goods, as well as a tally count of the actual goods in the ship's hold. (NB: This certificate is not to be confused with the more expensive certification that analyses the health and chemical make-up of the goods as attested by experts.)

It's very important to know your certificates! Make sure the certificate is to be provided in the English language. For example, if the intermediary is dealing with a bank in English, and produces SGS certification in Chinese, this could mean that delivery fails. Similarly, if a Russian-issued certificate is produced in English, but from an unknown authority rather than SGS as requested, then delivery could also fail. The intermediary needs to control the deal in an orderly manner. Since the buyer will nearly always ask for an 'SGS certificate of quality' when they often actually mean a 'PSI' certificate, the intermediary often needs to cover all important matters until they become experienced in knowing how and where they are able to edit and amend the terms and conditions of the contract. The following inspection condition on a FOB contract will suffice to ensure the intermediary has control of the deal:

10.2 Certificate of Inspection: Quantity

For the account of the seller: at the date of delivery the seller shall provide a visual on board inspection of goods and tally count certificate as conducted in the first instance by 'SGS' (Societe Generale de Surveilliance). Should this agency not be in operation in the country of origin then the seller shall provide certification as issued by BV (Bureau Veritas), SAYBOLT or GOVERNMENTAL AGENCY, whichever is available in the country of origin. The buyer hereby agrees to accept this certification and covenants to amend any condition on the credit to accommodate document issuance, as soon as it becomes apparent that it is necessary.

10.3 Certificate of Quality: Non-PSI Type

The goods offered have a certificate of quality which states that the goods are specifically 'fit for purpose' for use as attested by a world class inspection agency such as 'SGS' (Societe Generale de Surveilliance). If SGS does not operate in the country of origin then the seller shall in the second instance provide BV (Bureau Veritas) verification, SAYBOLT or GOVERNMENTAL AGENCY, whichever is available in the country of origin. The buyer shall accept the certification of quality and if necessary amend the condition of the credit to accommodate the issue of this secondary type of document. For the certificate to be issued the goods can be inspected anywhere except on board ship, whether immediately prior to the goods being delivered on board or inspected in the year of manufacture or production. The certificate is provided by the seller, for the account and cost of the seller, and is incorporated in the price of the goods. The buyer provides formal acceptance of the certificate of inspection by initialling and placing an 'X' in the check box below. If no initials or marks are apparent, the seller will issue a PSI certificate as defined below.

We accept the non-Pre-shipment Inspection Certificate of Quality type (PSI) (   ) Initials_____:

10.4 Certificate of Quality: PSI Type

This type of certificate of quality shows that the goods offered have been tested as being specifically 'fit for purpose' for use, as attested by a world-class inspection agency such as 'SGS' (Societe Generale de Surveillance). Should this agency not be in operation in the country of origin of the goods, then in the second instance the seller shall provide such certification as issued by BV (Bureau Veritas), SAYBOLT or GOVERNMENTAL AGENCY, whichever is available in the country of origin. In this instance the buyer shall accept this certification of quality and if need be immediately amend the condition of the credit to accommodate the issuance of this document. This certificate is issued for goods inspected on board the ship or, if the ship is late in arriving, immediately prior to the goods being delivered on board the named ship. This certificate shall be provided by the seller for the account and cost of the buyer and will not be incorporated in the price of goods offered. A further expense shall be recorded on the seller's invoice as a debit against the account of the buyer. The buyer hereby indicates acceptance of the certificate of inspection unless the initials and mark are indicated on the non-PSI certificate above.

The intermediary must include the above three clauses in contracts for all bulk FOB delivered goods or 'FCA' (Free Carrier) container type of transactions to establish fitness for purpose. In the case of container(s) deals the certificates are issued immediately prior to delivery (delivery being to the registered transport operator carrier who is taking the goods to the customs wharf, that is within 21 days of delivery). The carrier has no idea of the nature of the goods inside a container or indeed their value. Therefore the carrier will not take responsibility for goods damaged inside a container, but rather only 'damage caused to the container'. The insurance company usually deals with any claims relating to damaged containers unless, exceptionally, proof of the value of the goods is known and the carrier or its authorized agents are found to be negligent.

10.5 An Export Permit

10.6 An Original Seller's Invoice

10.7 Certificate of Origin

10.8 An *'In Rem'* Certificate of Quality which states that the goods are offered by a manufacturer or producer of an export compliant company or entity. If no such certificate is available an ISO (International Standards Organization) certificate issued by experts shall be provided, and will declare that the goods have been inspected by said experts within the last year and meet export standards.

10.9 PSI (Pre-Shipment Inspection): *'In Personam'* type. This is an on board inspection certificate which describes the quality, quantity and condition of the goods offered by the seller, issued by a globally recognized independent expert(s) carrying on the duty as an inspection authority. These inspection services are a cost for the seller's account contrary to the implications of Incoterms 2000 delivery rules. The price of goods offered shall accommodate this type of PSI certification. Should the end buyer taking possession of goods insist upon or make a request for any other form of inspection then this shall be secured by the seller. However the costs of such extra services shall be for the account of the buyer, including samples, if applicable, which, if requested, must be paid for in advance.

11. SPECIAL DOCUMENT PRESENTATIONS

11.1 Policy Proof of Interest Certificate

If an acceptable 'Pre-advised' credit is used to pay for the goods, the seller shall issue a document called the 'Policy Proof of Interest Certificate', which identifies the genuine manufacturer, owner or supplier of the goods. The buyer accepts this blank certificate model, and the procedures applied therein, as the process needed to verify that the goods are genuine.

As previously stated the Policy Proof of Interest (PPI) certificate must be issued in order to convert the pre-advised credit into an operational and active credit. The certificate must also be issued when a normal active documentary credit is provided for payment. It does not matter whether or not the buyer chooses to verify the information provided on the PPI document; the act of disclosure of the product verification information is all that is required.

> 11.2 The buyer shall accept this information within three days of disclosure, whether acceptance is provided explicitly or not. The PPI blank model shall be added to the end of this contract and, upon the financial instrument having been advised as accepted by the seller, shall be returned to the buyer carrying genuine disclosure of the seller's allocation and interests in the goods being sold.

> 11.3 If the information later proves to be false no protests will be entertained with regard to the suitability of the document once issued. Should it be proven that the information supplied by the seller is false, then the buyer shall be allowed to make claims of fraudulent and dishonourable intent against the seller, because the seller has not honoured the required obligations to deliver genuine verifiable information. In this event the buyer shall grant the seller a period of 48 hours within which to remedy the situation before the buyer declares a breach of the seller's conditions.

> 11.4 The seller shall be required to make a copy of the PPI certificate as an appendix to this contract, to fill in the details to disclose the supplier of the goods and to forward it from the advising bank to the issuing bank in electronic form, or to the issuing bank by hard copy courier, whichever comes first.

> 11.5 The buyer must read the blank copy of the PPI certificate contained herein, and accept the information yet to be applied on it in disclosing the supplier's information. The buyer must also adhere to the terms on the blank PPI certificate and is permitted to authenticate the information thereon once only.

We are now specifically reinforcing all further matters relevant to the PPI document here, especially in terms of scheduling and intent. Once the pre-advised credit is advised and accepted, the blank PPI certificate as offered on the contract is filled in and returned to the buyer's bank. The pre-advised credit is then made active and operational not carrying the pre-advised status. Other than the method as above, there is no other reasonably safe way a buyer/seller can meet the requirements of 'proof'. The type of proof being offered must be explained fully and accurately prior to accepting the pre-advised credit. Failure to do so will lead to a situation in which a pre-advised credit is issued and the offered 'proof' is poorly defined. This will allow the end buyer to obtain the supplier's details but the bank would refuse to make the credit active. Thus the intermediary actually ties the bank into an obligation not with what is advised on the body of the PPI, but by simply identifying that a certificate such as a PPI has been issued in accordance with the requirement of the credit. The information on the body of the PPI is for the end buyer's use only. It has nothing to do with the bank's obligations. This satisfies Article 4 of UCP600 that states that 'banks shall not get involved in matters of the sales contract'. The term PPI is a recognizable term used in international trade, just as disclosing and offering its contents is a matter of contract. In meeting the conditions of the credit the bank is only concerned that an identifiable document has been provided, rather than requiring to verify or even have knowledge of its content. The end buyer is not obligated to verify the content of the PPI. The seller cannot make it a specific condition of the contract that the end buyer must verify the content of the PPI, because if the end buyer decides not to verify the content of the PPI this could cause the deal to collapse. Therefore the seller only gives the end buyer the opportunity to verify the PPI as genuine unless proven otherwise. This is the only way ostensibly to 'prove' or provide verifiable 'evidence' that a real product, as secured by a buyer from a supplier in possession of those goods, is being offered with honourable intent.

12. INTERNET PROTOCOL

12.1 The buyer accepts full responsibility for service of documents and any or all communications transmitted electronically in the pursuance or issuance of this transaction. He shall not be able to use domestic laws pertaining to their own jurisdiction to negate either their intent or the legality of the documents when transmitted electronically whether initiated via the Internet or by any other means.

12.2 The buyer hereby accepts that signature of this internationally enforceable contract creates a personal legal obligation regardless of the domestic laws of their country.

13. SHIPPING

13.1 Nothing in this agreement shall negate or otherwise detract from the obligations relating to, *inter alia*, shipping, demurrage, delays, berthing and weather relating to delivery of the goods and which are in force at the date of signature of this contract.

13.2 The buyer hereby acknowledges that they are responsible for matters of shipping as per their contract with the carrier and must ensure that the bill of lading document and its terms and conditions comply with the international maritime shipping rules further defined as the 'Hague Rules' in the first instance or the 'Hague-Visby Rules' in the second instance.

13.3 If the seller is asked by the buyer to assist with the matter of securing the bill of lading on the buyer's behalf in a variant FOB transaction, then the seller will only provide such assistance of 'added services' or variation on a FOB transaction to the best of their abilities as per the implications and provisions of Incoterms 2000.

13.4 The seller shall not be held liable where this 'variant FOB' assistance fails to procure the required bill of lading, and in no circumstances shall this be construed to mean that the seller has failed to 'deliver'. The seller shall not offer such assistance with securing the bill of lading to a rented ship in relation to which there is a charterparty agreement.

In keeping with the spirit of Incoterms 2000, the seller reserves the right to assist the buyer in securing a bill of lading if so requested, but only from a carrier and endorsed by a shipowner.

13.5 The obtaining and securing of the bill of lading is the obligation of the end buyer.

13.5.1 Delays caused by the carrier are the fault of the carrier.

13.5.2 Delays caused as a result of not being ready to accept the goods, pay the freight and other carriage and import statutory charges and obligations therein, once the goods pass the ship's rail in the port of loading, are the responsibility of the buyer. The buyer shall also bear all the costs and added expenses affecting the seller's ability to perform, where the buyer's delays have incurred these added expenses and costs.

13.5.3 Delays in loading which result in the goods not being ready for loading shall be the responsibility of the seller. Any cost incurred for these delays will be added to the account of the seller as per Incoterms 2000.

13.6 At least fourteen (14) days before its arrival the buyer will provide the seller with an estimated ship arrival date and time at loading port.

13.7 The buyer will give the seller a revised arrival date and time once the ship is no less than forty-eight (48) hours from berthing at the local port. Thereafter the seller shall prepare the goods alongside ship ready for loading.

13.8 The seller shall make ready the said goods alongside ship ready for loading.

13.9 The entity causing and/or being at fault in matters of shipping bears the consequences of the fault, in accordance with the terms and conditions of the said bill of lading and/or Incoterms 2000 as appropriate (once goods are on board ship).

Intermediaries don't order ships, don't deal in shipping contract obligations and are only required to deliver in relation to the correct presentation of documents relating to the goods. The supplier may indeed pass shipping contract matters to the intermediary, but that is because as far as the supplier is concerned they are dealing with a 'buyer'. The supplier is indifferent to the fact that the buyer is not the end user or end buyer. Therefore any added conditions relating to these matters on the supplier's contract with the intermediary should not be of concern, as the intermediary has covered these conditions in their contract model for the end buyer's consideration.

14. NAME OF SHIP AND DATE OF ARRIVAL

14.1 In accordance with the provisions contained in the schedule of delivery contained within this agreement the date of delivery shall be the earliest date that the goods will be available for loading.

14.2 The buyer shall notify the seller of the name of the carrier within fourteen days of the arrival date of such ship at loading port.

14.3 The buyer and seller agree that the notification date applies from the said delivery date, less fourteen days before or more.

14.4 Regardless of any other concurrent matters of scheduling the above minimum stipulation shall mean that the buyer is required to initiate the processes needed to ensure that the carrier will be at the loading port on or within the required timeframe.

14.5 The buyer hereby agrees to begin initiating the process of securing the required carrier, as soon as the contract has been formally accepted by the parties and is legally binding.

The buyer has to inform to the seller (PIA) when the ship is due to arrive, and the PIA informs the supplier accordingly. Any delay in performance of their duties will incur considerable extra costs and consequences.

15. ARBITRATION

15.1 All parties to the contract shall endeavour to settle any contract dispute amicably in the first instance. Where such matters have failed to be resolved the arbitration rules as applied under the London Court of International Arbitration (LCIA) shall apply.

15.2 The appropriate venue shall be in the seller's country and state, as defined in this agreement.

16. LAW AND JURISDICTION

16.1 English language and English international commercial law shall apply.

16.2 Should a dispute arise as to the goods in possession this shall be answerable in the supplier's country and state, and the seller's obligation in defending the buyer's claim on behalf of the buyers shall become apparent if such claims are justified in the appropriate country.

16.3 Any disputes relating to the seller's obligations as defined in this contract (and as a secondary document the offer preceding this contract) shall be arbitrated in the following country and city: – Melbourne City, State of Victoria, Australia.

16.4 Where the seller is required to defend the claim made by the end buyer, in the supplier's country, the seller shall be obligated to meet the end buyer in the supplier's country and attend any proceedings but only on the condition that the end buyer agrees to be physically present in the country to litigate upon the matter in dispute.

If there is going to be a dispute with the buyer then it should be in the seller's country. The supplier will also insist that if the PIA was in dispute with them, that any arbitration hearings would take place in the supplier's country. If the buyer takes issue with only the seller then it will be in the seller's country. If the seller takes issue with the supplier on an end buyer's claim then the seller will need to travel to the supplier's country for these matters, so long as the end buyer also attends the hearing.

17. FORCE MAJEURE

17.1 Neither party shall be held liable for any default due to any act of nature, piracy, war, whether declared or not, strike, lockout, industrial action, epidemic, drought, flood, acts of terrorism, or fire or other event (*force majeure* event) which is beyond the reasonable control of either party. The seller shall not be held liable for delay or failure to perform any of its obligations under this agreement as a result of a *force majeure* event suffered by the seller's supplier or sub-contractor.

'Acts of nature' replaces 'acts of God', to ensure that there can be no ambiguity in the event of a dispute. Defining an 'act of God' is simply too broad in terms of any loss of goods when faced with the reality of a trading disaster. FTN is unable to find evidence of any successful claim made because of an apparent 'act of God'. Simply applying the term 'ICC *Force Majeure* shall apply to this contract', is not enough. The full term must be included in the body of the contract. Acts of 'terrorism' and 'piracy' are the latest FTN additions to the standard terms.

17.2 On the happening of a *force majeure* event the party relying on this clause is to give notice in writing of the fact within 72 hours of the event's occurrence.

17.3 Neither party is entitled to benefit from a *force majeure* event or frustration of the contract where that party has been responsible, in whole or in part, for delay or non-performance of its obligations under this agreement.

17.4 On the occurrence of a *force majeure* event experienced by either the buyer, the seller or the seller's supplier, the obligations of the parties shall be suspended for so long as the *force majeure* event makes performance under this contract impossible. The affected party will be entitled to a reasonable extension of time for performance which is in any event equal to the period of delay or stoppage.

17.4.1 Costs arising from the delay or stoppage will be born by the party incurring those costs.

17.4.2 The party affected by the *force majeure* event and so claiming shall endeavour and take all necessary steps to continue with their obligations under this agreement whether that constitutes bringing an end to the *force majeure* event or finding a way in which to bypass its effect.

17.5 The seller has the right to terminate this agreement if performance cannot be resumed within thirty (30) consecutive days of the occurrence of the *force majeure* event.

17.6 The invitation to continue with the transaction shall be given in writing as amended to the contract as applicable prior to the *force majeure* event, which once accepted within the thirty (30)-day period, both parties once more are bound by the terms and conditions of this agreement as amended.

17.7 In the event that the contract resumes after a *force majeure* event, each party shall be responsible for their own costs incurred as a result of the delay.

17.8 In accordance with clause 17.4 and 17.5 above the buyer is hereby notified that the seller may raise the legitimate matter of *force majeure* to discharge themselves from performance if performance becomes impossible as a result of a *force majeure* event experienced by the supplier or owner of the goods from whom the seller is obtaining documentary possession.

17.9 Notwithstanding the happening of a *force majeure* event the buyer will refrain from contracting with the third party as named on the PPI document in the appendix to this agreement for a period of six months from the date of this agreement. To do otherwise is a serious breach of contract for which the buyer will be held liable.

The offended party must take heed of this clause. One party can argue all they like, but if no rules are being broken then that party has no recourse. If the deal fails after the PPI has been provided, then at least the buyer has no right to approach the supplier for six months. If the deal collapses due to unforeseen events after which time the buyer goes ahead and uses the PPI information to secure a deal with the supplier there is a breach of contract and a possible cause of action, albeit a weak one. An intermediary is open to the risk of the deal collapsing due to unforeseen events both with the supplier and the end buyer. Although not explicit from any textbook or legal journal, experience tells us that the intermediary is vulnerable on four fronts, both from the supplier and end buyer, and from the occurrence of both deliberate and unavoidable events. Of course, the deliberate act to induce non-performance under the *force majeure* event is of greater concern to the intermediary. This kind of induced frustration differs greatly from the broad legal definition of the common law doctrine of frustration, or from the intention of the *force majeure* clause. So how is frustration actually defined? Frustration occurs when due to no fault of either party to the contract an unforeseen event or situation has occurred that has significantly altered the environment or situation that renders performance of the contract impossible. Frustration may occur after the offer has been accepted but is more likely to occur after the contract has been signed. *Force majeure* seeks to provide an option to continue the contract for a certain amount of time, whereas frustration may make the contract void almost immediately on the occurrence of the unavoidable event.

How could an intermediary encounter a *force majeure* event in a trade? Let's assume that the PIA, the intermediary, has a contract(s) in place to perform the delivery of sugar to Iraq. If the USA declared war on Iraq after the contracts were signed, and the intermediary lives in a country which supports the USA, they will not be able to perform their duties because of (a) an immediate embargo on the import and export of goods into or from Iraq or (b) no ship will be able to be secured to deliver the sugar because (c) if a supplier tried to use their own ship to deliver the goods both the goods and the ship could be confiscated or (d) the end buyer in Iraq may not be able to perform in which case neither can the intermediary, through no fault of their own.

In this scenario a supplier taking action against the PIA for breach of contract would most likely be wasting their time and money as the PIA would claim the defence of a *force majeure* event as their reason for non-performance. This is because the PIA's ability to perform in relation to their obligations with the supplier has dramatically and radically changed. This is the case even though the PIA is both geographically and personally removed from the war between the USA and Iraq – but then again the supplier's relationship with the PIA is not directly affected either. The test that the courts will apply is whether or not they are able to identify a dramatically and or radically differing situation that occurs after the contracts have been signed.

Let us look at another situation that relates specifically to the above contract, not just as it applies to the supplier but also to the end buyer. If the above situation occurred and there was a *force majeure* clause in the contract, the PIA could mount a defence by invoking the operation of that clause. This would also give the PIA the option to continue the contract within 30 days if the *force majeure* event passed. If there was no *force majeure* clause in the contract, the PIA, or anyone else affected, could indeed defend themselves using the doctrine of frustration. For example: a PIA is trading with a corporation (whether supplier or end buyer), which is represented by an import, or export manager. The PIA has obtained ostensible authority to secure the end buyer and funds, which to the PIA's surprise are issued quite quickly. The funds are lodged and the PIA is ready to issue the contract for acceptance as arranged and pre-dated. The contract arrives with the supplier and hours later the PIA receives an email which states: 'Dear PIA, we regret to inform you that due to unforeseen circumstances we are unable to service your order (a) our export manager has tragically died' or (b) 'we have discovered that the sugar has an unusual amount of pesticides' or (c) 'our company has gone into receivership' and so forth and so on. If the PIA claims that their inability to perform under the contract was due to frustration of the contract to the end buyer it may be accepted in the case of (c) but not in the case of either (a) or in most cases (b).

In (a) someone else from the corporation could have continued with the contract as nothing has radically changed to affect the capability of the corporation to conduct normal business. In (b) a corporation which sells many tons of sugar from different crop sources would not be able to extricate itself from the requirement to perform under the contract, unless the pesticide problem affected all of the sugar which was of the particular specification. For frustration to be claimed as a successful defence to non-performance, all sugar crops owned by the supplier would need to be affected. In (c) the legal person (the corporation) was solvent at the time the DLC was issued but then became insolvent, which is enough of a reason for a bank not to 'honour' its commitment to the PIA. So just as it affects the end buyer, it also directly affects the PIA's ability to perform with the supplier. The term 'honour' in the newly-established UCP600 DLC rules has major significance, especially in terms of fraud and frustration. The contract model above defines when a *force majeure* event can feasibly be claimed. Parties to the contract must be aware that an 'induced act of frustration' or false claiming of a *force majeure* event will not be tolerated. Unfortunately, it is the imposed act of frustration that the intermediary often encounters, particularly after contracts have been signed. Imposed frustration is an attempt to get out of obligations by forcing a 'get out' clause.

So the deal is active, all contracts are signed and the PIA waits for a DLC to arrive. When it does, suppose that it is totally different from that which was required by the contract. As a result the PIA's obligation to the supplier will be significantly delayed. The PIA attempts to force the end buyer to amend the credit as per the conditions of the contract. The end buyer in turn is taking advantage of the situation by demanding a lower price for the goods in return for making the changes to the credit. The PIA refuses, but the deal is so badly delayed that the supplier is now demanding to know what is happening. Luckily the PIA did not make the performance guarantee 'active' upon issuance of the buyer's financial instrument, but made the PG active upon the acceptance of the DLC, and non-acceptance was indeed communicated. The supplier may well instigate court proceedings against the PIA, and in turn the PIA will do the same to the end buyer.

In this situation the PIA has no other option but to fail to meet their obligations to the supplier and to test the matter in court. Although the supplier has the option to extend time, lower prices and even delay the contract they are not obliged to accept those changes. The proceedings against the PIA are for breach of contract. By way of a defence the PIA could claim a *force majeure* event caused by the end buyer having created an irrevocable situation, radically and dramatically different from the status quo – so much so that the PIA was forced to fail to perform in their obligations to the supplier. There was no way that the PIA could foresee this dishonourable act. Whereas other options were available to both principals in the deal, the PIA, as the middle principal, had no other option. The PIA simply could not declare that the end buyer was in breach of contract, because the PIA's obligations to the supplier would not be mitigated. In this type of situation, the PIA has to test to see if induced frustration will prevent the supplier from pursuing their claim, and then sue the end buyer for breach of contract.

This is why it is of fundamental importance for the PIA to sign the supplier's contract but retain it until such time as the financial instrument from the end buyer is both advised and accepted.

18. AUTHORITY TO ENTER INTO AGREEMENT

18.1 By contracting under the terms of this agreement all parties hereby confirm that they:

18.2.1 Are over 18 years of age and mentally competent; and

18.2.2 Have never be convicted or cautioned for acts of fraud;

18.2.3 Are neither a declared or undischarged bankrupt.

19. SUMMARY OF PROCEDURES

19.1 The buyers shall request an offer that, once accepted, instigates the issuance of the draft contract to which the following schedule of procedures shall apply.

19.1.1 (1) Draft contract is signed and returned to the seller from the buyer to imply a formal legal contracting situation.

19.1.2 (2) Financial instrument issued within contracted days to initiate acceptance.

19.1.3 (3) PPI Certificate defining 'proof of interest in the goods' is provided by the seller. The operational credit converts into an active credit.

19.1.4 (4) Performance Guarantee or LLD certificate is provided.

19.1.5 (5) Ship arrival date at loading port advised to seller.

19.1.6 (6) Goods are proven as being loaded on-board the buyer's ordered carrier with the issuance of the leading delivery document.

19.1.7 (7) Remaining documents advised within contracted days.

19.1.8 (8) Delivery completed, collection made at sight of the delivery documents.

19.1.9 (9) Next shipment loaded if revolving shipments have been ordered.

19.2 Applicable references to be used by all parties to the contract:

a) To identify an acceptable Top Class World Bank:

    'http://www.forbes.com/2006/03/29/06f2k_worlds-largest-public-companies_land.html' Forbes.com LLC (USA) [online]

b) To calculate distance assuming ship is sailing at 14 knots per hour.

    'http://www.distances.com' Part of the WN Network (USA) [online]

c) To calculate Weights and Measures.

    'http://www.onlineconversion.com/' Robert Fogt. 2008

d) To identify loading and unloading ports.

    'http://www.distances.com' Part of the WN Network (USA) [online]

A schedule is a very useful tool for identifying a party in breach of their obligations under the contract. Reference to reliable websites as points of reference is also useful. The more transparent a contract is, the better the understanding between the parties of the business at hand. If internet addresses are included by way of reference then for instance there would be very little excuse for an end buyer if they advised a letter of credit from a bank that is not listed on the referenced website.

If the buyer fails to observe the content of these websites then in the case of a serious breach of contract, the seller could argue that the buyer did not perform as defined under the reference page offered. The seller who fails to advise the acceptance of the buyer's DLC in accordance with UCP600 inadvertently implies that they have accepted the DLC. In not accepting the DLC the supplier must inform the advising bank that this is the case, or the contracting schedule and conditions will remain in force.

20. POLICY PROOF OF INTEREST CERTIFICATE (PPI)

20.1 In accordance with clause 11 above the following information defines the aforesaid 'Policy Proof of Interest Certificate', which is hereby exposed to the buyer and or buyer's bank as a 'Blank Model (PART A)' document bearing no information other than depicted.

20.2 The seller shall complete the model documents with the required information. A copy will be made and returned to the buyer and/or buyer's bank within 3 days of the acceptance of the buyer's financial instrument.

20.3 The information once provided is secured directly from the owner of the goods as purchased by the seller, which are consequently being resold to the buyer. Unless otherwise proven the buyer accepts the information unconditionally as being genuine, in meeting with the seller's obligation in accordance with the summary of the procedures in clause 19 above.

20.4 Paragraph 19.1 above provides the timeframe and scheduling for the performance of the contract.

20.5 The seller's 'proof of interest' in the goods is officially declared once the information regarding the owner in possession of the goods has been disclosed. Whether or not the buyer chooses to verify this information is of no concern to the seller.

20.6 The financial instrument shall be made active on satisfaction of the pre-advised condition, when the document entitled 'PPI policy proof of interest certificate' which contains this information is disclosed to the issuing bank.

20.7 The seller is not giving the buyer, buyer's bank or associated bank of the issuing bank permission to approach the supplier. Either the buyer or the issuing bank can verify the information provided.

20.8 If the buyer exercises this discretion and verifies the interests in the goods held by the seller, then the information requested of the supplier is strictly limited to verification that the goods are genuine and available as disclosed on the PPI certificate and nothing else. The seller's name, the nature of the goods and seller's interests therein are the only verifiable matters that the buyer should expect to receive.

20.9 The buyer hereby agrees not to request or make enquiries concerning sensitive information regarding, *inter alia*, price and the disclosure of the DLC number. Any such requests will not be tolerated under any circumstances.

20.10 The discretionary period within which the buyer is permitted to verify that such goods are genuine and available must be exercised within exactly 72 hours after the PPI certificate is surrendered to the issuing bank.

20.11 Any approaches made to the supplier for whatsoever reason after the expiry of the 72-hour timeframe and for a period of 12 months thereafter, whether or not the business at hand was successfully or unsuccessfully closed, shall be treated as a dishonourable act and a serious breach of conditions.

21. PPI CERTIFICATE

A blank PPI certificate is hereby offered below. This document will be completed and returned to the issuing bank as per the time provided in this agreement.

PPI: POLICY PROOF OF INTEREST CERTIFICATE (BLANK MODEL PART 'A')

IMPORTANT BANK PRESENTATION DELIVERY DOCUMENT

PPI Advised By: FTN Exporting, 'the seller'
Address:
Contact Number:
Seller's Advising bank:
Supporting Transaction Code:
For the Immediate Attention of:
Applicant's Issuing bank.
For the Account of the Applicant: (The buyer) Name:
Supporting Pre-advised Letter of Credit Number:
Date PPI advised:
Issued by Facsimile (   ) and/or PDF (   ):
In reference: Full Activation of Credit.
Supporting the purchase of goods defined as:
Attention Bank Officer – Name:

Dear Sir or Madam,

Please be advised that the named applicant, also referred to as the buyer, has issued a UCP600 pre-advised credit from your bank to our advising bank. We are required to present details to identify the supplier of the goods we are reselling to the applicant of the credit. This Proof of Interest (PPI) certificate is hereby offered as per our contracting conditions, in meeting with the pre-advised credit condition. Please be advised that the service of this disclosure meets our obligation regardless of whether the applicant confirms the validity of the information provided or not.

Accordingly we request that you revoke the 'pre-advised' status of the credit, thereby making the credit a normal active UCP600 irrevocable transferable documentary letter of credit (and therefore operational.)

Yours faithfully

Print Name:
Signed:
Dated:

The buyer and applicant of the issued credit shall by their own means and discretion using facsimile, email or other forms of telecommunication to confirm the details of the supplier as per the information provided below. Whether or not they choose to exercise this discretion has no effect on the activation of the credit.

PPI: SUPPLIER'S DETAILS:

The Supplier and owner of the goods are:
The name of the person representing the supplier and owner is:
Address:
Email:
Facsimile:
Phone Number:
Business Number:
Supplier's Website, if any:
Description of Goods:
Quantity:

End of PPI Certificate

Date sent to issuing bank:

Seller and Buyer Details and Declaration:

SELLER'S DETAILS

Name of the Seller: FTN Exporting
Name of person offering the goods: Davide Papa
Business Address:
Mailing Address:
All Communication Details:
Email:
Phone(s):
Facsimile:
Name of Bank:

Name apparent on Account: Davide Papa
Address:
Account Number:
SWIFT CODE:
Phone/Facsimile:

SELLER'S DECLARATION

I, Davide Giovanni Papa C/o P.O. Box 468 Carlton Nth, Melbourne, Victoria, 3054 Citizen of Australia, as an independent private commodity trader using the registered trading name of FTN Exporting do hereby sign and/or sign and seal this contract with good and honourable intent as seller acting on behalf of an undisclosed principal or various principals. This/these principal(s) shall be disclosed upon the acceptance of the buyer's financial instrument, in accordance with the terms of this agreement.

Print Name: Davide Andrew Giovanni PAPA
Date: 20 March 20--
Signature:

Seal:

BUYER'S DETAILS

Name of the Buyer:
Person taking possession of the goods:
Business Address:
Mailing Address:
All Communication Details:
Email:
Phone(s):
Facsimile:
Name of Bank:
Address:
Name apparent on Account:
Account Number:
SWIFT CODE:
Phone/Facsimile:

BUYER'S DECLARATION

I, _____ do hereby seal this contract with good and honourable intent as buyer taking both title and possession of the offered goods. I the buyer accordingly agree with all the terms, scope and conditions of this contract.

Print Name:
Date:
Signature:

Seal:

Once the trader feels confident enough to take the deal to the contracting stage then knowledge of this type of contract will serve its purpose. However one nagging problem persists as a major hurdle that only becomes apparent after the contract has been signed. It is probably the biggest trading trap of all. Issuing a correctly calculated and defined performance guarantee is a critical part of the trade that must never be ignored, and is explored in detail in the following chapter.

13

Performance Guarantee

Let us consider the scenario where the quotation for the goods was for US$200 per metric ton as secured from a real supplier via other intermediaries. The buyer/seller in their confused state thinks the price is highly competitive and adds US$20 per MT to the price for themselves. The buyer/seller issues a new offer reflecting this into the realm of the intermediary group, looking to secure an end buyer. On the so called seller's side there are three intermediaries each receiving the offer from the previous intermediary on that side of the string contract, who had each changed the price to include their own personal commissions. Finally the third intermediary connects with a so-called buyer's side intermediary looking to buy the very product being offered. The buyer now also begins to manipulate the price by adding their commission on top. Three other intermediaries on the buyer's side do the same until it reaches the final intermediary next to the end buyer who thinks their position is of great importance and call themselves a mandate (even though they're not) and adds a full US$20 per MT commission on top of the same offer. The buyer then gives the offer to an end buyer.

The end buyer accepts the offer (or so it seems) but the price of the goods has now reached a staggering US$310 per MT after everyone has added their own commissions, which vary from US$5 per MT to as high as US$20 per MT. Let us assume that the quantity being offered is 10,000 metric tons. The offer has reached the end buyer as issued except for the original issued price of the goods. Let's imply that a real supplier has issued the offer to the first intermediary with a 2 per cent performance guarantee. The end buyer accepts the offer, signs the contract and finally issues the DLC for US$310 per MT reaching someone holding the stated trading position of buyer/seller. Let us also assume that by some miracle the buyer/seller transfers the purchase value of the goods being US$200 per MT to the supplier, the US$110 per MT coverage being theirs and everyone else's portion of the commission in their account and under their control.

The supplier accepts the DLC for the total value as per their quote and offer for US$2,000,000 and accordingly issues a PG for the said offered value of 2 per cent (US$40,000). The end buyer however is expecting a PG value as applied to their purchase price of 2 per cent as well (US$62,000). The credit will fail to become operative if only US$40,000 is advised and the deal will collapse there and then. The end buyer will allege breach of contract and implicate everyone. Anyone who was involved in the deal scurries away to hide, phones are disconnected, and emails don't get answered.

Greedy and ill-informed intermediaries have killed the deal off. The end buyer would have been notified of the US$40,000 PG and it does not take long for their bankers to work out that the end buyer was paying US$310 for goods that were only worth around US$200 per MT. The end buyer is now also furious to find out that US$110 of their hard-earned cash was nearly going to end up in the pockets of intermediaries for doing nothing.

Multiply the above effect many times with many end buyers over many years. The result is that it is now nearly impossible to close deals today. There is no longer any confidence in these offers and, unless you trade correctly and deal only with genuine traders, the chances of ever closing a deal when mixing it with the millions of misguided traders on the internet today is virtually impossible. Even top traders will find it difficult to close these deals unless, by accident, an end buyer spends time to read your offer and realizes that the person making it seems to be applying strong trading principles which are very familiar to any end buyer who has imported goods in the past. Getting real principals to look at an offer or request is difficult to accomplish.

In our scenario the end buyer has the details of the supplier via the bank, because when a DLC is transferred this information automatically becomes apparent. The deal collapses and the end buyer eventually contacts the supplier directly and closes the deal for US$200 per MT. The end buyer then vows never to touch an intermediary deal again and continues ordering the goods from information supplied originally by intermediaries. A transaction for 10,000 metric tons is a small deal: multiply the effect of the PG issuance in a deal where the price is US$400 or US$500 per MT for quantities of 100,000 MT or more, and you can see how a very small variation in a PG will result in a huge gap between the values of the respective PG amounts.

If, as a well-informed intermediary, the PIA had taken control of the deal the situation where other buyers and sellers were also allowed to transact in the same deal would not have occurred. The PIA would have also kept all intermediaries informed, being very well aware that the PG rate would have needed to change. The PIA would have verified the goods with the supplier by making all the seller's side intermediaries including the implied seller to 'step back'.

If they failed to 'step back' the PIA would not have continued with the deal and would instead move on to another potential transaction very quickly. The PIA would also have ensured that the end buyer was quoted a fair price and that the commissions would not have spiralled out of control.

Issuing a Performance Guarantee

Let's look specifically at the issue relating to the PG. A PG under UCP600 may be issued in two ways:

1. By issuing an ISP98 SLC the supplier is declaring that they are issuing a credit that is allowed to be transferred more than once among a trading group.

2. The issuance of a UCP600 SLC, on the other hand, means that the PG can only be transferred once, just like the DLC used to pay for the goods. The supplier issues a transferable UCP600 SLC to the PIA who is able to transfer it once to the end buyer only. This is the preferred PG that would be used by the PIA most of the time, as the PIA would have not traded with an intermediate buyer standing between themselves and the end buyer.

The performance guarantee is often referred to as a performance bond, again highlighting the lack of trading knowledge among internet traders. The 'bond' is not so different to that which applies in criminal law where a 'bond' (usually financial) is an assurance that the defendant will return to court on bail to answer charges at a later date. Failing to appear means forfeiture of the bond. The assurance given to the court by a bond to the court has been breached and the defendant can be arrested and imprisoned pending a court appearance. In addition a further penalty may also be imposed for breaking the bond. A 'performance bond' (PB) could be used in a deal where delivery is based on 'ex ship' as defined under Incoterms 2000 where the assurances given apply to 'bond' with the goods, until the goods arrive in the contracted condition into the possession of the end buyer, in their port of discharge. This is irrelevant as far as the intermediary is concerned, as intermediaries should not trade in these types of 'ex ship' deals or similar. In an ex ship deal the goods and not the documents must arrive before delivery is said to have occurred. As previously stated intermediaries should not deal in possession of goods but only title or delivery documents.

If an intermediary decided to buy the goods with their own money for physical sale later on, they would not be acting within the role of the intermediary but rather a supplier doing business directly with a corporate importer, distributor or wholesaler in a two-party deal that may allow the use of a performance bond.

The performance guarantee is related to 'performance' as it applies to the specific activities of the international trade intermediary, broker or agent. Since intermediaries cannot deal in possession of goods, the performance in this case is 'delivery' and only relates to the act of securing the title or leading delivery documents of the goods being offered within a certain timeframe. In a CIF deal the goods pass the ship's rail in the port of loading and all the delivery documents referred to in the contract and DLC are issued to the PIA. The PIA in turn endorses them over to the end buyer within a specific timeframe. When the required documents are delivered on time, then the required 'performance' has occurred and the performance guarantee is no longer enforceable. The ship leaves the loading port and the purchased cargo arrives many weeks later into the possession of the end buyer who has the title documents for the goods.

The intermediary must ensure that all the required delivery documents arrive at the bank within the specific timeframe. If this timeframe is breached, the end buyer will also receive the performance guarantee value even though actual 'delivery' still occurs sometime later, outside the required timeframe. If in an FOB deal the ship does not arrive in time for the delivery date, but the seller has ensured that the goods are ready for loading at the designated place, then the buyer cannot claim the PG due to the seller's lack of 'performance' because the seller has 'performed' as per their contracted obligation. In a CIF deal the goods have to pass the ship's rail on the requisite delivery date or earlier (but not later).

Once the delivery documents arrive at the issuing bank, UCP600 implies that examination must occur within five days. The leading delivery document once dated is said to be the shipment date. Regardless of what happens, the shipment date infers that all documents must be presented with 21 days of issuance and before the credit expires. Otherwise the documents will be treated as stale, and the bank will not accept presentation. Stale documents would cause the performance guarantee to be called upon.

The shipment date is also used when establishing the breach of the delivery date, as it compares to the date on the contract. If documents were missing or marked incorrectly at presentation time, then this too could also cause the performance guarantee to be collected upon unconditionally by the end buyer. If the contract provides a specific delivery date and the delivery is late the performance guarantee can be called upon. As per UCP rules, the nature of business relating to the financial instrument is totally different to that of a sales contract. Unlike a DLC used to pay for goods a SLC does not require any documents to be collected upon. A simple breach of a required action will cause the SLC PG to be called upon unconditionally: all that needs to be shown is that delivery of the goods is late.

Thus to the intermediary 'performance' and 'delivery' are strictly associated with the production of title documents on time, within the DLC expiration period. Once this happens you can collect on the financial instrument. Intermediaries deal exclusively in documents. The presentation of all the documents and the format of all such documents are of critical importance and cannot afford to be ambiguous in any way. When a trader obtains quotations, offers and contracts which make reference to ambiguous trading terms which are apparently indifferent to Incoterms and UCP600 rules then this itself is an early warning sign which suggests that the offer should be dismissed at the earliest opportunity.

So we have seen that the absence of a performance guarantee in a deal makes for an easier transaction for the intermediary, and that a PG is not as common as misguided online intermediaries would have you believe. When the PIA sources goods directly from a supplier they should always ask for a PG of under 2 per cent. If the supplier informs the PIA that they can give a quotation but without the required PG, the PIA often then attempts to simply resell the goods making it clear that the goods are offered at that price without a PG. On the other hand if the supplier offers a PG to the PIA then the PIA can choose whether or not to offer a PG in the first instance when reselling, and simply wait for the end buyer to request one. If this happens, no matter what the PG amount secured by the PIA is, the PIA must always offer a lesser value to the end buyer. In any event, the PG for the end buyer can never be for more than the PG value secured by the PIA and must always be issued at a lesser rate by a minimum of 0.25 per cent. If the supplier agrees to offer you 1.5 per cent as a PG then the PIA would initially offer no PG to the end buyer, but if need be could offer 1 per cent or even up to 1.15 per cent as a PG value.

You must ensure that there is a gap between the two PG amounts. Previously FTN Exporting advised that the maximum acceptable commission on a bulk deal was around 2.5 per cent. We imposed this in order to give a workable set of guidance parameters to new traders. We still need to watch the PG gap, but 5 per cent is now allowable as a commission rate to a maximum of 10 per cent with 7 per cent being the medium average range for non-container type deals. If an end buyer often purchases goods at US$250 per MT and the intermediaries as a group manage to secure the goods for US$200 per MT, then in effect it would not be inappropriate to offer such goods to the end buyer at US$220 per MT. Everyone in the deal gets an allocated portion of the commission. The end buyer would not be too concerned to learn that intermediaries are sharing US$20 per MT on such a deal, especially when they are paying US$30 per MT less than the amount they were paying previously.

In such a situation the PIA could easily work out the minimum and maximum parameters of the PG rate well in advance of having to negotiate it with the end buyer.

In our trading scenario if the PIA was offered or managed to secure, for example, a 2 per cent PG from a supplier, and the PIA was sharp enough to issue their offer carrying a 1 per cent PG then the deal would have been safe from collapse because of an improper PG rate (assuming it was a proper deal in the first place).

The supplier could have issued the US$40,000 UCP600 transferable SLC and the end buyer, if they accepted the offer with the 1 per cent PG, would have expected to receive only a PG of US$31,000. This in turn would have easily also protected all commissions. As a matter of fact if the end buyer was not impressed with a 1 per cent PG then the PIA could have offered 1.25 per cent PG (US$38,750) and still be safe. If the end buyer still wanted more, then the PIA could have reduced all commission rates to a lower level in order to offer a lower price to the end buyer as further incentive to get the buyer to accept the offer that would have allowed an even higher PG to apply.

The PIA must control the 'PG gap' at all times, and where possible try and get some kind of PG from the supplier but offer none or a very small PG to the end buyer in the first instance. The unequivocal rule here is never to offer the PG rate as collected from the supplier.

Warning: some intermediaries have suggested that those trading in the position as a PIA could have taken US$20,000 of their own money to make up the gap between the PG values. This is unwise and very impractical, not to mention dangerous. What happens if there is a PG gap of US$200,000 or US$300,000? Don't assume intermediaries could get these funds and even if they could, the chances of losing a PG without the deal in hand closing is great.

In any case the PIA could not simply add in the difference. The PIA has to keep the SLC PG as issued from the supplier and issues a full SLC at the new PG rate for the full amount that needs to be serviced from their own pocket. A back-to-back transaction is not acceptable here as banks don't accept an SLC as being equal in tender to cash. If the PIA issues a PG with their own funds, which is a risky thing to do, the following could happen: the supplier could indeed perform to the PIA, but it is the PIA who had made a mistake with the end buyer which by default caused the PIA to lose the PG outright, without having any right to recoup it from the supplier's PG. If the deal collapses later, the seller has lost the PG and will be liable for a breach of contract arising from both ends of the transaction.

An intermediary should never fund their own PG, no matter how small the amount. A few collapsed deals in a short period of time where no commission was earned could financially ruin the intermediary especially if the PG SLC was secured using collateral. It is therefore imperative that you never offer a PG first then attempt to accept a DLC for payment of goods. A PG is automatically and unconditionally payable upon the breach in 'delivery' having occurred, and scam artists know very well the situation in which they could legally walk away from a deal after collecting the PG without having any intention of opening their own DLC in the first place.

The scam involves convincing the supplier that they are a real end buyer. Once convinced, the supplier then is tricked first into opening the PG to the so-called buyer. The supplier then waits for the DLC to be opened for the goods being purchased, but instead the buyer ends up arguing on some point about the contract and starts making unfair demands. The moment the supplier indicates that they will not comply with such unfair demands the deal collapses. Legally this means that the supplier has indeed failed 'delivery' and voila! the buyer is allowed to collect on the supplier's PG. The supplier spends time and money trying to bring the culprits to court for breach of contract and, not surprisingly, they are nowhere to be found and are having a good time living off the supplier's lack of due diligence.

A DLC is always provided first, before the active PG. Even if it is suggested that a non-active PG be issued first, which is made operational when the DLC is issued, the same scam is in play. A non-operational PG is advised and a DLC for far less than the required amount is advised, which could automatically activate the PG. If an argument erupts the DLC, carrying a very short validity date, is cancelled. Because the supplier failed to perform on delivery, the end buyer is legally entitled to the PG payment. Remember, the bank cannot become involved in matters of the sales contract. The buyer opens a credit for 1,000 dollars instead of 100,000 dollars that activates the PG then the supplier will refuse delivery until a proper DLC value is issued. The DLC expires, delivery has failed and the end buyer unconditionally gets to keep the supplier's PG.

14

Delivery

The term 'delivery' is clearly defined by Incoterms 2000. As we know intermediaries do not deal in physical possession of the product being purchased and sold as they deal in the title and delivery documents of the goods. In a EXW, CIF, CFR, FAS or FOB bulk deals, or including deals involving full container loads (FCL) as defined by the equivalent trading acronym CIP or FCA, delivery means 'delivery of documents' relating to the goods. Delivery for most deals is initiated by ensuring the goods 'pass the ship's rail' in the port of loading (except for FAS and FCA deals). This action among other things activates the most important 'delivery' document being the clean on board 'shipped' or 'received' marine bill of lading where appropriate.

In the case of an aircraft being used for transportation, the equivalent document to the marine bill of lading is an 'airway bill' (of lading). Similarly 'delivery' is said to have been initiated once the goods are on board the aircraft and the doors are sealed as, unless there is an emergency, once this occurs it is nearly impossible to stop the aircraft from departing and/or have the doors reopened. This 'closed door' policy is also used in certain passenger airlines. The airway bill of lading is issued on the understanding that once the goods are on the plane, delivery has occurred. Once the doors are sealed they cannot be reopened until the aircraft has arrived at the destination port. The captain of a plane acts in the same position as the master of a vessel.

This book deals mostly with shipping of bulk 'FOB Incoterms' goods, and to a lesser extent CIF transactions. Intermediaries learning a carrier's FOB method would learn the other delivery methods over time, thus as mentioned before intermediaries should begin by trading in FOB bulk goods. This gives the intermediary the required base premise upon which all other trade deliveries are formed: the platform to a CIF deal is built upon the base of an FOB deal.

'Delivery' is a confusing term to intermediaries because most believe they are indeed required to deliver the physical goods to the end buyer before their part of the transaction is closed. Many end buyers are also confused by the same term, especially those importing goods for the first time.

There are exceptions to the definition of 'delivery' and FOB is the primary method that intermediaries should concentrate on and need to perfect. It is however appropriate to give a brief mention to the other delivery terms.

In a delivery ex ship (DES) transaction, which so many end buyers ask for but seldom get, the ship must arrive at destination port with the goods to imply 'delivery'. Intermediaries cannot deal with these transactions because documents in this 'delivery' are not enough; in order for the supplier to collect on the end buyer's documentary letter of credit the goods must be delivered. The problem here is one of arrival. If an intermediary were to get involved in an ex ship deal then they could become heavily embroiled in controversy at the time of arrival, especially if the end buyer decides to play hardball by rejecting the goods unfairly in an effort to obtain further financial incentives and gains from the supplier. If the buyer does not attend to collect and inspect their goods when the ship berths, the supplier may not be able to collect upon the financial instrument, thus creating frustration and delays at the time when the deal is supposed to close.

Intermediaries should not deal in 'delivery ex ship' (DES) deals. Naturally after trading for a long time some intermediaries may gain the required knowledge to trade in all delivery applications including DES, but that is a matter for that individual intermediary at the time. Intermediaries must study FOB Incoterms 2000 after reading this book and those who wish to broaden their knowledge on the subject should enquire at a large bank. Many banks have their own publications regarding international trade. If you're an account holder you may not have to pay for a copy of their publication. A bank's own publication will reinforce, in a more technical way, that which has already been taught in this work as it applies to a two-party transaction and will usually make reference to Incoterms 2000 and UCP600 throughout. The following Top 100 world class UCP600 bank has good free publications available to download in PDF form: http://www.westpac.com.au/internet/publish.nsf/ Content/BBIT+Export+Services Westpac Banking Corporation (Australia) (online).

A grasp of the procedure in this book will make study of more complex matters of international trade much easier.

Using Strict Delivery Terms

In an FCA deal the goods pass over the ship's rail and it is at this point that the marine bill of lading will be marked as 'received'. In a CIF deal the BOL is defined as being 'shipped'. In a container deal the term FOB term is replaced with the term FCA (Free Carrier).

In an FCA deal, the ship may be required to remain in the loading port for weeks awaiting final container lifting. For example the exporter arranges physical delivery of the goods to a Container Freight Station (CFS) for example, on Monday. By Tuesday it is loaded on board a ship and takes up 'free' space on it in consideration of freight charges. The bill of lading is signed and returned to the shipper, which shows that the container is officially registered 'on board' a named ship in possession of the carrier. But there are another 300 containers that still need to be loaded and, because of bad weather conditions and other unforeseen delays, it may take another ten days to complete the loading of the carrier before it can set 'sail' (NB: Although technically no longer the case, nor has it been for generations, romanticized shipping terms such as 'set sail' are still used. Similarly the BOL is still referred to as a 'SS BOL' – steam ship bill of lading.) The bill of lading is simply endorsed as being 'on board', in other words, the bill of lading is issued to confirm that the exporter's container has been officially 'received' by the carrier.

The intermediary could include a clause in the contract for either FCL or bulk FOB shipments to the effect that the leading delivery document is the received clean on board bill of lading marked as original and issued as a single original copy. The provisions of Incoterms only require 'evidence' that the goods are on board. As we have already seen the intermediary should ideally deliver the first 'available' delivery document that provides on board evidence. A CFS receipt that the goods are in 'possession' of a carrier would not meet the requirements of Incoterms that the goods are 'evidenced' as being on board ship.

The carrier owners cannot comment on the actual goods inside the container. The container is sealed so whether or not the goods inside the container are 'clean' on board has no bearing in relation to whether or not the goods are damaged inside the container. The only assurance given at this time is that the container, which presumably contains the goods being exported, is on board the ship. If the container arrives at the destination port and the goods are not as ordered, not fit for purpose, or are damaged this is a matter to be settled between the end buyer and the supplier as per the provisions in the contract of sale. In a Bulk FOB and CIF transaction the opposite is true. For example, 25,000 metric tons of sugar loaded on board the 'free' offered space of the carrier in consideration for freight will either produce a clean bill of lading, or one which is subject to a 'clause' that states, for example, 'Approximately five hundred bags of sugar received torn open'. The issuing bank will refuse to allow collection upon the credit where the bill of lading is not issued as clean. The applicant for the credit expects to receive goods that are as described, fit for their purpose and of satisfactory quality.

A 'charterparty' occurs if a party that does not own a ship hires one instead. Intermediaries should not deal with charterparty 'BOL' when CFR or CIF deals are contemplated. If a 'rented' ship carries on board a variety of non-container bulk goods and is going to various ports along a specific route, then the nature of business is specific to the person chartering the ship and their customers accordingly. Intermediaries deal in delivery documents that the bank must receive and then examine. These documents must not relate to a single customer's order amongst others, but must only pertain to one customer purchasing bulk goods and to which the bill of lading has been issued accordingly. In other words the intermediary's method of doing business is with one bulk carrying ship, one bill of lading and one customer buying and taking possession of the goods. As an example: the buyer informs you that they have found a ship being loaded in Brazil and heading for New York and they have reserved the space so that 2,000 MT of sugar they have ordered from you can be put on board this ship. Obviously the intermediary even if asked to do so is not going to secure the bill of lading as being a part of the delivery and DLC presentation process and may secure it on behalf of the end buyer on the understanding that it is done on a personal level not attached in any way to the process of delivery or presentation of documents.

The date on the received bill of lading is said to be the date the goods have been received on board the nominated ship. It is from this date that the banks will accept these documents for examination. As long as the documents are not 'stale' on arrival banks using UCP600 will have five days to examine them. A bank will refuse to examine documents under UCP600 that arrive more than 21 days after the 'received' or 'shipped' on board date.

The following example provides a 'shipped' status for a CIF transaction. The bulk goods are loaded on board a 'Suez Max' class ship. This ship prepares to depart, the bill of lading is issued as clean and dated on the shipment date. The ship departs to deliver the goods to the end buyer. The end buyer is actually being told that 'their' goods and nobody else's goods are loaded on board a named ship in a specific loading port which is now heading towards the buyer's destination port. The shipped documents must arrive before the ship arrives at the destination port. The documents bearing title to the goods must be presented within 21 days of the 'shipped' date.

For example, the shipped date presented on the bill of lading is the 10th of March. This is the date the ship was meant to have arrived at the port ready for loading. However the bill of lading is marked as 'goods clean on board' 15 days later. This means that the main title document being the BOL (bill of lading) must arrive at the bank within the next five days. The BOL is presented, filled in, to the ship's master by the supplier. The master of the ship acts on behalf of the owner of the carrier. Via the owner's representatives the master checks the goods against the BOL and endorses it accordingly. The date on the shipped bill of lading, as far as the intermediary is concerned, is also the delivery date. Once the documents are presented 'clean' as stipulated on the credit then the intermediary has closed the deal upon collection of the delivery credit.

15

Delivery and Commission Payments

The following scenario is based on UCP600.

The PIA is the middle controlling intermediary in a specific deal. John helped the PIA to secure a genuine supplier, and as a result John's commission is protected and will eventually be paid by the PIA. Mary assists the PIA to secure an end buyer, thus Mary is similarly protected by the PIA. After two months of hard negotiations the PIA has received an irrevocable UCP600 transferable pre-advised credit from the end buyer's bank – the issuing bank – into their account, defined as the account of the 'beneficiary' of the advising bank.

The PIA checks the credit and finds it in order and accepts the credit by issuing a document 'bank to bank', which discloses the owner in possession of the goods so that the end buyer has an opportunity if they wish to verify that the goods are genuine. As we have seen, the document is the Policy Proof of Interest certificate. This action has the immediate effect of activating the pre-advised credit into a normal transferable credit (as advised by the issuing bank to the advising bank) along with the required transfer fee. The PIA transfers the exact amount of funds required to 'buy' the goods from the supplier to the supplier's bank. The difference in the buying and selling price remains in the account of the PIA, as commission. This commission is paid to Mary and John in their allocated shares.

The supplier issues a transferable UCP600 SLC performance guarantee to the PIA as per the contract, which is transferred to the end buyer. The PIA pays for the transfer fee in this instance because the deal has passed the crucial DLC stage and has been accepted by the supplier. In comparison to the credit used to pay for the goods this fee is considered very small and affordable by most. The supplier now waits for notification of the buyer's ship, as secured from a shipowner or a charterparty. Remember this is an FOB deal. Intermediaries are not concerned with these issues that are the responsibility of the end buyer, specifically matters of the shipping charter.

The ship finally arrives and any issues of demurrage are dealt with between the carrier and the end buyer. The ship berths and laytime commences. (Laytime can be expressed in laydays and is the amount of time the shipowner allows for the cargo to be loaded and/or discharging to be undertaken.) This is where the supplier must cause the goods to cross over the ship's rail to bring delivery into effect. The usual practice here is that an agent or freight forwarder secured by the supplier ensures that the goods do get on board the named ship. The supplier issues the required 'evidence' to the PIA, which proves that the goods are on board. This is obtained from their forwarders as serviced by the ship's officer.

Under international trade law, there is a document that is defined as being 'first class evidence' other than the BOL that can be secured officially to record that the goods are on board the ship. Even if the intermediary is asked by the buyer to assist in securing the BOL, this assistance has nothing to do with 'presentation' documents that the intermediary is required to produce. Intermediaries should first secure the ship's mate's receipt as per the contract of sale. If the end buyer insists that the seller secures the bill of lading instead then this must be included in the contract, which must also include provisions for failure to secure it. Presentation of delivery documents must still be the main priority.

Assume everything goes well and the PIA receives all the hardcopy delivery documents in good order by post, either directly to the PIA or to their advising bank. If the documents arrive at their advising bank, they are all collected and passed onto the PIA who simply sends them by courier directly to the end buyer or their issuing bank. Alternatively these may be sent by the advising bank for forwarding, in either hard copy and/or electronic format, to the issuing bank. If the advising bank loses the documents it has a 'no fault' clause under UPC600, which indemnifies the bank from any resultant loss. Before the PIA forwards these documents the supplier's invoice is replaced with their own to reflect the price paid by the end buyer.

Under UCP600 the issuing bank (and not the advising bank) has five days to examine the documents and accept them. When the issuing bank accepts the documents the advising bank is notified of this, which also has the effect of formally providing this information to the supplier's bank. The supplier has successfully applied for collection on their financial instrument as per the URC 522 rules and this act now means that the original issued total credit amount is able to be collected upon from the PIA. Therefore the portion of funds not transferred (attached by its L/C number to the transferred portion) can also be collected upon by the PIA personally. Therefore the PIA applies for collection. Fees are charged and the issuing bank negotiates with the advising bank that in turn allows collection by the PIA.

The PIA keeps their portion of the allotted commission in the same account. Once the PIA has successfully collected their own secured commission the other intermediaries, upon receiving specific instructions from the PIA, now each submit their own 'pay orders' to their respective bank for authentication and collection against the account of the PIA. The PIA is not paying intermediaries from their pocket. The PIA is also getting paid a commission upon the successful closing of the transaction. Thus a commission pay order is first issued as a personal guarantee and, once accepted, the personal guarantee is returned and endorsed by the PIA. By the time the deal closes the PIA has already issued the pay order to each protected member as a UCP600 SLC. The member then only needs to submit the corporate SLC for collection to apply once the specific condition has been met as defined on the SLC. The intermediary will need to take sufficient identification to the bank to collect the commission. For example the SLC may state for security reasons: 'Please pay on presentation upon the bearer providing a passport or other identifiable statutory form of identification acceptable to the bank.'

The intermediaries receive their commission at the same time as the PIA. Intermediaries collect their own commissions, but the PIA is now obligated to stay with the transaction and follow the goods to their final destination. The PIA had issued the SLC as a promissory note early in the deal knowing that it might take at least five weeks and up to 12 weeks to close the deal. As soon as it became apparent that clean presentation was imminent, the PIA endorsed the offered promissory note that had turned the promissory note into an SLC.

The loaded ship heads towards the port of the end buyer and arrives some four weeks later. The end buyer presents their title documents. They already have the bill of lading as sent from the supplier, which is the most important delivery document in obtaining possession of the goods. It is the buyer's shipment, thus the bill of lading once endorsed is handed over to the buyer and not the intermediate buyer/seller, even if the PIA is asked to assist in the securing of the BOL.

The goods are unloaded and it takes ten days to store them in the buyer's warehouse. When unloaded the last lot of the goods reveals torn bags, which denotes that the supplier had used inferior packaging. Photographic evidence, an affidavit and a witness statement from an independent witness, that is not a member of the buyer's own firm, confirms the damage to the goods. The end buyer further claims a rejection of the goods because of the change in packaging which did not become apparent until the last batch was unloaded.

Once the PIA hears the news of the damage the PIA has two options. Firstly, if the quantity damaged is small and the commission was sufficient, the PIA would apologize and negotiate a refund and would send it via SWIFT out of the PIA's commission immediately in an effort to keep this potentially long-term customer happy. In the alternative, if it is a large amount being sought by way of remedy, the PIA would mitigate the loss on behalf of the end buyer with the supplier. The PIA would also seek remedy as the buyer directly from the supplier. Once this remedy is obtained, the PIA would remit the compensation to their end buyer.

This is a simple insight into how the commission is secured against the backdrop of a complete transaction. At each point in the transition bankers, shippers, suppliers and forwarders will all offer advice and guidance on the complexities of these types of matters. This example should give intermediaries a good idea as to how commissions are earned and when they are paid out.

But there are other questions that need to be addressed in relation to the intermediary's role: what if the certificate of origin was not sent to the PIA, and time is running out to meet the letter of credit expiry date after which documentary presentation will become 'stale'? The PIA has a contract with the supplier so it is imperative that they put pressure on the supplier, who runs the risk of not getting paid either. The PIA knows that the bank has nothing to do with the contract with the supplier. The bank is only concerned with the document presentation meeting with the requirement of the credit. Therefore it is advisable to seek advice from the advising bank to see what they can suggest. A bank will help once they can sense a deal being near to closure. In these circumstances the nominated or advising bank usually asks for a waiver from the issuing bank relating to 'discrepant documents'.

There is therefore a degree of discretion when a deal is near closure. The intermediary seeks the advice of their bank in relation to 'waivers' and 'notices' that could allow the issuing bank to offer an indemnity to the end buyer in allowing the bank only to accept documents which are in hand. If the PIA does not try to mitigate any unexpected events regarding the DLC, the bank will still proceed with presentation (even though failure of the deal is apparent). Doing nothing could result in heavy losses being incurred. There is not much point in asking the bank's advice before a DLC is secured: banks get thousands of requests daily from intermediaries who do not know what they are doing and often the bank won't even reply. Seeking such advice when a DLC is close to being honoured will result in good service and advice.

In the scenario above the end buyer could have advised the issuing bank to accept the delivery documents 'as they are' (after further research has found that the end buyer does not need the certificate of origin to allow the goods to enter their country and that the import permit they obtained, coupled with the export permit which was presented correctly, is all that was needed). The end buyer may not be aware of this, so the intermediary might need to bring this information to their attention. If an intermediary has no idea what they are doing, they ruin their own chances of closing a deal. The intermediary who wants to trade seriously must gain a solid grounding in knowledge, experience and practice – simply reading this or any other international trade documentation is not enough.

Confidence and Knowledge

Once the intermediary has the basic outline of the entire deal and knows what is needed to close a deal successfully other issues can be rectified simply by establishing who is responsible for what and approaching them for advice and assistance. If an intermediary were only to study trading academically for 12 months, then practical experience would still be necessary. Intermediaries, especially those new to the business want to begin to trade immediately: once the definitive concepts are grasped a trader can learn along the way. It is imperative that the intermediary understands the concepts relating to commission early on, because interactions with other traders is a vital part of the whole process from the very start.

The trader acting in the role of the PIA must exhibit leadership qualities at all times. Other traders need to feel confident in their dealings with the

PIA and will need to know immediately how the PIA is going to protect their interests (commissions) so as to allow the PIA to take control of a deal. This allows all other matters of the deal to be attended to without having to argue about issues relating to commission. So many other issues have to be contended with before any such commission payment becomes relevant. Take control of the deal, make everyone step back quickly to you and address any concerns regarding commission at the earliest opportunity so that they are no longer an issue.

Standby Letter of Credit Model

Let's look at an SLC (standby letter of credit) as used for the payment of a performance guarantee. This SLC is advised as an ISP98 instrument and is issued by a bank. The beneficiary may make the demand for payment so long as certain conditions are met. Check the specific conditions needed to collect on this SLC:

TRANSFERBLE STANDBY LETTER OF CREDIT

Issuing Bank:	BANK OF CHINA Hong Kong
Date of Issue:	2nd Day of December 2006 HKD
Standby Letter of Credit No :	4567 777888999777
Date of Advising:	02/12/2006 HKD
Expiration Date:	30 Days from Date of Issue
Credit Applicant:	H.K.D Import/Export Co. LTD H.K
Beneficiary of the Credit:	FTN Exporting 309 Rathdowne Street Carlton North 3054 Melbourne Australia
Total Amount:	US$200,000.00

Advising Bank: WESTPAC Bank
                                        305 Collins Street Melbourne 3000
                                        Victoria Australia
                                        Swift: WESAU3444

As requested by the Applicant, we hereby irrevocably and unconditionally (except as stated herein) undertake to pay the Beneficiary on their first demand in writing at our counter the sum of US$200,000.00 (TWO HUNDRED THOUSAND UNITED STATES DOLLARS). This is subject to the demand in writing being accompanied by the Beneficiary's written and signed statement that the amount demanded is due and owing between the Beneficiary and the Applicant and the demand in writing bears the Applicant's signed confirmation that it is correct and the Applicant's signature(s) thereon is (are) verified by us as a full Identifiable signature.

This standby letter of credit is payable unconditionally upon first demand.

Paid to the counter of the advising bank.

Payment under this standby letter of credit shall be made to the Beneficiary pursuant to their demand in writing as stated above without set-off and free from any deductions, charges, fees or withholdings of any nature now or hereafter imposed, levied, collected, withheld or assessed by the Hong Kong government or any political subdivision or authority thereof or therein.

This standby letter of credit shall remain valid from 02/12/20-- until 02/01/20--. The demand in writing, if any, under this standby letter of credit may be presented to us at our counter between 10/12/20-- and 16/12/20-- (15 days before the expiry date. Both dates inclusive to Hong Kong date line, such defined date(s) hereafter shall be referred to as the 'Presentation Period'). Any demand under this standby letter of credit presented to us outside the presentation period shall be considered invalid and shall not be honoured by us.

We hereby engage with the Beneficiary that their demand in writing made strictly in compliance with the terms and conditions of this standby letter of credit as expressly stated herein shall be duly honoured by us on presentation in accordance with the terms and conditions of this standby letter of credit.

This standby letter of credit shall be subject to International Standby Letters of Credit Procedures Publication 98 (ISP98) as defined by the ICC, Paris France.

Let's consider the SLC that has not been issued by a bank, the type used for the payment of commissions. In all transactions the protected intermediaries must receive an individual pay order, unless other arrangements have been made. No master pay order is allowed. For the first time under UCP600 an intermediary is allowed to issue a personally created 'corporate' DLC or SLC that is fully supported under UCP600.

To use the previous example Mary and John have informed the PIA that they have the information by way of a signed offer or good quotation that clearly identifies they have a genuine end buyer. Mary is the closest to the PIA and is nominated to be a PI of the PIA. Mary is asked to collect and provide a copy of the details of all intermediaries being protected by the PIA. Mary provides details about herself and one other intermediary named John: she furnishes the PIA with both her and John's names, addresses, contact telephone numbers and full bank account details. The PIA makes each a promissory note and attached draft copy of a SLC UCP600 supported commission pay order, and issues it to each intermediary via facsimile or PDF email. Each intermediary makes a copy of the pay order, hand signs it and returns it as accepted. This document once returned serves to prove to the taxman that such money was required to be paid for services to the people named. It is also a promissory note guaranteeing the beneficiary that once the nature of business closes, the pay order becomes collectable. A promissory note holds in most countries especially in the USA and England to be a legally-binding 'promise', and is certainly a superior document to any NCND agreement or any other kind of pay order.

Mary and John now surrender the quotation or offer which discloses the end principal buyer. The PIA concludes the business with the principal keeping the PI well informed. The PI in turn ensures all other intermediaries involved in the transaction are fully informed. In this case only John is involved. Stepping back procedures in our example occurred without a hitch. Weeks later, when delivery is imminent and clean presentation of the documents is accepted, the PIA issues the draft SLC copy as an original hardcopy SLC by courier mail to each intermediary carrying the original signature and seal of the PIA. When the PIA has the funds cleared in their bank account, an email or facsimile issued by the PIA confirms that the SLC may be presented to each member's bank for official collection, the 'commission confirmation slip'. The issuing bank will contact the PIA as each claim is made so that the PIA can formally confirm the authenticity of each payment of the said commission value. Payment is then made by SWIFT straight into the account of the named beneficiary.

Here is an example of a commission promissory note and supporting draft corporate pay order, issued at the stepping back stage.

STANDBY PRIVATELY ISSUED LETTER OF CREDIT – DRAFT COPY

To: (Bank of Beneficiary)

For personal collection by beneficiary only using original hardcopy

Any apparent changes or ambiguous marks on this credit shall render the credit null and void. The draft copy shall be for the files of the beneficiary. The original, as marked with a stamp bearing the term 'original' hand signed hardcopy credit issued by courier mail shall be the operational instrument. Collection shall be applied for at the bank of the beneficiary upon the confirmation slip attached becoming active. All fees and bank charges for authentication and collection are for the account of the beneficiary.

Issued by:	FTN EXPORTING
	25 Lygon Street Carlton
	3000 Melbourne Australia
Date of Issue:	2nd Day of March 20— AUD
Private Stand-by Letter of Credit No:	1812002
Supported by Bank issued SLC No:	4567 777888999777
Date of Advising:	12/03/20— AUD
Expiration Date:	10 Days from Date of Issue
The Applicant:	Davide G. A. Papa
Beneficiary of the Credit:	MARY EXPORT LTD
	30 Windermere Street
	Essex, England UK
Per:	Payment of Consultancy Services rendered in relation to business transaction code 11PIAETH001

Total Amount:	US$100,000.00
Name of Issuer's Bank:	WESTPAC Bank
	305 Collins Street Melbourne 3000
	Victoria Australia
	Swift: WESAU3444
Account Name:	Davide Papa
Account Number:	123-456-7898
Phone:	61 03 93473333

The Issuer does hereby irrevocably and unconditionally (except as stated herein) undertake to pay the Beneficiary on their first demand in writing at the Issuer's bank counter the sum of US$100,000.00 (ONE HUNDRED THOUSAND UNITED STATES DOLLARS). This payment is subject to the demand in writing being accompanied by the beneficiary's written and signed statement that the amount demanded is due and owing between the beneficiary and the Issuer and the demand in writing bears the issuer's original signed confirmation slip.

This privately issued standby letter of credit is payable unconditionally upon first demand to the counter of the issuer's bank for withdrawing from the Issuer's account.

Payment under this standby letter of credit shall be made to the beneficiary pursuant to their demand in writing as stated above, without set-off and free from any statutory deductions, charges, fees or withholdings of any nature now or hereafter imposed, levied, collected, withheld or assessed by the Australian government or any political subdivision or authority thereof or therein.

This standby letter of credit shall remain valid from 02/12/20-- until 02/01/20--. The demand in writing, if any, under this standby letter of credit may be presented to us at our counter between 10/12/20-- and 16/12/20-- (15 days before the expiry date. Both dates are inclusive to the Australian date line. These defined date(s) hereafter shall be referred to as the 'presentation period'). Any demand under this standby letter of credit presented to us outside the presentation period shall be considered invalid and shall not be honoured by us.

We hereby engage with the beneficiary that their demand in writing, made strictly in compliance with the terms and conditions of this standby letter of credit, shall be duly honoured by us on presentation in accordance with the terms and conditions of this private standby letter of credit as allowed under UCP600.

This standby letter of credit shall be subject to International Standby Letters of Credit Procedures Publication as defined UCP600 2007 as defined by the ICC, Paris France.

Signed By the Issuer:

Date:

Seal.

CONFIRMATION SLIP AND NOTICE OF COLLECTION DEMAND

DATE OF ISSUE:

SUPPORTING SLC CREDIT NUMBER: 1012001

I, Mary Smith of Mary Export LTD as the named beneficiary to the credit, do hereby make demand for rightful collection of the said sum, for which I now engage the services of my bank to initiate collection of funds to my bank account on my behalf. The Issuer has allowed for collection to be authorized by signature. I hereby provide the acceptable identification to verify that I am the rightful beneficiary of this sum and can lawfully collect it.

Beneficiary Demanding Payment: Print Name

Signed by the Beneficiary:

Date:

Confirmation issued by:

Authorization of the Issuer:

Date Seal:

Email:

Facsimile:

Phone Number:

(Copy lodged with issuer's bank for authentication purposes C/o – Facsimile: 61 03 9456 899 Westpac Melbourne Australia)

Study the structure of both types of SLC; the bank-issued and the corporate type. An SLC must not be used to pay for goods as presentation documents are not relevant as to whether or not payment can be collected. They are however ideally suited in relation to performance guarantees and commission payments. The promissory note or personal guarantee and intent of the PIA is evident by the 'draft' issued, which provides that collection can only be applied for upon a certain event occurring, such as production of a document. In this case it is the issuance of a hardcopy signed document with the stamped term 'original' on it, along with a signed confirmation slip and demand notice. Such an event will not happen unless the PIA has the funds cleared in their account. If an intermediary tries to collect on the value of the SLC without the confirmation slip and demand notice then no funds will be paid, and they may be arrested on suspicion of fraud. The SLC, once issued, is an irrevocable undertaking – not dissimilar to the PIA presenting a personal cheque. An intermediary can freely issue draft copies; but only once they have a very clear understanding that a potential transaction is in play, and that stepping back procedures must need to occur in order to test the veracity of the principal. However under no circumstances shall the original SLC and confirmation slip be provided unless the funds are in the account ready for collection. Information given by intermediaries must be accurate from the onset as once the draft SLC advice is issued no changes can be applied.

Taxation and Commissions

The laws on taxation vary from country to country and the rules of your home or domiciled country always prevail. It is, however, worth noting the following factors in relation to taxation on commission payments.

As an international trade intermediary you are conducting business. As with any other business tax is payable based on gross income less deductibles. If you make money from selling commodities then you will need to pay personal income tax, but more importantly if a PIA trades incorrectly they may find themselves liable for income tax on the whole amount of commission being protected once the sum has been secured.

Intermediaries are only concerned with one sum: 'net and clear commission'. The PIA on the other hand earns and secures a 'gross commission' from which the intermediary commissions are paid. For this and other reasons it is very important to keep copies of all paperwork relating to commissions, which show the figures the PIA has secured and that which is yet to be disbursed to the protected intermediaries. In order to pay their protected intermediaries, the PIA first issues 'commission pay orders' as a kind of pro forma invoice.

Once a deal has closed successfully each intermediary signs the commission pay order and returns it to the PIA. The intermediaries are in effect submitting an invoice for 'services rendered' in assisting the PIA with the deal. Each intermediary, on receiving their commission payment, has an obligation to pay tax on their earnings as per the laws of their country. But if a PIA fails to provide accurate information to prove that the transfers took place, they could in fact find themselves with a tax bill for the total gross amount. Further, the authorities are likely to take all the information submitted in relation to the gross profits claimed on a successfully closed deal, and verify the claims overseas. If the authorities attempt to verify the information with the entity that responds with different information or does not respond at all, then this can be used as evidence against a defendant in a court of law.

The total commission amount when the PIA receives it is a 'gross' sum, which reverts to being a 'net' taxable amount once it is divided into its individual amounts and paid to each intermediary. URPIB 600 now incorporates provisions relating to procedures for issuance of commission pay orders and payments. The PIA issues a pay order which acts as an 'invoice for consultancy fees' as well as a personal guarantee, which is called an 'Irrevocable Intermediary Pay Order and Guarantee' (IPG). Once the PIA issues the invoice as per the conditions of the pay order, each intermediary signs and returns it to the PIA within a certain timeframe as instructed. The pay order then becomes operational at a specified time and the intermediary simply presents the original copy (which has been delivered by courier mail) at their own bank for collection. This IPG application as issued earlier and subsequently later is converted to a SLC (standby letter of credit) is issued at the point in the deal when the delivery documents are presented to the PIA in a clean state, that is once delivery has occurred.

When the PIA lodges their yearly tax return, they disclose a figure that constitutes gross earnings (all the intermediary commissions together which they have received, including their own) then deducts each invoice evidenced by a copy of each SLC pay order. This leaves the PIA with a before tax profit.

The email or facsimile copy of the pay order provides proof that the PIA is personally guaranteeing to secure and collect each intermediary's commissions should the deal close. The SLC subsequently sent by courier to the intermediary allows them to collect their own commission. Once this is done, the intermediary becomes responsible for payment of all collection fees, GST and income tax as per their jurisdiction.

If an intermediary is caught trying to avoid paying taxes on this income the relevant authorities in one country will attempt to obtain information from the payee of the commission, because most authorities would not have the power to secure confidential information from the bank of the intermediary without a court order. As a result there may be very little chance to obtain the information from the bank of the payee due to confidentiality laws, depending on the laws of the country in question. The authorities would ask the payee to confirm the payment and the amount and be asked to provide a letter from their bankers further to verify the amount transferred. If the payee does not offer the required documents, then the intermediary involved could be in legal trouble. If the required documents are provided then the authorities have the right to bypass local confidentiality laws to verify at the very least the contents of the bank issued letter. Some intermediaries have or think that offshore accounts are the answer, but as already stated the authorities start with the person paying the commission.

16

INCOTERMS 2000 Explained Further

We highly recommend to those wanting the full version of Incoterms 2000 or UCP600 to purchase books from the ICC online or perhaps from an ICC affiliated branch office in your own countries. The full version will be especially useful for those who understand this book and want to continue to improve their knowledge in the long term. Only the relevant and important parts of Incoterms are offered here and presented in a simplified form. It is preferable in the early years of trading to deal in FOB Incoterms for bulk shipments, thus it is FOB bulk delivery that is covered in the most detail. The business of containers and other delivery applications are only briefly defined.

Delivery Terms Adopted for Intermediary Use

EXW (Ex Works): Be careful when dealing with this term. It may appear as though it is a simple trading method but there are a lot of potential problems associated with it. Both parties agree to a point of sale and pick-up, generally the factory floor or a specified boundary. The delivery date is fixed and the supplier is physically required to make the delivery at the place named on the contract. Once the delivery is made, collection on the payment instrument can be effected. If the buyer is late to obtain possession of the goods after title has been surrendered, and the goods have been placed at the designated place then, unless the goods are stored securely, they are likely to vanish! Collection can be effected once the goods are delivered. The title in the goods, in the form of an invoice, is surrendered along with a few other basic documents as agreed on the contract. The L/C is then cleared for collection. Defining these borders is a problem at times. For example, if you purchased crude oil from Russia, but you failed to identify or arrive at the pick-up point 500 miles away from the refinery – the pipeline pick-up point is defined as the supplier's 'boundary' even though the factory is nowhere in sight. General types of documents are those that are produced at factory floor level – the supplier's invoice, preferential certificate of origin (if asked for at buyer's cost) and perhaps an ISO factory certification. EXW dealings are not really suitable for an intermediary in the majority of cases. Distant buyers prefer FOB or CIF most of the time.

FCA (Free Carrier): This applies as a container term. In bulk goods sales FCA is similar to FOB. Unless they are able to set up an expensive well-staffed office, intermediaries should keep away from buying and selling only 'Full Container Loads' (FCL). To be successful at this type of sale, you need to initiate weekly sales on a continual basis to make these FCL trades worthwhile. An office environment fully staffed with trained traders, who completes 10–15 deals every week, is a different matter. In the absence of this, however, it is strongly suggested that intermediaries keep away from container deals unless dealing in at least 20 FCL for each order. Free Carrier is a very popular container delivery method, when an end buyer is dealing directly with a supplier, but less so when dealing with an intermediary. The supplier calls for the carrier's shipping agent to deliver an empty container for loading. The FCL or less than full container (LCL) is then filled and passed to the carrier's designated point of delivery. Designated point of delivery most commonly requires that the FCL must be delivered to the carrier's designated 'Container Freight Station' inside the customs port, where 'delivery' is initiated.

FAS (Free Alongside Ship): FAS is an excellent trading method for intermediaries. Obviously FCL of 'wood chips' is not going to be a worthwhile commodity to trade as the resulting commissions are simply too small in comparison with the effort needed to close such a deal. What about 5,000 MT bulk quantity that is already stored outdoors near the loading wharves? Once the buyer's ship arrives, as long as the goods are 'loaded' on the ship's tackle or loaded on shore cranes, 'delivery' is said to have occurred. The goods don't have to pass the ship's rail to meet the definition that the goods are 'owned' by the buyer. The seller has to ensure that the goods are able to be loaded, physically or mechanically to comply with the requirement of 'delivery'. If the ship is far off shore due to, for example, shallow waters close to the point of loading, then the seller bears the cost of 'barges' in getting the goods to the ship's tackle. A forwarder's receipt of the exporter or supplier from the loading wharf, and other documents once presented, initiates the process of 'presentation'. This is an ideal transaction, which could be initiated from a close proximity to the intermediary's home market. The intermediary gets to contract stage, accepts the payments for the goods and actually physically supervises the loading of the purchased goods. An intermediary finding local home markets a few hours or even less away from place of operations is a good way to start learning the matters of getting goods sold and loaded.

FOB (Free on Board, Named port of Shipment): The goods are loaded on board a carrier's 'space' free of charges in consideration of freight, from a named port of shipment. FOB deals are great for intermediaries, especially when mastering the ways of international trade. 'Named port of shipment' distinguishes 'FOB Incoterms' from FOB as used in the USA as per its own Uniform Commercial Code (UCC). USA exporters may use both terms but unless otherwise stated 'FOB' on its own implies the UCC definition will be the standing applicable delivery rule. Intermediaries must learn to specify 'FOB Incoterms, named port of shipment' as standard practice. A full CIF deal incorporates EXW, FAS to FOB, from which CFR and CIF eventuate. Mastering CIF means you have mastered the full realm of trading possibilities as applicable to most intermediaries. Later, with confidence and experience, the intermediary can attempt the most popular delivery application of CIF.

Let's examine Incoterms 2000 FOB method and the obligations and responsibilities of the trading parties. The supplier must communicate the following to a 'PIA' as buyer, of which the PIA then applies accordingly to their end buyer as seller.

The FOB seller must:

a)   Supply the goods that conform to the sales contract, and supply the required 'Evidence' of conformity as per the contract (documents).

Note: LOI/ BCL and POP are nonsense deals as proven by Incoterms: 'Proof of Product' (POP) only becomes a ruling requirement once delivery has been initiated (as per PPI). Note that the correct term in reference is 'evidence' not proof. You simply cannot 'prove' goods by passing information to others in a string contract. In fact the intermediary cannot really provide proof of goods they have no possession of and will never even see. What can be given is evidence of the goods. The official so-called proof comes after the goods have been delivered and that if the seller has got no money 'first' to obtain and to arrive at the provable 'status', then no such 'proof' is possible or indeed required to be given beforehand. Intermediaries' Proof of Product is indeed applicable as to proving that the goods are loaded on board ship, but do not prove the existence of the goods prior to loading. Prior to loading the PPI is given to prove proprietary interest in the goods being sold. An intermediary 12,000 miles away does not even know if the goods exist, so how can they provide real 'proof'? Even if they could provide proof without securing the DLC for payment, what about circumvention? Incoterms states that evidence of the goods must be supplied 'on board' as agreed upon on the contract – so in fact the terms of the contract must provide all the conditions regarding the goods and evidence of them. Incoterms also provides the matter of procedures as required to initiate delivery.

b)   Deliver the goods on board the named ship of the buyer, which must arrive at the named port of shipment as per the schedule on the sales contract. Customary port procedures apply. Once the goods are delivered on board the seller must also notify the buyer without delay.

Note: The named port of shipment must be on the contract and the buyer must ensure the named ship arrives on time at the named port. This is why the BOL is related to the end buyer and the carrier. It is the end buyer who must book their own ship in an FOB deal. Shipping and BOL matters have nothing to do with a contract used by intermediaries, yet so many contracts on internet trading sites make inappropriate references to these matters. Unless the intermediary is working as a PI under the guidance of the PIA, or other highly qualified teacher, or has long standing experience they will not offer to secure the BOL.

c)   Obtain at their expense and indeed their risk all governmental authorizations, export permits and/or licences necessary for the export of such goods.

Risks? Yes risks! What happens if the middle seller is dealing with a supplier who thinks they are able to export the goods. However after the payment instrument is advised and transferred to the supplier they realize that the export permit for the goods cannot be initiated due to some domestic policy or laws applicable to their own country. This is another reason why the offer and contract must specify clearly the full requirement(s) of the buyer/seller. This way if the deal fails, then it will be the supplier's fault that they will lose their performance guarantee (rather than yours). There is an implied obligation that the seller should also advise the end buyer that they (the end buyer) will be required to ensure that import permits can be secured, as stated on the actual offer. This allows the end buyer to seek appropriate advice prior to signature of the contract.

    d)   Bear all costs and risks of the goods until the goods pass over the 'ship's rail' at the port of loading. Thus all appropriate formalities including taxes, wharf charges, inspections, export permits and the like are for the account of the 'seller', except those which are applied to the account of the end buyer as implied.

Note: For intermediaries this term, as provided by Incoterms, is ambiguous. It is not entirely correct that the point where the goods become the property of the end buyer is said to occur when the goods cross over the 'ship's rail' at port of loading. International courts have thoroughly tested the meaning of the 'passing of risk'. The courts have found that there is, if not a legal, then at least a moral obligation on the part of the seller to have the goods not just pass the ship's rail but also to ensure that the goods are indeed on board 'clean' of damage. For example the goods pass the ship's rail and are stowed below deck, upon which packaging tears open on many of the goods, not after passing the ship's rail, but each time the goods were placed in the ship's hold. The seller has passed the ship's rail test, but failed the test to deliver 'clean on board'. The whole objective of the seller is to deliver 'clean on board' goods. No buyer is intentionally going to buy damaged goods. The intent of the end buyer is to expect that the goods being purchased are going to be at least delivered 'clean' on board. In effect the goods in an FOB deal passing the 'ship's rail' in a sound state, may nevertheless result in a qualified bill of lading, without the 'clean' endorsement. The documents presented will not reflect that the goods were 'received clean on board'. Therefore the requirement for collection will not be satisfied. Although the seller is not required to produce the clean on board bill of lading, they are required to ensure that the goods are delivered 'clean on board'. This means that the 'mate's receipt' or 'forwarder's receipt' could be used to meet delivery obligations as far as the intermediary is concerned, but so long as the goods have indeed passed the ship's rail at the port of loading in a 'clean' state this will fully satisfy the meaning defined in Incoterms. The matter of damaged goods is settled once the goods are unloaded and, even though the goods passed the ship's rail as clean, the seller is still obligated to rectify any damage which was apparent at the time of loading.

Another potential area of concern is 'inspections'. The supplier bears the cost of 'inspections' for the PIA, accordingly the PIA ostensibly does the same by default for the end buyer. If the supplier has paid for 'inspections' three months earlier for goods already stored at a local warehouse, then the supplier will claim that they have indeed paid for 'inspections'. What if the end buyer is insisting that the PIA obtains a pre-shipment on board inspection of goods? The supplier may rightfully refuse to pay for this added expense, insisting that they have complied with the meaning within Incoterms.

The intermediary must therefore ask for a PSI certification of quality and quantity from the supplier right at the beginning, when obtaining the offer. If none is forthcoming, the PIA still offers the PSI certificate to their end buyer and ensures that the supplier obtains the required PSI certification but that it is added as an expense to the PIA. The PIA mitigates this expense by adding up to 5 per cent onto the quote given to their end buyer. The intermediary applies the above variation from the start so as not to stall the end buyer's side of the deal.

e) Bear at their own expense the cost of the customary packaging of the goods, unless the goods do not normally require such packaging.

Note: Goods can be sold in huge quantities, and therefore bulk wheat for example can be bought in one-ton bags, or loose, or in 50-kilo bags. Where the goods are loaded directly into the ship's hold, and if the goods are to be sold packed into smaller units, then appropriate packaging will need to be used. Buying sugar, for instance, for local market consumption will not need such expensive packaging as sugar that is being sold overseas. If the sales contract fails to state the type of packaging, some remedy may be sought in that an exporter who often exports these types of goods should have applied the customary packaging for the goods. Nevertheless the buyer may insist that for the sake of cutting costs they don't want, for example, 'Five Ply Kraft' paper lined bags. The buyer may choose instead to have an inferior three-ply non-lined version but if the goods become contaminated during the long sea voyage, there may only be limited recourse for the end buyer upon taking possession of the goods. Intermediaries are to specify packaging in exactly the same terminology used by the supplier. If an intermediate 'buyer/seller' makes excessive or indeed ambiguous claims about packaging on an offer, which does not reflect the truth and the goods arrive contaminated or damaged, then the 'buyer/seller' could be held liable for making a deceptive claim on the offer or contract. In the first instance intermediaries shall not request any change of packaging that the supplier insists must prevail for the type of goods being exported. This includes changing of weight and units. If goods are sold in one kilogram packets, then this should not be represented as being 10 metric tons of goods but rather that the goods are 10,000 kilograms of sugar in one kilogram packets. Intermediaries must never convert weight to accommodate the end buyer's request. The description of the goods remains the same during purchase and sale.

f)   Bear at their own expense the cost of any checks required, for example quality, quantities, tallies, and weights and measures, which in part form the necessary requirement of delivery.

Note: Think about the ship's rail and the passing of risk from seller to the buyer. Incoterms has clearly defined the term 'quality' as already stated by the issuance of an *'in rem'* certificate versus the *'in personam'* certificate. Incoterms is only stating that quality assurances are to be provided without specifying as to the type. As an example, part of the documentation presentation the end buyer requires is an SGS certificate, which defines the quality of the goods being purchased at loading time (PSI: pre-shipment inspection). One might presume, interpreting Incoterms, that this expense is a cost for the seller. It may be appropriate that an ISO rated standard *'in rem'* quality certificate is issued to confirm the consistent production of DVD players from China. The quality assertions are related to the way the goods are made and not as to the quality of the actual unit. The quality of one sample unit indicates that all such units are the same quality and that the issuance on the *'in rem'* certificate is a cost for the seller but this is not the case: it is for the buyer. Inconsistency in quality that may occur in, for example, Russian re-combined blended crude oil (RECMD). A PSI certificate may be issued if requested by the end buyer if they do not accept a standard state or government endorsed 'GOST' quality certificate (CIS country quality standards certification including Russia, Belarus, Ukraine, Kazakhstan, Azerbaijan, Uzbekistan among others), or even a SGS certificate already paid for prior to loading. The end buyer, and not the seller, meets the cost of the PSI certificate. Therefore intermediaries must be careful when using the term 'quality'.

If the supplier has already incurred the huge expense of third party certification not in line with the buyer's wishes, they will often not accommodate a further added expense of certification simply because the buyer has asked for it. If they are forced to comply then the price of goods will rise. If this is going to happen, then in fact the offer has become qualified, as will the contract. For example, the supplier has agreed to offer, let's say, a SGS certificate but later at the time of loading the buyer insists that the certificate was to be provided at the loading time – this will create a serious problem if the SGS certification offered was for goods inspected at a tank farm near the port of loading, weeks before the ship arrived. The supplier has met with the conditions of Incoterms, and won't readily accept the idea that further expenses need to be incurred.

The intermediary must ascertain the type of certificate being offered and ensure that it is this type that is offered to the end buyer. Alternatively the intermediary could offer the buyer in the first instance a PSI certificate with the price of this incorporated into the offer. Test the supplier with such a request and if the supplier says no then at the very least, the buyer/seller has applied the extra charge to the goods in order to allow the supplier to secure a PSI for the account of the buyer/seller. Should the supplier surprisingly agree to incur the expense of a further PSI certification, then the buyer/seller could offer a discount on price to their buyer when the seller's invoice is presented. The supplier would undoubtedly be impressed with this unexpected discount and would probably be very happy to do business with the same buyer/seller again.

To reiterate: if the DLC states that one of the documents which is required to be presented is simply described as an 'SGS certificate of quality' then presentation will not be affected, regardless of the argument raging between the principals to the contract. Under such circumstances the principals in dispute will need to settle these matters amicably or through arbitration.

g)   Bear at their own expense for the cost of clean documents in proving delivery of goods on board the vessel.

Note: As already stated in respect of the clean on board BOL in a FOB deal the supplier or their agent provides the BOL to the ship's master for endorsing which, once returned, is presented to the end buyer directly and not to the intermediary. The supplier is responsible for all fees and charges in obtaining the delivery documents as defined, in particular those 'proving' that the goods are 'clean' on board. The supplier also bears the expense of issuing other delivery documents required by the buyer. Therefore the supplier pays for documents being issued and bears all applicable costs to the intermediate buyer as well. The buyer as seller then endorses the delivery document to their end buyer, the same way as a supplier would endorse a clean on board bill of lading over to the end buyer in a CIF transaction.

h) Provide the 'certificate of origin' at the buyer's request (buyer's expense).

The supplier obtains the certificate of origin, but only if asked to do so by the buyer. The intermediary applying this condition to the contract has to be careful here. If the end buyer has not asked for this certificate from the seller, and the intermediary seller as buyer asks for one from their supplier, then the supplier will obtain the certificate of origin at the expense of the buyer/seller. When the intermediary buyer/seller attempts to do the same by transferring the cost to their end buyer's account, the end buyer may indeed protest and refuse to allow the debit to be added to their payment instrument because (and rightly so) they never asked for the certificate in the first place.

It is imperative that when the intermediary seller gives a quotation or offer to the end buyer the certificate of origin is stipulated as a delivery document required for presentation. It is the end buyer who should indicate the acceptance or rejection of that certificate. Usually the certificate of origin is needed in any event as customs in most countries legally require it to be produced when taking possession of goods. A preferential certificate of origin is issued from the exporter's country. When a non-preferential certificate of origin is issued it is done so from the consulate of the country to which the goods are being exported. If the end buyer requests one be sure to stipulate which type of certificate is going to be issued.

i) Render 'assistance' to the buyer in obtaining the bill of lading at the buyer's risk and expense, and any appropriate documents as defined in the rules.

Note: The above procedure is the correct one for FOB delivery. 'Named port of shipment' is often incorrectly stated on countless offers made by internet traders. The carrier is ordered and chartered by the end buyer. The end buyer has to ensure that the ship is at the port of loading at the scheduled time as per the contract. The supplier must ensure that the goods are ready to be loaded on board the ship as provided by their contract with the intermediate buyer/seller. Once the goods are loaded on board as 'received', a 'received bill of lading' is issued directly into the hands of the end buyer and not the intermediate 'buyer/seller'. The obligation of the intermediary is only to have the goods loaded 'Free on Board' taking up the ship's free space which is provided, free of storage charges, for consideration of freight. Once loading has been accomplished the intermediary has met their obligations as far as delivery is concerned. But as stated earlier the 'ship's rail' obligations do not completely release the intermediary as they may provide further assistance to the end buyer in obtaining the 'bill of lading'. Such 'assistance' is allowed as an 'FOB Variant'. This is defined as 'FOB with Added Services'. 'Every assistance shall be granted to the end buyer in obtaining the bill of lading' – again this is an ambiguous statement. The issue is not whether the bill of lading is provided on board either 'clean' or not, or even whether or not the bill of lading has been issued at all, but rather: has the intermediary rendered 'assistance' in every way to the end buyer in obtaining the bill of lading? Once this assistance has been exhausted, regardless of whether the bill of lading is issued or not, 'delivery' is allowed to occur to the benefit of the intermediate seller. The intermediary shall only assist in BOL matters if requested to do so. Even if they fail to secure the BOL with the assistance of the seller then at the very least the seller has met their obligations under Incoterms.

Let us consider the provisions of Incoterms 2000 from the perspective of the buyer. Again the 'buyer' means the 'end buyer' taking actual possession of the goods as opposed to the 'intermediate buyer' (you), claiming only documentary title to the goods.

The FOB Incoterms buyer must:

a)   At their own cost, charter a named vessel or reserve space on board a shipowner's named vessel and provide the seller in good time, the name of the ship, loading berth and delivery dates of the vessel.

Note: Therefore the above is the responsibility of the end buyer. The end buyer must also provide the seller's full details so that the seller is able to meet the required deadline in getting the goods to the designated port of loading. If the details of the ship are provided accurately and the ship berths at the designated place only to find the goods are not ready for loading, this is a direct breach of the supplier's obligations and they are responsible for all the resulting carrier's costs. These can be from US$3,000 per day. By default if the supplier is late then they are answerable to their immediate buyer/seller. The intermediary who provides pages and pages of ambiguous carrier obligations on a contract could not bind himself to shipping terms and conditions with which the supplier was not prepared to comply. Therefore the intermediary shall maintain the following position in a trade:

In all matters of shipping obligations and responsibilities the person creating or causing fault in relation to these matters bears the consequential loss and who in effect shall be required to bear all costs associated with creating or causing failures of obligations and responsibilities as defined under Incoterms 2000.

If an act or omission of the supplier affects shipping matters, the supplier is obligated to the controlling intermediary to remedy the situation who in turn transfers the remedy to their end buyer.

b)   Bear all costs once the goods pass the ship's rail at the port of loading, and pay the price of the ordered goods as provided on the sales contract.

Note: The time to pay the purchase price of the goods is at the point when they have cleared the ship's rail. The ship has not left the loading port and the seller has already been paid, even the PG has been cancelled, because delivery has been successfully initiated. As far as getting paid is concerned, matters of shipping are simply no longer relevant to the buyer/seller.

c)   Bear all extra costs incurred if the buyer's named vessel failed to arrive on a stipulated date or within a particular period, including bearing the risk of damage to any goods that have been waiting alongside the berth prior to the ship's arrival.

If the buyer's ship has not arrived on time but the seller has not delivered on time either, the goods are still not at the designated port. What happens? The end buyer triumphs. You cannot claim anything unless your part of the delivery obligation has been fully met.

d)   Should the buyer fail to name the vessel on time, or to indicate a specific arrival date on time, or make requests for a different delivery port of loading on time, then all additional expenses associated with these issues shall be borne by the buyer, so long as the identifiable goods have been duly appropriated as per the sales contract.

If amendments are notified on time then the supplier should accommodate the buyer's requests, in accordance with the requirement that the 'seller is to assist the buyer in obtaining the BOL'. That means if the seller has initiated delivery and made the goods ready for loading but the end buyer then causes a delay, it is the end buyer who will pay the extra expenses involved. An example of this is if the end buyer has obtained a poorly staffed or maintained charter ship, and the ship arrives at the out marker of the loading port only to find that the port cannot handle the ship's draught. The extra expense would be in getting the ship to dock in an appropriate port and to arrange for the goods to go to that port ready to be loaded on the ship.

  e) Pay all charges incurred in obtaining the bill of lading.

Note: 'Marine' is added to the term BOL to confirm that it applies to a ship and not an aircraft, which uses an 'airway bill of lading'. If a contract requires a 'clean marine bill of lading' to be presented and the credit stipulates 'bill of lading' with or without the reference of 'clean' or 'marine' then you could have problems at presentation time. This is especially so in the case of a 'through bill', which is where both a shipping bill and airway bill are required to get the goods to their final destinations (as often happens with some central African countries).

  f) Pay all costs and associated charges in obtaining the certificate of origin, consular documents, and further demands under Incoterms 2000.

Note: This matter is the seller's obligation. Of particular importance is the certificate of origin which the buyer may need in relation to import customs regulations.

The intermediate buyer/seller should adopt the delivery rules accordingly.

  As far as the intermediary is concerned, they are the buyer to the supplier and the seller to the end buyer. As such all obligations of the supplier are simply endorsed and/or transferred to the buyer to apply to their own client, the end buyer. All obligations of the seller to the supplier work on the same basis once secured from the end buyer. We have included CIF Incoterms 2000 in short form, in the next chapter, for the purpose of comparing the rules to the advised FOB application. Intermediaries are strongly advised not to attempt to transact in a CIF deal until the FOB application has been learned and used extensively in trading scenarios.

17

CIF INCOTERMS 2000

CIF – Cost Insurance and Freight 'Named Port of Destination' Bulk

The duties of the seller are to:

a)   ship the goods contained in the contract;

b)   procure contract of carriage by sea and arrange for the goods to be delivered to the disclosed destination;

c)   obtain insurance at current rates for the benefit of the buyer;

d)   make out an invoice which usually debits the buyer for the price of the goods, or actual incorporated price of the goods, commission charges, freight and insurance premium, and credits the buyer with freight charges that the buyer will need to pay upon goods arriving at the destination port; and

e)   tender all the documents to the buyer so they may know what freight needs to be paid or to recover such loss of goods if they do not arrive due to the goods being lost in transit.

The duties of the buyer are to:

a)   accept the conforming documents tendered by the seller, at which time the seller is entitled to be paid;

b)   accept the goods at the destination port and bear all costs and charges, excluding freight and insurance, for expenses in the transit of the goods to the buyer's port, including all unloading costs, 'lighterage' and wharf charges;

c)   bear all risks from when the goods pass the ship's rail at port of loading;

d)   pay the cost and charges in obtaining the certificate of origin;

e)   pay all import customs, taxes and tariffs; and

f)   pay for all expenses in obtaining statutory importation documents.

Incoterms 2000 clearly spells out the obligations of the buyer and seller as in CIF transactions. Intermediaries should not attempt to trade in CIF or CFR (cost and freight) transactions until they have experience in and mastered trading in FOB transactions. The main issue regarding CIF transactions is understanding how to apply debits and credits.

Below is an example of a seller's invoice as issued from the supplier to the PIA, and then from the PIA to the end buyer. We have used a CIF invoice, which is not dissimilar to an FOB invoice except the matters of debits and credits are addressed differently.

Assume the invoice from a supplier to the PIA reads:

Total value of goods price:	$200,000.00
Certificate of origin is:	$7,000.00
Insurance:	$2,000.00
Freight:	$90,000.00
Sub total:	$299,000.00 CIF
Less freight:	$90,000.00
Total payable:	$209,000.00

The quotation given by the PIA to the end buyer was for the DLC and was issued to support a value of $325,000.00.

On receipt of the supplier's BOL and other required documents the PIA replaces the supplier's invoice with their own, incorporating commissions on the seller's invoice that will be forwarded to the end buyer. Because of this the PIA should never, by accident, allow the supplier's invoice to travel to the issuing bank. The PIA needs to make a copy of the supplier's invoice on their own letterhead, changing only the price of the goods to include the commission – thus the price of the goods now would be $226,000. Freight of $90,000 is added as well as all other expenses ($9,000) to produce an invoice with a sub total equalling $325,000. The freight is credited back to the end buyer. This will result in a total payable amount of $235,000. The end buyer allows the $235,000 to be collected. '$209,000' is transferred for collection. The PIA now has exactly $26,000 of commission left in their account.

When the ship arrives, the buyer pays the 'freight' charge from the funds in their account as per the quotation, which included the freight rates. This is why 'ASWP' freight rates simply cannot work. What happens if the PIA quoted $325,000 'ASWP' for the goods and the end buyer accepted this quotation, but when the supplier produced their invoice, freight rates were an additional US$150,000?

Even if the BOL is marked as 'Freight Pre-Paid' (as misguided internet traders often do), the reality is that a bank examining the presented delivery documents is required to disregard such a term. Even if a supplier provides the PIA with an 'ASWP' quote (which isn't a good quotation at all), then the PIA must ask the supplier to stipulate the freight rate. Unlike an FOB trade, the PIA has to secure a 'shipped BOL' where the name of consignee is applied to 'order' and where 'notify party PIA' would be applied on the BOL.

18

Endorsed Versus Blank Endorsed Delivery Documents

The BOL matters (below) that were in force under UCP500 are now also relevant to UCP600. Only very experienced intermediaries should attempt a CIF deal.

In a CIF deal, where both the insurance contract and shipped marine bill of lading is secured, these documents become transferable but not as a 'negotiable instrument' in the true sense. The need to 'transfer' these documents plays a different role in law than that which is defined when using the term 'negotiate upon'. One may negotiate the price payable for a car, and regardless of the accepted price the title is transferred to the new owner once the price has been agreed. In banking terms negotiation upon the value of the financial instrument can only truly happen once delivery has occurred. At this time the financial instrument becomes valuable due to the issuing bank allowing collection to occur. The financial instrument's value may be 'discounted' from one banking institution to another.

As we know intermediaries cannot obtain actual possession of goods but only documentary title to those goods. The term 'leading delivery document' is a better term to use than 'title document' because, in the true sense, the leading document is in fact not a true title document at all. While the documents travel among the realm of the intermediaries, they are only endorsed over to the name of the next person in the string contract. The very last person accepting the bill of lading endorses it without putting another name on it. In this case the BOL is said to be 'blank endorsed', and puts a stop to any further transfer, which means that the last person is the one who is able to claim actual title to the goods as a final 'acceptance' of the title of those goods. A transferable bill of lading is consigned 'to order' meaning that where no consignee is named the carrier will take a specific 'order' as to who they are to release the cargo to.

When 'Frank' the shipper/supplier sells goods to 'Harry', Frank's title to the goods must be transferred to Harry. Harry is selling the same goods to Mary and endorses the BOL to Mary. Mary signs and accepts the BOL without endorsing it over to anyone else, at which time the BOL is said to be 'blank endorsed'. Thus the term 'endorsed' has a different meaning to the term 'blank endorsed'.

The carrier will deliver the goods to the person holding the blank endorsed BOL. This has to happen to meet with the issuing bank's delivery document 'presentation' requirements. The handing over of the actual goods is still dependent on the carrier first being paid for freight, because maritime shipping laws define that the carrier has not earned such freight (the charge associated with delivery of the cargo) until the goods have been physically delivered to the buyer's destination port. Thus in effect a lien is held over the goods in the possession of the carrier until the freight is paid. The shipper provides the BOL to the master of the ship. The master now waits for the tally clerk to inspect the goods and to record what has been loaded on board. A ship's mate's receipt is issued by the 'ship's officer' as first class evidence of what is on board. The mate's receipt is compared with the shipper's BOL advice and if it matches, the BOL is said to be 'clean' on board. The shipper, Frank, now endorses the BOL in his name on the rear of the BOL form, over to Harry the intermediary 'buyer/seller' of the goods. Harry in his name now endorses the bill of lading, on the rear of the form, over to Mary who is named accordingly. Mary, being the person who has actually paid for the goods (or her appointed mandated agent), accepts the bill and endorses it in her name without endorsing it further to any other named person. Therefore Mary holds the blank endorsed BOL and is the genuine 'title' holder of the goods. When Mary surrenders the 'title' to the goods, the carrier will present a freight invoice to Mary for payment, with the funds that are already in her account because of the credit applied on the seller's invoice.

On the BOL there is a space in which the consignee is entered. Instead of entering this information, the word 'order' is entered instead. The presence of this one word allows the BOL to be 'transferred'. If the consignee's name is put in the space instead of the word 'order' then the BOL cannot be transferred and the buyer/seller will face a collapsing deal. Below the consignee's name there is a space that says 'notify party' on which the shipper has put Harry's name because he is 'buying the goods'. Therefore Harry gets the BOL as the party being notified, but the back of the BOL form identifies to whom Harry is endorsing the BOL. Each trader has the capacity to make an 'order' to endorse the BOL to the other.

If a shipowner is issuing the BOL, then certain international maritime rules apply on the BOL regarding the goods and carriage. These are mostly defined as the Hague Rules. Some countries use an amended version of these rules, which are known as the Hague-Visby rules. In a 'charterparty' shipping agreement (where a ship is being 'rented' from a shipowner) different rules may apply. Although under UCP600 intermediaries are now allowed to deal in charterparty shipping in a CIF transaction, FTN Exporting strongly advises that intermediaries only use a shipowner's endorsed BOL. This ensures that the safest kind of 'title' document is being handled at all times.

The very few challenges that FTN Exporting has received over the years have involved intermediaries who have not studied the practicalities of trading but who have simply obtained a copy of Incoterms or any other set of rules without understanding that issues pertaining to the BOL, as explained above, are simply not apparent from these rules.

19

Case Study

This case study is designed to show the correct procedures required to close an intermediary trade. Although fictitious, it correctly describes timeframes, rules and methods that would be required in a real trade. For the purpose of this example, assume there were no problems and the trade was successfully completed (a rare event!). This case study proves that deals cannot 'close in 24 hours', and demonstrates why a real trade takes at least 80 days to close. The contract model provided in the case study can be modified for other bulk FOB deals.

The Scenario

FTN Exporting CEO Mr 'Pia' has an enquiry in his inbox to buy sulphur. The enquiry is comprehensive and free of ambiguous or improper trading terms and after some due diligence, Mr Pia is convinced that there is the potential to proceed with the matter. In this case, there are five parties involved in the string contract, as follows:

> *The End Buyer*: Mr Akimoro: China
>
> *An Intermediary (PI, End Buyer's Side)*: Mr Ben Ling: USA
>
> *Buyer/Seller and Controlling Intermediary*: Mr David Pia, CEO FTN Exporting Australia
>
> *An Intermediary (PI, Supplier's Side)*: Mr Stephen Yong: Malaysia
>
> *A Supplier:* Mr Carl Ville: Georgia Sulfur Corporation USA

David Pia is the controlling buyer/seller, and keeps both sides of the deal separate. Mr Ben Ling and Mr Akimoro are on the buyer's side, and will not have any contact with Mr Stephen Yong or Mr Carl Ville.

Mr Pia is acting 'on behalf of an undisclosed principal(s)' so he is not required to disclose the identity of his Supplier to his end buyer – or vice versa.

The deal is supported by INCOTERMS 2000, URC522 COLLECTION RULES, UCP600 LETTERS OF CREDIT RULES, ICC RULES OF AGENCY, AND URPIB FTN EXPORTING'S OWN IN-HOUSE RULES as found on www. itsi.itgo.com.

MONDAY 9 FEBRUARY 2009

Mr Pia opens an enquiry from a Mr Ben Ling in the USA. It reads as follows:

> Dear Mr Pia,
>
> We require a quotation for the following item.
>
> Bulk Sulphur:
>
> Grade/Specifications: Bright yellow in form of granules or prill or pellets, about 2–4 mm. Purity: 99.9% min, Ash: 0.05% max, Moisture: 1% max, Acid: 0.0003%
>
> Carbon: 0.05% max, As: 0.0001% max, Se: 1ppm max, Chlorides: 50 ppm max.
>
> Quantity: 10,000 MT. FOB
>
> Regards
>
> Mr Ben Ling
> Ben Ling Trading Ltd
> www.benling.com

Mr Pia has amassed specifications of many commodities over the years and checks his own files for the specifications of the sulphur in question. The specification provided on Mr Ling's email is the same as the specification Mr Pia has from a manufacturer in the USA.

Mr Pia now 'googles' 'Ben Ling Trading Limited' and also uses Yahoo to do the same. There are only a few results, each of which is on the site http://www. alibaba.com. Mr Pia is able to deduce from this information that Mr Ling has not been trading for long. The longer an intermediary is in business, the greater number of search engine results they generate. A visit to Mr Ling's website confirms that he is an intermediary. There are no LOI/ICPO/BCL/NCND/ ASWP/MPA/FFDLC or other incorrect terms on the website, and Mr Ling also refers to 'INCOTERMS 2000' which is a very positive sign.

Mr Pia is satisfied that he is able to commence a deal with Mr Ling. Over the years Mr Pia has developed relationships with a few suppliers. He already knows a Mr Ville of the USA who is employed by the Georgia Sulfur Corporation as their export manager. Although they have never closed a deal together, both parties/entities are amicable to each other because Mr Pia and Mr Ville have been in email dialogue every now and then.

Pia emails Mr Ville and enquires as to whether he has sulphur for sale, and if not, whether he knows someone who does. Although Pia has the direct details of a possible supplier in Mr Ville, the original introduction of Mr Ville to Pia was made by Mr Stephen Yong of Malaysia. In these circumstances it is proper to ask Mr Yong, as a representative of Pia, to approach Mr Ville for a quotation for sulphur. Pia has acted in such a way as to show any other party who becomes involved in the deal that he is in control as the buyer/seller.

Mr Yong is familiar with URPIB and the correct procedures for international trade intermediaries. He knows that he will need to 'step back' at the required time and trusts Pia to act honourably at all times, in particular in relation to commissions. Mr Pia prepares a *RFQ* (Request for a Quote) for Mr Ville via Mr Yong as follows. Pia MUST obtain *Ostensible Authority* to buy the goods before he can make an offer to Ben. Pia cannot offer to sell goods from a quotation given by another intermediary or 'buyer/seller' unless Pia is allowed to verify the supplier directly (that is, the intermediary between Pia and the supplier allows Pia to contact the supplier). (Note: Most ill-informed intermediaries don't understand the importance of stepping back, or why Pia needs to verify the goods. Problems also arise if a buyer/seller makes an offer to another buyer/seller, as Pia is not allowed to transfer the letter of credit more than once, and only directly to the supplier as being non-transferable.)

Pia sends an email to Stephen Yong:

Dear Stephen,

Do you remember Mr Ville of GSC USA? Could you please check the following RFQ below then forward it to him for his consideration? I wanted to involve you at this early stage because GSC was originally your client. As usual all your interests remain protected by me and everything travels from Mr Ville to you and then to me until failure or success of the deal is recorded. You are nominated as my 'Primary intermediary' on the supplier's side.

Thank you

Pia

Attached to the email is a RFQ in PDF form that Stephen will forward to 'his client' after checking its contents and price calculations. The RFQ looks like this:

FTN Exporting
PO BOX 30 Carlton Nth 3054 Melbourne Australia

Email:	General ftnexporting@yahoo.com
Private email:	ftnexportingceo@bigponds.com
Telex: FTN37AU Facsimile:	(61 03) 9347 0003
Private Office Phone:	(Applied on final contract only)
Video/Voice Cell Ph Sat/Sun:	(Applied on final contract only)
OFFICE HOURS:	Monday to Friday 6 am to 5.00 pm AEST

Trade Educators, Buyer and Sellers; Established 1988

Above contact information is strictly confidential.

All calls taken by appointment only.

Principals may not contact each other prior to exchange of signed contracts.

REQUEST FOR A QUOTATION: 'RFQ'

TO: Georgia Gulf Sulfur Corporation
         1729 Dow Street
         Valdosta, Georgia, USA 31601

Attention: Mr J. Ville

Authorized Representative of buyer FTN Exporting:
Mr Stephen Yong: Malaysia email: syong_ftnexporting@yahoo.com

BUYER: FTN EXPORTING C/o- CEO: Mr Pia

www.ftnexporting.com

Date of issued 9th February 20— AEST

Validity *4 days* from above date.

Confidential

Dear Sir,

We enclose the following procurement offer for your consideration.

PRODUCT WANTED: SULPHUR

Transaction Code: 10FTN-GSC-0208-S

First Delivery: 10th May 20— OR SOONER –/+10 days.

Description: Sulphur.

Sulfur- S: Non-metallic atomic number 16.

Form B: MONOCLINIC. Prismatic, Pale Yellow Crystals capable of change in forming FORM A Sulphur below 94.5C: - MP 119C: BP 444.6C: Flash p 405F (207C), Auto Ignition 450F: Ref Index 2.038: Soluble in water.

Quantity up to 10000 MT per Month for 4 months or more –/+10%

Loaded for bulk transport via buyer's chartered ocean carrier.

Export grade packaging 50 kilograms poly sealed bags.

SPECIFIC GRADE:

Sulphur: Bright yellow in form of granules or prill or pellets, about 2–4 mm.

Purity: 99.9% min, Ash: 0.05% max, Moisture: 1% max, Acid: 0.0003%

Carbon: 0.05% max, As: 0.0001% max, Se: 1ppm max, Chlorides: 50 ppm max.

Quantity: Up to 10,000 MT Per month for 6 months +/–10% FOB Incoterms

Preference type order- In Pellets, Granules or Lump-

PG: Supplier will be required to offer 1.50% UCP600 bank issued SLC as a Performance Guarantee upon a full UCP600 non-transferable irrevocable DLC (non-cumulative revolving) being advised and accepted from a top 100 world ranked bank-Rules of Trade: UCP600, URC522, INCOTERMS 2000.

Procedures: (1) Quotation (2) Offer (3) Contracts (4) FTN deposits active payment first (5) Supplier deposits active PG (6) Delivery initiated first shipment (7) Collection at Sigh is attempted (8) Next shipment initiated.

SUPPLIER'S ADVICE Confirmation slip

Please return VIA EMAIL

Please provide details including exact product specifications, port of loading, Packaging, quantity, name of bank for depositing our UCP600 financial instruments, agency providing analysis inspection certification and Final assured price at FOB or FAS for a period of 15 days from quotation issue.

We await your response.

Kind Regards

Mr Stephen Yong

Per :- David Pia
CEO: FTN and AGI FTN Exporting
www.ftnexporting.com

Note: The first delivery date is in 90 days' time. This is a safe delivery date to quote for most transactions. If the first delivery date is requested as being sooner than this, this creates greater risks in relation to the PG and could in fact cause the deal to collapse. For these reasons you should not attempt to close a deal within 60 days. The quotation should be directly from a supplier (not an intermediary) and should also be valid for at least ten days. In the above example, Pia has asked for the price to be valid for 15 days.

While Pia is waiting for the offer from Mr Ville (via Mr Yong) Pia sends a holding email to Mr Ling on the 'end buyer's side', in which he tells Mr Ling he will need to 'step back' because Pia cannot transfer the DLC more than once. Mr Ling is new to trading and does not know about the substantial transfer fees that will need to be paid before the DLC can be transferred. Mr Ling accepts Pia's requests, as otherwise there is no deal. In return Pia bears the full legal responsibility of this side of the deal including guaranteeing Mr Ling's commission should the deal close.

Dear Mr Ling

Thank you for your email regarding sulphur. Please be advised that your quotation is being prepared and will be forwarded to you within four days. Please also note the following:

You will remain as our temporary representative until failure or success of the transaction is recorded. You are nominated as FTN Exporting's 'Primary intermediary' for this side of this one deal only. All correspondence from FTN Exporting to you must be passed on without change or amendment to your end buyer taking possession and paying for the goods, and vice versa.

We will protect your commission rate and payment, and invite you to note the presence of your name on the quotation that we will send to you for submission to your end buyer. This is the strongest intermediary protection you can hope to obtain so early in the transaction. At this early stage we estimate that, if the deal closes, your commission will be US$3.00 per MT. However this is merely an estimate and will be confirmed by the issuance of an irrevocable pay order, which will be sent to you after contracts have been signed and at the time payments are secured for goods by FTN Exporting.

You shall forward the quotation (or offer) unchanged to your client. If the quotation is accepted your client should fill in the required details on the form and return the offer/quotation to FTN Exporting. This will disclose the identity of your client to us, and a full contract will follow thereafter for you to send to your client.

Your client is not permitted to approach us now or in the future without your involvement.

If you feel you cannot accept our procedures please confirm this at your earliest convenience in order for us to terminate the proposed trade.

In return for your participation and in the interests of transparency we shall ensure that you remain appraised of the progress of the deal until failure or success has been recorded.

Regards

Mr Pia
CEO FTN Exporting

Pia did not have to write an 'introduction' to Stephen, because Stephen has been attached to FTN Exporting for many years and is regarded as an asset to FTN Exporting. If Mr Ling refuses to accept these procedures, Pia may attempt to sell the sulphur on the open market instead.

DAY 4 – MORNING – OFFICE FTN EXPORTING

Mr Pia receives a reply from Stephen Yong regarding the sulphur quotation. The supplier GSC has provided the quotation and other information. Pia is able to make a formal offer to Mr Ben Ling who has also replied positively to the 'letter of introduction' and accepted Pia's procedures.

Pia has the ostensible authority to buy the goods. He sends the official offer to Mr Ling and then prepares a procurement offer to buy from GSC (and has 15 days to reply to GSC). Therefore he needs to make the timescale within which the end buyer performs much shorter than the 15-day validity period with the supplier. Pia makes the offer to the end buyer valid for five days. That way, if it is rejected he will send another offer to them with a validity date of three days, which still gives him seven days to find an end buyer on the open market if all else fails. Pia is preparing a formal offer to Mr Ling to send to his client but first he sends a quick email to Mr Yong.

> Dear Stephen,
>
> Thanks for the quotation. Keep in contact with GSC and answer any questions they may have. I need at least 4/5 days to get a response from our end buyer, before I can confirm the quotation and issue a formal offer to buy. Will advise asap.
>
> For your further information; US$574 per MT FOB is a good price. This time around I will add only a 2 per cent commission rate on top of the buy price and offer to sell the goods at US$584 per MT. I won't apply the usual 5–7% commission rate on this deal because I want to give the lowest price to a potentially new client, and because it's such a short string contract. In the spirit of FTN's URPIB rules of disbursements:- US$4.00+ per MT is allotted for myself. US$3.00+ per MT is allocated to you and US$3.00+ per MT is reserved for FTN's primary intermediary to the end buyer, a Mr Ben Ling from USA. No others are involved in this deal.
>
> Kind Regards
>
> David Pia

Stephen gets Pia's email and keeps in contact with GSC with 'small talk' during the next few days while Pia's secures the 'buy side' of then transaction. Stephen knows he must keep GSC's interest in supplying the goods alive. Stephen has learned well over the years and is a 'buyer/seller' in his own right. However, in this instance it is Mr Pia's deal so Stephen simply acts as a sourcing intermediary in this transaction (albeit that he is a PI in this trade). If Stephen was taking full legal responsibility for the transaction for the deal, then Pia would hold the position of 'sourcing intermediary'.

DAY 4 – AFTERNOON – FTN OFFICE – OFFER TO BEN READY

Finally, after four to five hours of preparing and checking the formal offer to Ben Ling, Pia is ready to send it by email in a PDF format. Pia sends the following offer to Ben Ling for his client to consider, while protecting Ben's own interests. If Pia were to circumvent Ben Ling and the deal closed, what better evidence would there be than to have a copy of an offer and contract with his name on as well as the names of the principals (that is supplier and Pia, or end buyer and Pia)? It is *prima facie* evidence of Mr Ling's involvement in a deal that has closed. Mr Ling would therefore sue for damages for his loss of profits.

Only one intermediary from either side of the deal should have their name added to the contract. Therefore others are in a weaker position but hopefully are persuaded by the sourcing intermediary whose name is on the contract (the primary intermediary) that their interests are protected. This primary intermediary also keeps each sourcing intermediary updated as to the progress of the deal, so that Pia is able to get on with trying to close the deal without being distracted by intermediaries anxious to know when they are going to get paid.

Offer sent to Ben Ling to forward to his client.

FTN Exporting
PO BOX 30 Carlton Nth 3054 Melbourne Australia

email:	General ftnexporting@yahoo.com
Telex: FTN37AU Facsimile:	(61 03) 9347 0003
Private Office Phone:	(Applied on final contract only)
Video/Voice Cell Ph Sat/Sun:	(Applied on final contract only)
OFFICE HOURS:	Monday to Friday 6 am to 5.00 pm AEST

Trade Educators, Buyer and Sellers; Established 1988

Above contact information is strictly confidential when advised.

All calls taken by appointment only.

Principals may not contact each other prior to contract signature.

Offer to Sell: Sulphur – Subject to final contract

FTN Representative: The named person below is authorized to act on behalf of FTN Exporting. The buyer must not approach FTN Exporting directly without the prior permission of this representative.

Representative: Mr Ben Ling: Fish Market Road California 90122; USA

EMAIL: benling@yahoo.com

I, David Pia, CEO of FTN Exporting of 37 Elgin St Carlton, Melbourne, Australia 3054 as seller do hereby offer the following goods with good and honourable intent.

Details of the Product Offered:

SELLER: FTN EXPORTING c/o- CEO: David Pia
            www.ftnexporting.com

Date of issued: 13th February 2009 AEST

VALIDITY *5 DAYS* FROM ABOVE DATE at 12.01 PM AEST

PRODUCT OFFERED: SULPHUR

Transaction Code: 10FTN-GSC-0208-S

First Delivery: 10th May 2009 as per final contract, and every month thereafter for a total of 4 consecutive months of deliveries -/+ 5 DAYS

General Uniform Base Specification.

Product Wanted: Sulphur.

Description: Sulphur- S: Non-metallic atomic number 16.

Form B: MONOCLINIC. Prismatic, Pale Yellow Crystals

Capable of change in forming:

FORM A Sulphur below 94.5C: - MP 119C: BP 444.6C: Flash p 405F (207C), Auto Ignition 450F: Ref Index 2.038: Soluble in water.

SPECIFIC GRADE OFFERED:

Sulphur:	Bright yellow in form of granules or prill or pellets, about 2–4 mm.
Purity:	99.9% min, Ash: 0.05% max, Moisture: 1% max, Acid: 0.0003%.
Carbon:	0.05% max, As: 0.0001% max, Se: 1ppm max, Chlorides: 50 ppm max.
Quantity offered:	10000 MT-/+10% (Metric Ton) per Month, one shipment.

Loaded for bulk transport via ocean carrier:- 4 months minimum.

FULL SELL PRICE OFFERED FOB:

For Granules: US$584 PER MT FOB

PACKAGING POLY SEALED BAGS OF 50 KILOGRAM NET WEIGHT EACH

US$5,740,000 per shipment value

Total Contract value 4 months: US$22,960,000.00

Origin: USA as first choice.

Option: Should for any reason USA be unable to deliver on time seller has option to secure goods from Odessa Ukraine.

PAYMENT: At price of goods being offered: UCP600 Transferable Irrevocable Documentary letter credit payable 100% at sight of clean delivery presentation documents – issued from a top 300 world ranking bank. All cost of transferring the DLC for the account of the buyer in accordance with the 'unless' clause of Article 38 UCP600.

Payment: FTN Exporting will accept a 'NON Transferable' but CONFIRMED DLC instead at the same price of goods. All credits to be issued as non-cumulative revolving guaranteeing 4 shipment value as taken one shipment at a time.

PERFORMANCE GUARANTEE/LDD: Seller offers 'Late Delivery Discount' of US$6.00 per MT to the buyer, on sellers invoice as a credit favouring the buyer if delivery is late – As defined on final contract:

Note: Buyer must be the person paying for the goods and taking possession of goods being ordered and not another intermediary.

Minimum Rules of Trade: UCP600, URC522, INCOTERMS 2000.

Delivery as per INCOTERMS (FOB)

1) Government certificate of quantity.

2) Certificate of origin.

3) Standard certificate of quality.

4) Export permit.

5) Seller's invoice defining credit for freight and debit for certificate of origin.

STRICT PROCEDURES:

1) Quotation.

2) Provisional Offer/Negotiation/Formal offer issued – Buyer accepts.

3) Draft Contract issued/Buyer's Acceptance.

4) DLC Payment made by Buyer. Seller indicates acceptance.

5) Delivery is initiated/Documents as per contract.

6) Collection of DLC at sight as per each delivery.

Final Contract must be signed within 15 days of offer date in order for the first delivery date to apply. The offer is not legally binding until the final contract is signed. It is the buyer's duty to ascertain matters of import taxes, and import permit requirements.

First delivery date: 19th May 2009

Offer made by: David Giovanni Pia

Date: 14th February 2009

CEO: FTN and AGI

FTN Exporting

ARBN:B1468892F

www.ftnexporting.com

BUYER'S ACCEPTANCE:

I/we the buyer(s) taking final possession of goods do hereby accept this offer, which does not constitute a legally binding situation unless and until such time as the contract has been signed. Please therefore issue the draft contract.

We hereby accept email communication up to draft contract stage and understand that after this final contracts will be issued in hard copy.

Date of return of this document to seller:

Name of Import manager:

Corporate Name:

Corporate Address:

Facsimile/Phone:

Email address:

Website (If any):

Name of Bank issuing Credit:

Country:

Confirm: Transferable type of Bank DLC will be issued:(   )

Confirm: Non-transferable but confirmed type of DLC will be issued:(   )

Confirm Final Quantity:

Confirm: Delivery is for _____ consecutive months

Any other relevant information that the seller should know please add below:

Good and honourable intent governs this transaction at all times.

Print name: _____

Print corporate registration number: _____

Dated:

Signature:

Seal:

The buyer should complete and sign this offer, retain a copy and return the completed document to FTN Exporting via Mr Ling in JPEG or PDF format, before the expiry of the validity date.

PIA is now preparing to make an offer to 'buy' from the supplier to ensure the 15-day validity requirement is met with time to spare. In this case Pia will ensure that the offer is not made legally binding until signature of the final contract (although if Pia was 100 per cent sure of the end buyers intent then the offer to 'buy' from the supplier would have been made legally binding from the outset). Pia will wait for the buyer's acceptance before issuing the 'procurement offer' (the offer to buy from the supplier).

Trading Schedule to Date:

Buyer to Buyer	Seller to Supplier
Enquiry from Buyer: 9th Feb	Supplier Reply 14th: Valid 15 days
Offer sent 5 days Validity: 13th Feb	
Acceptance must return: 18th Feb	Supplier's buy offer issued: 5 days valid

DAY 9 – MORNING – FTN OFFICE – ACCEPTANCE FROM END BUYER

Ben Ling returns the end buyer's offer as accepted: it is unaltered and fully completed. Upon receiving the end buyer's acceptance, Pia sends the offer to buy sulphur to the supplier via Stephen Yong.

Pia is setting up the deal to buy from the supplier and to 'flip' the contract over by selling the same goods to the end buyer. The end buyer is now waiting for a draft contract from Pia. Pia is waiting for the offer to be accepted by the supplier. The most critical element at this stage is obtaining the funds from the end buyer. This dictates the timescale for the rest of the procedures. The offer to the supplier mirrors the end buyer's offer, except the offer to buy from the supplier is geared to heavily favour Pia and not the end buyer. The document that was sent to the supplier is detailed below:

FTN Exporting
PO BOX 30 Carlton Nth 3054 Melbourne Australia

email:	General ftnexporting@yahoo.com
Telex: FTN37AU Facsimile:	(61 03) 9347 0003
Private Office Phone:	(Applied on final contract only)
Video/Voice Cell Ph Sat/Sun	(Applied on final contract only)
OFFICE HOURS:	Monday to Friday 6.00 am to 5.00 pm AEST

Trade Educators, Buyer and Sellers; Established 1988.

Above contact information are strictly confidential when advised.

All calls taken by appointment only.

Principals may not contact each other prior to signature of the contract.

Offer to Buy: Sulphur – Subject to final contract

FTN Representative: The named person below is authorized to act on behalf of FTN Exporting on the nature of business applied. Supplier of goods offered by below representative must not approach FTN exporting without permission of the below said representative.

Representative Name: Mr Stephen Yong

EMAIL: syong_ftnexporting@yahoo.com

I, David Pia CEO of FTN Exporting of 37 Elgin St Carlton, Melbourne, Australia 3054, as buyer do hereby make this procurement offer with good and honourable intent.

Details Product Sought:

Buyer: FTN EXPORTING c/o- CEO: David Pia
        www.ftnexporting.com

Date of issued: 18th February 2009 AEST

VALIDITY 5 DAYS FROM ABOVE DATE at 12.01 PM AEST

PRODUCT Sought: SULPHUR

Transaction Code: 10FTN-GSC-0208-S

First Delivery: 10th May 2009 as defined on final contract, and every month thereafter for a total of 4 consecutive months of deliveries –/+ 5 DAYS

General Uniform Base Specification.

Product Wanted: Sulphur.

Description: Sulphur- S: Non metallic atomic number 16.

Form B: MONOCLINIC. Prismatic, Pale Yellow Crystals capable to change in forming.

FORM A Sulphur below 94.5C: - MP 119C: BP 444.6C: Flash p 405F (207C), Auto Ignition 450F: Ref Index 2.038: Soluble in water.

SPECIFIC GRADE OFFERED:

Sulfur: Bright yellow in form of granules or prill or pellets, about
2–4 mm.

Purity: 99.9% min, Ash: 0.05% max, Moisture: 1% max, Acid: 0.0003%

Carbon: 0.05% max, As: 0.0001% max, Se: 1ppm max, Chlorides:
50 ppm max.

Quantity offered: 10000 MT–/+10% (Metric Ton) per Month, one shipment
monthly

Loaded for bulk transport via ocean carrier: 4 months minimum contract of
supply.

FULL PURCHASE PRICE OFFERED FOB:

For granules: US$574 PER MT FOB

PACKAGING POLY SEALED BAGS OF 50 KILOGRAM NET WEIGHT
EACH

US$5,740,000.00 per shipment value

Origin: USA as first choice.

PAYMENT: At price of goods being offered: Transferable UCP600
Irrevocable Documentary letter credit payable 100% at sight of clean
delivery presentation documents as advised from a top 300 world
ranking bank. Credit issued as non-cumulative revolving 2 shipments
in advance -

PERFORMANCE GUARANTEE: Seller requires an ISP 98 SLC to a
2.0% value of each shipment, issued as non-cumulative revolving
upon acceptance of the buyers financial instrument for payment of the
goods.

Minimum Rules of Trade: UCP600, URC522, INCOTERMS 2000.

Delivery as per INCOTERMS (FOB)

1) Government and SGS certificate of quantity.

2) Certificate of Origin.

3) Standard Certificate of quality.

4) Export Permit.

5) Seller's Invoice defining credit for freight and debit for certificate of
origin.

STRICT PROCEDURES:

1) Quotation.

2) Provisional Offer/Negotiation/Formal offer issued – Buyer accepts.

3) Draft contracts issued/Buyer's acceptance.

4) DLC Payment made by Buyer. Supplier indicates acceptance/PG advised.

5) Delivery is initiated/Clean Documents are presented as per contract.

6) Collection of DLC at sight as per each delivery allowed.

Final contract must be signed 15 days from offer date at the latest. Offer not legally binding until final contract is signed. It is the buyer's responsibility to ensure that they meet all requisite import taxes and import permits.

Procurement Offer made by:

David Giovanni Pia

Date: 19th February 20—

CEO: FTN and AGI

FTN Exporting

ARBN: B1468892F

www.ftnexporting.com

BUYER'S ACCEPTANCE:

I/we the buyer(s) do hereby accept this offer, which is not legally binding until the contract has been signed. Please issue the draft contract. I/we agree to accept email communication to draft contract stage, after which hard copies shall be required (final contract). I/we further agree to use the same web site references applications as provided on the offer and contract.

Date of returning to Supplier: 19th February 20—

Name of buyer: David Pia

Corporate Name: FTN Exporting

Corporate Address: PO Box 30 Carlton Nth 3054 Melbourne Australia

Facsimile/Phone: PH: 61 3 93334444 FAX: 61 3 9444333 Cell 610415322222

Email address: ftnexporting@yahoo.com

Website (If any): www.ftnexporting.com

Name of Bank Authenticating Credit: West Pac Banking Corporation

Country: Melbourne City Australia

Please add any further relevant information below:

Supplier will assist buyer in obtaining BOL as an Buyer added expense.

Good and honourable intent governs this transaction at all times.

Print Name: David Pia

Print corporate registration number: ABRN: F889998N:

Dated: 19th February 20—

Signature: David Pia

Seal: *****FTN******

Supplier's Declaration:

I/we the below named supplier have confirmed the acceptance of this offer subject to signature of final contract.

Date of confirmation:

Name of supplier:

Address:

Contact details

Signature

Seal

End of offer:

DAY 14 – MORNING – OFFICE FTN EXPORTING

The supplier has accepted the procurement offer, and Pia can now issue the draft contract to the end buyer via Stephen Yong. The end buyer will then have the opportunity to review the contract prior to signing it so that when the final contract is issued the deal can proceed without delay.

Sixteen days have passed since Ben Ling first asked for a quote.

DAY 16 – MORNING – OFFICE FTN EXPORTING.

The end buyer has a draft contract in their possession. Pia receives the supplier's contract, which has a 21-day validity period. The supplier's contract is highly technical and it is obvious to Pia that the supplier has employed commercial lawyers to draft it. The critical elements of the supplier's contract mirror the terms of Pia's contract with the end buyer. Pia has spotted a couple of small issues on the supplier's contract; one of which is inconsistent with the original signed offer; and one of which is in fact inconsistent with Incoterms. Pia is conscious of the risk factor however these mistakes are minor in significance and he cannot afford to cause the deal to stall at this late stage. If the supplier challenges Pia later on, Pia will simply refer to the offer in his own defence and also to the relevant passages of Incoterms to add credence to his case. It is not uncommon for a supplier or even an end buyer to accept an offer bearing certain rules that are not in the contract. Many suppliers use a standard contract model, which is expensive to alter using their lawyers. Often the supplier will see that there are differences but will issue its own contract hoping that the other party misses or waives the differences. All parties – the end buyer, Pia and the supplier – have a common aim, which is to ensure that the deal closes successfully. If things go wrong later on, the contract will be scrutinized and the issues picked over.

The supplier's contract is signed and dated prior to the arrival of the buyer's signed and dated contract. It is very important that the supplier's contract shows an earlier signature from the buyer's contract. However, Pia will not send the supplier's contract back until the buyer's financial instrument is in his bank and accepted. Once the contract is signed and in the supplier's possession this is legally binding, whereas the supplier can't claim that there has been a breach of contract if the signed contract is not yet in their possession.

DAY 20 – FTN OFFICE – EMAIL

The buyer has informed Pia that he wishes to proceed. Pia issues a blank contract to the buyer via fax or internet, while at the same time fills in, signs, seals and sends by overnight courier two hard copies of the contract to the buyer. The end buyer does the same from their end to Pia.

DRAFT CONTRACT

Contract of Sale UCP600 F.O.B.

Supporting Incoterms 2000 'F.O.B Named Port of Shipment'

UCP 600 DLC Applies

Internet Trading Compliant

PARTIES

SELLER

FTN Exporting, ABN: F345623

Authorised Representative: David Pia

P.O. BOX 30 Carlton North, 3054 Melbourne, Victoria, Australia.

BUYER

Imperial Chemicals Import Export Limited of 300 Shanghai Road, Shanghai, China (Limited Liability Company)

Authorised Representative: Mr Akimori Akimoro

On this the 24th day of February in the year 20—

TRANSACTION CODE: 10FTN – GSC- 0208-S

WHEREAS:

The Seller is a private independent intermediate seller acting without disclosure of any other principal, as defined under the ICC International Rules of Agency, and;

The Buyer or End Buyer is a corporate or individual entity paying for and taking both documentary and physical possession of the goods.

NOW, THEREFORE, IT IS AGREED AS FOLLOWS:

1. DEFINITIONS

1.1 Date of issue: The date of this agreement, and therefore the validity commencement date, shall be the date on which the Seller issues this Agreement to the Buyer.

1.2 Buyer: Buyer taking documentary title and physical possession.

1.3 Seller: A private independent intermediate seller and vendor of the goods.

1.4 Supplier: The manufacturer or other supplier of the goods to the seller.

1.5 PPI: The instrument by which the letter of credit will cease to have a 'pre-advised' status and become a fully operational transferable documentary letter of credit.

1.6 All times as per (AEST) Australian Eastern Standard Times and Dates quoted are as per Australian Eastern Standard Times (AEST) and are taken from 12.30 PM.

1.7 Days shall have their ordinary meaning of 24 hours and that there are 7 in every week.

1.8 Months shall be defined as a period of 30 consecutive days.

1.9 Years shall constitute 365 consecutive days.

2. VALIDITY AND CONTRACT ACCEPTANCE

2.1 This contract is not valid until such time as an offer has been accepted in relation to the purchase of the goods.

2.2 This agreement shall be valid for a period of fifteen days from the date of issue. The date of issue is the date on which the Seller issues this Agreement to the Buyer as defined under 'Validity Date'.

2.3 Should this Agreement not be signed within the stipulated timescale the contract shall become invalid and not legally binding.

2.4 All times as per (AEST) Australian Eastern Standard Times and Dates quoted are as per Australian Eastern Standard Times (AEST) and are taken from 12.30 PM.

2.5 This contract cannot be entered into unless and until the Seller has accepted the Buyer's signed offer.

2.6 Once signed and dated the Buyer must return this contract to the Seller via facsimile transmission, and in addition a scanned Portable

Document Format (PDF) or other electronic copy of the document must also be transmitted via electronic mail.

2.7 The time and date of transmission and acceptance of the contract by the Buyer shall be deemed to be at the time and date when the Buyer sent the document.

2.8 The arrival of either the facsimile copy, bearing handwritten signatures and/or the PDF format copy bearing the term 'original' shall mean that the intent of the Buyer is to proceed, as being legally bound by the terms and conditions of this contract.

2.9 Good and honourable intent shall govern the parties to this contract at all times.

3. PRODUCT TO BE SOLD

3.1 SULPHUR OF SPECIFIC GRADE:

Sulphur: Bright yellow in form of granules or prill or pellets, about 2–4 mm. Purity: 99.9% min, Ash: 0.05% max, Moisture: 1% max, Acid: 0.0003% Carbon: 0.05% max, As: 0.0001% max, Se: 1ppm max, Chlorides: 50 ppm max.

3.2 ORIGIN – UNITED STATES OF AMERICA

As per clause 17 below, in case of serious delay or unforeseen events the Seller has the right to secure goods from another port or country, of equivalent quality to the goods offered in this agreement in accordance with the specification below.

3.3 SPECIFICATIONS, GRADE, PACKAGING

The goods shall be provided in accordance with the specifications as to quality and description. The official record of quality will be provided by a government or government authorized agency and shall carry the analytical content of the goods being sold 'in rem' as per the warehouse stock; and not as certified under a separate pre-shipment inspection certificate which, if sought, shall be secured by the seller at extra cost to the buyer.

The sulphur will be packed in export quality double heat sealed plastic bags. One of the layers shall be a liner, such as polyethylene, and the outer bag shall be polypropylene.

3.4 QUANTITY

10,000 Metric Tons, plus or minus 10 per cent.

3.5 SHIPMENT LOTS

The total quantity of the goods being sold is:

40,000 Metric Tons (MT) per 4 shipment lots, each shipment carrying:

10,000 MT –/+10% as delivered over 4 consecutive monthly periods. Final shipment to be adjusted to account for the final tally of delivered quantities. The Buyer accepts that each shipment delivery may have a variable range of on board goods between zero and 1000 MT being delivered at any one time. Collection upon the financial instrument is based on the final tally count as per the Ship's mate's receipt or Ship's forwarders receipt, whichever is presented first.

3.6 PRICE

The FOB price shall be *US$584.00 (five hundred and eighty-four United States dollars)* per Metric Ton.

The total value of each average shipment lot is; *US$5,840,000: (Five million, eight hundred and forty thousand United States dollars)*

The contract value of the said goods is US$23,360,000.00 (Twenty-three million, three hundred and sixty thousand United States dollars)

Price Escalation: PRICE ESCALATION CLAUSE:

This price is fixed and shall apply for the whole term of this contract.

4. DELIVERY

The price of the goods is offered as FOB (Free on board) Incoterms 2000 'Named port of shipment'. The Seller offers no variants of FOB in this Agreement.

The goods being offered are not permitted to be resold in the following countries: (1) Iran (2) Nth Korea (3) Cuba.

5. PERFORMANCE GUARANTEE

5.1 In accordance with the offer as agreed the Buyer hereby accepts a suitable Performance Guarantee in the form of a 'LDD' (Late Delivery Discount). In the event that late delivery occurs this discount shall be a credit on the seller's invoice to favour the buyer at a present value and rate.

5.2 LATE DELIVERY DISCOUNT VALUE

US$6.00 for each shipment that has failed delivery.

6. DUTIES OF THE BUYER

6.1 It is of primary importance that the Buyer assists the Seller in all matters. The Buyer must not in any way hinder the Seller in ensuring that the goods are delivered within the scope, terms and conditions applied in the contract.

6.2 The Buyer shall be required to open a letter of credit to the seller within 7 days of signature of this agreement. Bank issued Payment Required: An irrevocable Transferable UCP 600 Confirmed pre-advised operational documentary letter of credit unrestricted, issued as transferable.

6.3 The Buyer hereby accepts that signature of this internationally enforceable contract creates a personal legal obligation regardless of the domestic laws of their country.

6.4 The Buyer, having paid and obtained the title to the goods shall be entitled to possession of them in accordance with the terms and conditions of this agreement.

6.5 IMPORT LICENCE AND TAXES

The Buyer(s) hereby confirm that they have prior to signature of this Agreement secured the import licence or permits required for the successful purchase of the goods.

7 DUTIES OF THE SELLER

7.1 The Seller has purchased or is holding a contract for purchase or has the ability to purchase the interest in the goods offered from an undisclosed source(s) prior to offering the goods to the Buyer. The Seller is offering clean title and interest in the goods free of liens at an agreed price. The Seller will transfer their interests and title to the goods or required parts thereof to the buyer without obtaining possession of the actual goods.

7.2 The Seller has forthwith used a high degree of sourcing ability, skill and expertise in being able to offer a product to the Buyer for reasonable gain and the Buyer has obtained the lowest fair price for such goods as a direct result of the Seller's ability, skill and expertise.

7.3 The Seller shall ensure that all matters of quality and warranty of the goods follow the goods, for the benefit of the End Buyer.

7.4 The obligations to ensure quality and warranty shall be the responsibility of the Seller.

7.5 The seller shall be responsible for all matters up to final delivery. 'Delivery' is as defined by Incoterms 2000.

7.6 The Seller shall ensure above all else that the goods are delivered per the terms of the contract – the most important obligation as it is for the Buyer to pay for them.

SELLER'S WARRANTY OBLIGATIONS

7.7 The Seller declares with good intent that the goods being sold are fit for purpose and of merchantable quality and that if the Producer, Manufacturer or Supplier of the goods is at fault for delivering goods which are of a defective nature from the point of manufacture the Seller is responsible for any such reasonably defined defects in the goods.

7.8 The Seller will initiate procedures to remedy those defects for the Buyer taking final possession of such goods, within a period of 90 days after such goods having come into the possession of the Buyer.

7.9 All claims of such defects and/ or damage must be made within 28 days of the Buyer obtaining possession of the goods.

7.10 The Seller has obtained the implicit and specific right to transfer the warranty obligations, upon resale of the goods once only, and the manufacturer or owner of such goods has agreed to endorse this.

8. PROCEDURE IN THE EVENT OF DEFECTIVE GOODS

8.1 The procedure for claiming a remedy for the supply of defective goods shall be as follows:

8.2 The Buyer shall first give notice to the Seller of such defects in writing providing detailed information about the claim and proof of the same, sworn under affidavit or other acceptable statutory authority declaring that the goods did arrive in a state other than ordered, and that such goods are defective or damaged in such a way as to indicate that the Supplier or Manufacturer of the goods is at fault.

8.3 Photographic evidence of the damage shall also be provided where appropriate. Should a notice be communicated to the Seller by facsimile transmission, JPEG or email the Seller shall attempt to rectify the defect on behalf of the Buyer in the first instance to the mutual satisfaction of both once the evidence provided has been authenticated proving that the goods were delivered by the manufacturer or supplier in a sub-standard condition.

8.4 The Buyer shall allow any authority representative of the Seller visually to inspect the damage to the said goods in the Buyer's country and/or premises and report the same to the Seller.

8.5 The benefits conferred by the warranty are in addition to all implied warranties and other rights and remedies available to the buyer in respect of the goods being purchased under the Trade Practices Act and/ or similar state or territory laws of the country from which the goods are being exported. This is in addition to statutory provisions under the Hague-Visby international shipping rules and in conjunction with the English Sales of Goods Act 1979 (as amended) which provides the law in relation to the carriage of goods, where such matters incorporate damage caused to goods that fall to be remedied by the Carrier, as defined by the terms and conditions on the back of the Bill of Lading form.

8.6 The Seller shall be required to remedy the damage or defect on behalf of the Supplier once such evidence has been established in determining that the Supplier or manufacturer is at fault for selling the damaged or defective goods.

9. PAYMENT

9.1 The buyer will open a Bank issued irrevocable Transferable UCP600 confirmed pre-advised operational documentary letter of credit unrestricted, issued as transferable within seven (7) days of signature of this agreement.

9.2 The Credit shall be issued and become payable 100 per cent at sight upon presentation of the required delivery documents as specified under Incoterms 2000.

9.3 At Sight: present the required 'Title/Delivery documents' for the issuing bank to examine: 5 days is allowed for examination of the documents to take place. If after such time all the delivery documents are presented 'clean' the issuing bank will allow collection to proceed with the financial instrument used to pay for such goods.

9.4 The credit shall be opened as operational, and the Seller shall serve a document, which advises 'Proof of Interest' in the goods being offered, as per the terms of the contract. Once the proof of interest in the goods is disclosed, the pre-advised credit reverts to being a normal active operational transferable credit, which carries with it the confirmation if applicable. The Document bearing the heading 'Policy Proof of Interest Certificate' (PPI) as defined on the contract in blank form shall be the only document which, once such disclosure information has been applied to it as surrendered to the issuing bank of the Buyer, shall cause the pre-advised credit to revert into a fully active irrevocable transferable letter of credit. The term 'bank' must now also be apparent.

9.5 The actual contract price shall include the costs of bank charges and fees, including transfer charges, pre-advisement fees and conversion of the pre-advised credit into an operational credit. The Buyer, as the applicant of this credit, bears these costs. Such costs and added expenses are to be issued from the issuing bank to favour the seller's account within 3 days of the disclosure of the PPI Certificate.

9.6 The transfer fee only shall be returned as a credit to favour the Buyer on the Seller's invoice. The Buyer hereby agrees with the Seller that such charges shall be the cost applied to the actual goods, which the Buyer will pay for on behalf of the Seller. This is in accordance with Article 38 of UCP600 Paragraph (c): in that the Buyer has 'agreed upon' the Seller paying for such fees once the credit becomes transferable and after proof of goods has been disclosed via the issuance of the PPI Certificate.

9.7 If the Buyer or their bank is unable to issue a confirmed pre-advised credit, then a normal active credit shall be advised instead without affecting the overall basic terms and conditions of issuance, in accordance with UCP600. If the second credit is not issued by a top 100 world ranked bank, then the credit must also be issued as confirmed.

9.8 When the delivery documents are successfully presented the rules of collection apply as provided by URC 522 (ICC Uniform Rules of Collection Publication 522).

9.9 In the case of multiple shipments, the credit is issued as 'Non-Cumulative Revolving'.

9.10 The Non-Cumulative Revolving value of the financial instrument lodged for payment shall be clearly defined on contract in United States Dollars or Euros. Final debit or credit amount is dictated by the tolerances on each set of delivery documents, presentation of which is defined specifically on the Seller's invoice. This includes all credits and debits related to subsidies and the necessary expenses of each party to the contract, as defined under Incoterms 2000.

10. DELIVERY DOCUMENTS 'FOB Named Port of Shipment'

10.1 In accordance with the delivery requirements provided by Incoterms 2000 the Seller will serve, in hard copy or electronic format, the following documentations for authentication and presentation:

10.1.1 Provision of Leading Primary Delivery Document is a condition of financial instrument presentation. In the first instance this must be a Clean on Board Ship's Mate's Receipt signed on behalf of the Ship's Master or Ship Owner evidencing that the ordered goods are on board the named vessel of the Buyer.

10.1.2 All the abovementioned documents shall indicate, amongst other things, the quantity of goods on board. Should the secondary document be presented in lieu of the 'Ship's Mate's Receipt', the Buyer shall agree to notify their bankers to accept one of the alternative documents and issue an amendment to the credit at the expense of the Buyer within 24 hours of presentation of an alternative delivery document.

10.2 An Export Permit

10.3 An Original Seller's Invoice

10.4 Certificate of Origin

10.5 An 'In Rem' Certificate of Quality as issued by SGS or Societe Generale De Surveillance.

10.6 An ISO Certificate of manufacturing

10.7 CERTIFICATE OF INSPECTION: QUANTITY –

For the account of the Seller: At the date of delivery the Seller shall provided a visual on board inspection of goods and tally count Certificate as conducted in the first instance by 'SGS' (Societe Generale de Surveilliance). Should such an agency not be in operation in the country of origin then in the second instance the Seller shall provide such certification as issued by BV (Bureau Veritas), SAYBOLT or GOVERNMENTAL AGENCY, as per such service being available in country of origin. The Buyer shall accept such a certification and if need be immediately amend any condition on the credit to accommodate any such document issuance, once such becomes apparent.

10.8 CERTIFICATE OF QUALITY: NON-PSI TYPE –

The goods offered have a Certificate of Quality which states that the goods are specifically 'fit for purpose' for use as attested by a world-class inspection agency such as 'SGS' (Societe Generale de Surveilliance). If SGS does not operate in the country of origin then the Seller shall in the second instance provide BV (Bureau Veritas) verification, SAYBOLT or GOVERNMENTAL AGENCY, whichever is applicable in the country of origin. The Buyer shall accept the certification of quality and if necessary amend the condition of the credit to accommodate the issue of this secondary type of document. For the Certificate to be issued, the goods can be inspected anywhere except on board ship: immediately prior to the goods being delivered on board, goods inspected in the year of manufacture or production. The Buyer indicates that they accept the Certificate of inspection by initialling and placing an 'X' in the check box below. If no initials or marks be apparent, the Seller will issue a PSI Certificate as defined below.

We accept the non-Pre-shipment Inspection Certificate of Quality type (PSI) (   ) Initials: _____

10.9 CERTIFICATE OF QUALITY: PSI TYPE

This type of Certificate of Quality shows that the goods offered have been tested as being specifically 'fit for purpose' for use, as attested by a world-class inspection agency such as 'SGS' (Societe Generale de Surveillance). Should this agency not be in operation in the country of origin of the goods, then in the second instance the Seller shall provide such certification as issued by BV (Bureau Veritas), SAYBOLT or GOVERNMENTAL AGENCY, whichever is available in the country of origin. In this instance the Buyer shall accept this certification of quality and if need be immediately amend the condition of the credit to accommodate the issuance of this document. This Certificate is issued for goods inspected on board the ship or, if the ship is late in arriving, immediately prior to the goods being delivered on board the named ship. This Certificate shall be provided by the Seller for the account and cost of the Buyer and will not be incorporated in the price of goods offered. A further expense shall be recorded on the Seller's invoice as a debit against the account of the Buyer. The Buyer hereby indicates acceptance of the Certificate of Inspection unless the initials and mark are indicated on the Non-PSI Certificate above.

11. SPECIAL DOCUMENT PRESENTATIONS

11.1 POLICY PROOF OF INTEREST CERTIFICATE

If an acceptable 'Pre-advised' credit is used to pay for the goods, the Seller shall issue a document called the 'Policy Proof of Interest Certificate', which identifies the genuine Manufacturer, Owner or Supplier of the goods. The Buyer accepts this blank certificate model, and the procedures applied therein, as the process needed to verify that the goods are genuine.

11.2 The Buyer shall accept this information within 3 days of disclosure, whether acceptance is provided explicitly or not. The 'PPI' blank model shall be added to the end of this contract and, upon the financial instrument having been advised as accepted by the seller, shall be returned to the buyer carrying full genuine disclosure of the Seller's allocation and interests in the goods being sold.

11.3 If the information later proves to be false or untrue no protests will be entertained with regard to the suitability of the document once issued. Should it be proven that the information supplied by the Seller is false then the Buyer shall be allowed to make claims of fraudulent and dishonourable intent against the Seller, because the Seller has not honoured the required obligations to deliver genuine verifiable information. In this event the Buyer shall grant the Seller a period of 48 hours within which to remedy the situation before the Buyer declares a breach of the Seller's conditions.

11.4 The Seller shall be required to make a copy of the PPI certificate as an appendix to this contract, to fill in the details to disclose the Supplier of the goods and to forward it from the advising bank to the issuing bank in electronic form, or to the issuing bank by hard copy courier, whichever comes first.

11.5 The Buyer is obligated to read the blank copy of the PPI certificate contained herein, and accept the information yet to be applied on it in disclosing the Supplier's information. The Buyer must also adhere to the terms on the blank PPI Certificate and is permitted to authenticate the information thereon once only.

12. INTERNET PROTOCOL

The Buyer accepts full responsibility for service of documents and any or all communications transmitted electronically in the pursuance of this transaction. The buyer shall not be able to use domestic laws of their own jurisdiction to negate either their intent or the legality of the documents when transmitted electronically whether that is via the Internet or by any other means.

13. SHIPPING

13.1 Nothing in this agreement shall negate or otherwise detract from the obligations relating to, inter alia, shipping, demurrage, delays, berthing and weather relating to delivery of the goods and which are in force at the date of signature of this contract.

13.2 The Buyer hereby acknowledges that they are responsible for matters of shipping as per their contract with the Carrier and must ensure that the Bill of Lading document and its terms and conditions comply with the International Maritime shipping rules further defined as the 'Hague Rules' in the first instance or the 'Hague-Visby Rules' in the second instance.

13.3 If the Seller is asked by the buyer to assist with the matter of securing the Bill of Lading on the Buyer's behalf in a variant FOB transaction, then the Seller will only provide such assistance of 'added services' or variation on an FOB transaction to the best of their abilities as per the implications and provisions of Incoterms 2000.

13.4 The Seller shall not be held liable where this 'variant FOB' assistance fails to procure the required Bill of Lading, and in no circumstances shall this be construed to mean that the Seller has failed to 'deliver'. The Seller shall not offer such assistance with securing the Bill of Lading to a rented ship in relation to which there is a charterparty agreement.

13.5 The obtaining and securing of the Bill of Lading is the obligation of the End Buyer.

13.5.1 Delays caused by the Carrier are the fault of the Carrier.

13.5.2 Delays caused as a result of not being ready to accept the goods, pay the freight and other carriage and import statutory charges and obligations therein, once the goods pass the ship's rail in port of loading, are the responsibility of the Buyer who shall also bear all the costs and expenses for the Buyer unless otherwise provided for under the terms of this agreement.

13.5.3 Delays in loading which result in the goods not being ready for loading shall be the responsibility of the Seller. Any cost incurred for these delays will be added to the account of the Seller as per Incoterms 2000.

13.6 At least fourteen (14) days before its arrival the Buyer will provide the Seller with an estimated ship arrival date and time at loading port.

13.7 The Buyer will give the Seller a revised arrival date and time once the ship is no less than forty-eight (48) hours from berthing at the local port. Thereafter the Seller shall prepare the goods alongside ship ready for loading.

13.8 The Seller shall make ready the said goods alongside the ship ready for loading.

13.9 The entity causing and/or being at fault in matters of shipping bears the consequences of the fault, in accordance with the terms and conditions of the said Bill of Lading and/or Incoterms 2000 as appropriate (once goods are on board ship).

14. NAME OF SHIP AND DATE OF ARRIVAL

14.1 In accordance with the provisions contained in the schedule of delivery contained within this agreement the date of delivery shall be the earliest date that the goods will be available for loading.

14.2 The Buyer shall notify the Seller of the name of the carrier within 14 days of the arrival date of such ship at loading port.

14.3 The Buyer and Seller agree that the notification date applies from the said delivery date, less 14 days before or more.

14.4 Regardless of any other concurrent matters of scheduling the above minimum stipulation shall mean that the Buyer is required to initiate the processes needed to ensure that the Carrier will be at the loading port on or within the required timeframe.

14.5 The Buyer hereby agrees to begin initiating the process of securing the required Carrier, as soon as the contract has been formally accepted by the parties and is legally binding.

15. ARBITRATION

15.1 All parties to the contract shall endeavour to settle any contract dispute amicably in the first instance. Where such matters have failed to be resolved the arbitration rules as applied under the London Court of International Arbitration (LCIA) shall apply.

15.2 This clause shall be enforced in the appropriate venue in the Seller's country and state, as defined in this agreement.

16. LAW AND JURISDICTION

16.1 English language and English international trade laws shall apply.

16.2 Should a dispute arise as to the goods in possession this shall be answerable in the Supplier's country and state, and the Seller's obligation in defending the Buyer's claim on behalf of the buyers shall become apparent if such claims are justified in the appropriate country.

16.3 Any disputes relating to the Seller's obligations as defined in this contract (and as a secondary document the offer preceding this contract) shall be arbitrated in the following country and city: Melbourne City, State of Victoria, Australia.

16.4 Where the Seller is required to defend the claim made by the End Buyer, in the Supplier's country, the Seller shall be obligated to meet the End Buyer in the Supplier's country and attend any proceedings but only on the condition that the End Buyer agrees to be physically present in the country to litigate upon the matter in dispute.

17. FORCE MAJEURE

17.1 'Neither party shall be held liable for any default due to any act of nature, war, whether declared or not, strike, lockout, industrial action, epidemic, drought, flood, acts of terrorism, or fire or other event (*force majeure* event) which is beyond the reasonable control of either party. The Seller shall not be held liable for delay or failure to perform any of its obligations under this agreement as a result of a force majeure event suffered by the Seller's supplier or sub-contractor.

17.2 On the happening of a *force majeure* event the party relying on this clause is to give notice in writing of the fact within 72 hours of the event's occurrence.

17.3 Neither party is entitled to benefit from a force majeure event or frustration of the contract where that party has been responsible, in whole or in part, for delay or non-performance of its obligations under this agreement.

17.4 On the occurrence of a *force majeure* event experienced by either the Buyer, the Seller or the Seller's supplier, the obligations of the parties shall be suspended for so long as the force majeure event makes performance under this contract impossible. The affected party will be entitled to a reasonable extension of time for performance which is in any event equal to the period of delay or stoppage.

17.4.1 Costs arising from the delay or stoppage will be borne by the party incurring those costs

17.4.2 The party affected by the force majeure event and so claiming shall endeavour and take all necessary steps to continue with their obligations under this agreement whether that constitutes bringing an end to the force majeure event or finding a way in which to bypass its effect.

17.5 The Seller has the right to terminate this agreement if performance cannot be resumed within 30 (thirty) consecutive days of the occurrence of the force majeure event.

17.6 Should the Seller be the party affected by the *force majeure* event, the said Seller has the option to continue with the performance of the contract within this period on the clear understanding that all added expenses and consequences arising from the appropriate enactment of the *force majeure* clause are made for the account of the Buyer taking possession of goods offered.

17.7 Should the Buyer be the party affected by the *force majeure* event, the Buyer has the option to continue with the performance of the contract if invited to do so by the Seller within the 30-day period on the clear understanding that all added expenses and consequences arising from the appropriate enactment of the force majeure clause are made for the account of the Buyer taking possession of goods offered.

17.8 The invitation to continue with the transaction shall be given in writing as amended to the contract as applicable prior to the force majeure event, which once accepted within the 30-day period, both parties once more are bound by the terms and conditions of this agreement as amended.

17.9 In accordance with clause 17.4 and 17.5 above the Buyer is hereby notified that the Seller may raise the legitimate matter of force majeure to discharge themselves from performance if performance becomes impossible as a result of a force majeure event experienced by the supplier or owner of the goods from whom the Seller is obtaining documentary possession.

17.10 Notwithstanding the happening of a force majeure event the Buyer will refrain from contracting with the third party as named on the PPI document in the appendix to this agreement for a period of six months from the date of this agreement. To do otherwise is a serious breach of contract for which the Buyer will be held liable.

18. LEGALITY

By contracting under the terms of this agreement all parties hereby confirm that they:

Are over 18 years of age and mentally competent.

Have never be convicted or cautioned for act(s) of fraud.

Are neither a declared or undischarged bankrupt.

19. SUMMARY OF PROCEDURES

19.1 The Buyer shall request an offer to which, once accepted, instigates the issuance of the draft contract, to which the following schedule of procedures shall apply.

19.1.1 (1) Draft contract is signed and returned to the Seller from the Buyer to imply a formal legal contracting situation.

19.1.2 (2) Financial instrument issued within contracted days to initiate acceptance.

19.1.3 (3) PPI Certificate defining 'Proof of interest in the goods' is advised by the Seller. The operational credit converts into an active credit.

19.1.4 (4) Performance Guarantee (if applicable) is provided.

19.1.5 (5) Ship arrival date at loading port advised to Seller.

19.1.6 (6) Goods are proven as being loaded on-board the Buyer's ordered Carrier with the issuance of the leading delivery document.

19.1.7 (7) Remaining documents advised within contracted days.

19.1.8 (8) Delivery completed, collection made at sight of the delivery documents.

19.1.9 (9) Next shipment loaded if revolving shipments have been ordered.

19.2 Applicable references to be used by all parties to the Contract:

a) To identify an acceptable Top Class World Bank. http://www.forbes. com/2006/03/29/06f2k_worlds-largest-public-companies_land.html.

b) In matters of distance assuming ship is sailing at 14 knots per hour. http://www.distances.com.

c) In matters of Weights and Measures. http://www.onlineconversion. com.

d) UCP600 applicable banks may be found on. http://www.ftnexporting. com.

e) In matters of identifying loading and unloading ports. http://www. distances.com.

19.3 SHIPMENT SCHEDULE:

19.3.1 Shipment Date(s):

a) Financial instrument must be accepted by the seller within 3 days of receipt.

b) 40 days shall be allowed for goods to be made ready at port of loading.

c) 7 days shall be allowed for document presentation, for a total timeframe not exceeding the said schedule dates. In all, not more than 50 days should pass from the date of the financial instrument issuance to the date the first delivery is initiated by the Seller.

The agreed delivery schedule is as follows. For the avoidance of doubt, any delivery that is not complete on or before these dates will entitle the Buyer to the applicable Late Delivery Discount.

a) First shipment loading and delivery completed on or before: 8th of May 20—.

b) Second shipment loading and delivery completed on or before: 8th of June 20—.

c) Third shipment loading and delivery completed on or before: 8th of July 20—.

d) Final shipment loading and delivery completed on or before: 8th August 20—.

20. POLICY PROOF OF INTEREST CERTIFICATE (PPI)

20.1 In accordance with clause 11 above the following information defines the aforesaid 'Policy Proof of Interest Certificate', which is hereby exposed to the Buyer and or Buyer's bank as a 'Blank Model (PART A)' document bearing no information other than depicted.

20.2 The Seller shall complete the model documents with the required information. A copy will be made and returned to the Buyer and/or Buyer's bank within 3 days of the acceptance of the Buyer's financial instrument.

20.3 The information once provided is secured directly from the owner of the goods as purchased by the Seller, which are consequently being resold to the Buyer. Unless otherwise proven the Buyer accepts the information unconditionally as being genuine, in meeting with the Seller's obligation in accordance with the summary of the procedures in clause 19 above.

20.4 The Seller's 'Proof of Interest' in the goods is officially declared once the information regarding the owner in possession of the goods has been disclosed. Whether or not the buyer chooses to verify this information is of no concern to the Seller.

20.5 The financial instrument shall be made active on satisfaction of the pre-advised condition: when the document entitled 'PPI Policy Proof of Interest Certificate' which contains this information is disclosed to the issuing bank.

20.6 The Seller is not giving the Buyer, Buyer's bank or associated bank of the issuing bank permission to approach the Supplier. Either the Buyer or the issuing bank can verify the information provided.

20.7 If the Buyer exercises this discretion and verifies the interests in the goods held by the Seller, then the information requested of the Supplier is strictly limited to verification that the goods are genuine and available as disclosed on the PPI Certificate and nothing else. The Seller's name, the nature of the goods and Seller's interests therein are the only verifiable matters that the Buyer should expect to receive.

20.8 The Buyer hereby agrees not to request or make enquiries concerning sensitive information regarding, inter alia, price and the disclosure of the DLC number. Any such requests will not be tolerated under any circumstances.

20.9 The discretionary period within which the Buyer is permitted to verify that such goods are genuine and available must be exercised within exactly 72 hours after the PPI Certificate is surrendered to the issuing bank.

20.10 Any approaches made to the Supplier for whatsoever reason after the expiry of the 72-hour timeframe and for a period of 12 months thereafter, whether or not the business at hand was successfully or unsuccessfully closed, shall be treated as a dishonourable act and a serious breach of conditions.

21. PPI CERTIFICATE

A blank PPI certificate is hereby offered below. This document will be completed and returned to the issuing bank as per the time provided in this agreement.

PPI: POLICY PROOF OF INTEREST CERTIFICATE (BLANK MODEL PART 'A')

IMPORTANT BANK PRESENTATION DELIVERY DOCUMENT

PPI Advised By: FTN Exporting defined as 'The Seller'

Address

Contact Number

Seller's Advising bank:

Supporting Transaction Code:

For the Immediate Attention of:

Applicant's Issuing bank.

For the Account of the Applicant: (The buyer) Name:

Supporting Pre-advised Letter of Credit Number:

Date PPI advised:

Issued by Facsimile (   ) and/ or PDF (   ):

In reference: Full Activation of Credit.

Supporting the purchase of goods defined as:

Attention Bank Officer – Name:

Dear Sir or Madam,

Please be advised that the named applicant, also referred to as the Buyer, has issued a UCP600 pre-advised credit from your bank to our advising bank. We are required to present details to identify the Supplier of the goods we are reselling to the applicant of the credit. This Proof of Interests Certificate (PPI) is hereby offered as per our contracting conditions, in meeting with the pre-advised credit condition. Please be advised that the service of this disclosure meets our obligation regardless of whether the applicant confirms the validity of the information provided or not.

Accordingly we request that you revoke the 'pre-advised' status of the credit, thereby making the credit a normal active UCP600 irrevocable transferable documentary letter of credit (and therefore operational.)

Yours faithfully

Print Name:

Signed:
Dated:

The Buyer and applicant of the issued credit shall by their own means and discretion using facsimile, email or other forms of telecommunication confirm the details of the Supplier as per the information provided below. Whether or not they choose to exercise this discretion has no effect on the activation of the credit.

PPI: SUPPLIER'S DETAILS:

The Supplier and owner of the goods are:

The name of the person representing the Supplier and owner is:

Address:

Email:

Facsimile

Phone Number

Business Number

Supplier's Website (if any):

Description of Goods:

Quantity:

SELLER'S DETAILS

Name of the Seller: FTN Exporting

Name of person offering the goods: David Pia

Business Address:

Mailing Address:

All Communication Details:

Email:

Phone(s):

Facsimile:

Name of Bank:

Name apparent on Account: David Papa

Address:

Account Number:

SWIFT CODE:

Phone/Facsimile:

SELLER'S DECLARATION

I, David Pia C/o P.O. Box 468 Carlton Nth, Melbourne, Victoria, 3054 Citizen of Australia, as an independent private commodity trader using the registered trading name of FTN Exporting do hereby sign and/or sign and seal this contract with good and honourable intent as Seller acting on behalf of an undisclosed principal or various principals. This/These Principal(s) shall become disclosed upon the acceptance of the Buyer's financial instrument, in accordance with the terms of this agreement.

Print Name: David Pia

Date: 26th February 20—

Seal

Signature:

BUYER'S DETAILS

Name of the Buyer:

Person taking possession of the goods:

Business Address:

Mailing Address:

All Communication Details:

Email:

Phone(s):

Facsimile:

Name of Bank:

Address:

Name apparent on Account:

Account Number:

SWIFT CODE:

Phone/Facsimile:

BUYER'S DECLARATION

I, _____ Citizen
of _____ , as an Independent commodity trader using the registered
trading name of _____ , do hereby sign and/or sign
and seal this contract with good and honourable intent as Buyer taking
both title and possession of the offered goods. I the Buyer accordingly
agree with all the terms, scope and conditions of this contract.

Print Name:

Date:

Signature:

Seal:

End of Contract

Trading schedule to date:

Buyer to Buyer	Seller to Supplier
Enquiry from Buyer: 9th Feb	Supplier Reply 14th: Valid 15 days
Offer sent 5 days validity: 13th Feb	
Acceptance must return: 18th Feb	Supplier's buy offer issued: 5 days valid
Contract sent to Buyer: 23th Feb	
Supplier's contract arrives: 25th Feb	

DAY 25 – FTN OFFICE – EMAIL

Pia and the end buyer exchange signed hard copies of their contract, which they fax to one another and exchange hard copies by courier. The receipt of the facsimile copy shows the intent of the parties and allows the deal to continue while both parties are waiting for the hard copies to arrive.

The buyer's final instrument must arrive in the account of the seller as stipulated on the contract.

DAY 35 – FTN OFFICE – EMAIL

Pia has an accepted credit in his bank which is ready for transfer and sends the signed contract to the supplier by fax and overnight courier. The date on the contract shows that for a very short time prior to reselling the goods Pia 'owned' the goods which is important if the trade ever descends into litigation. Although this isn't a prerequisite to the trade's success, it does reinforce the fact that Pia has purchased the goods, and resold them as a *bona fide* 'buyer and seller' rather than merely an 'intermediary buyer/seller'.

DAY 40 – FTN'S ADVISING BANK

The credit was successfully transferred to the accepting bank. Pia has studied UCP600 and uses this knowledge to ensure that the bank's export manager follows the procedures.

The supplier's bank has accepted Pia's transferred financial instrument and now it is only a matter of time before the delivery documents are issued to Pia or his bank for final blank endorsement over to the end buyer. At this point the supplier will, depending on the nature of the instrument, issue a bill of exchange against Pia for only the value of his seller's invoice, and attach it to the delivery documents. When these documents arrive Pia also needs to ensure that he has provided a 'seller's invoice' marked as 'original' to go to the buyer's bank with the delivery documents he has prepared, that represent the buyer's buy price (unless a confirmed credit is used in which case payment is actually effected at Pia's bank there and then – the advising bank is reimbursed by the issuing bank). When this happens, Pia's work is complete and letter of credit collection procedures will commence in accordance with URC522. The bank has five days in which to examine the documents. If all the documents are in order, the supplier gets paid. Pia retains the difference between the value of the credit and the supplier's payment as commission, portions of which are then allocated to the other intermediaries. Mr Ben Ling and Mr Stephen Yong then present their UCP600 in-house SLCs at their respective banks in order to collect their share of the commission.

The delivery dates on the supplier's contract matches the delivery dates on Pia's contract with the end buyer. Therefore as long as the deliveries continue to occur, the money will continue to flow from Pia's account to the supplier as per the 'revolving credit'.

When the goods actually arrive with the end buyer, the end buyer gives the customs official the delivery documents, pays for all tariffs and import taxes, and freight charges as per FOB Incoterms and then takes delivery of the goods. If there are any small defects with the goods, and it is an issue with the actual supply of the goods rather than damage which occurred while the goods are in transit, Pia would be able to compensate the end buyer from his own commission. However, if the defects are serious, Pia is also required to seek compensation or remedy from the supplier on behalf of the end buyer.

This is the reason why 'ex ship or arrival' deals are not appropriate for intermediaries, because in these types of deals documents cannot be used to denote 'delivery'.

In effect once the DLC has been transferred, then the intermediary only needs to follow instructions and produce the required documents as stipulated on the contract. Once this has been completed successfully, the deal effectively closes by itself.

Under UCP600, 'Silence' means that Pia's bank endorsed draft has been accepted, and 'clean' documents means that this 'acceptance' has occurred.

However, if the commission rate is too high the issuing bank may reimburse the advising bank on the sale of the goods but may not allow collection on the commission portion left over. If the 'consultancy fee' is reasonable and the end buyer got a good and fair deal, then collection would most probably be allowed to occur. To ensure you mitigate any challenge it is imperative that you communicate that the 'Seller acting on behalf of an undisclosed principal' from the start of any deal, including on the contract with the buyer. Applying the letter 'C' at the end of delivery terms FOB or CIF may also help if a dispute arose about the commission payment as it would show that the end buyer knew that they were contracting with an intermediary looking to make gains on the goods, rather than directly with the supplier of the goods.

This brings us back to the very start of the transaction. The way the intermediary commences the deal will govern the way the rest of the deal transpires. A bad start to a deal is highly likely to impact on the latter stages and it could become difficult to collect your hard-earned commission. Finally, contrary to the view of some intermediaries, the end buyer will only allow Pia to collect the amount of the issued DLC value. This means Pia has to record the total amount of the DLC on his seller's invoice. If Pia's invoice is less than the DLC value Pia loses his commission: if it's more, then the bank has up to five per cent discretion to allow the excess charge to apply without seeking the permission of the end buyer to do so. In effect there will be a gap in value between Pia's and the end buyer's value on the seller's invoice. This gap is put on the seller's invoice as 'Consultancy fees and operating expenses' and is the total commission amount.

FTN EXPORTING

This Corporate in house Documentary Letter of Credit is issued supported by UCP600 Rules (Uniform Custom and Practice for the Issuance of a Documentary Credit as per Publication 600)

Date of Issue   :
Expiration Date   :
Type: Irrevocable and Non Transferable.
Name of Issuer:(The Applicant)
Business Address (No PO Box Allowed)   :
Phone   :
E- mail   :
Advising Bank in Support of Payment
Collection applied against the account of the issuer at;
Name of Bank   :
Address   :
Account Name   :
Account Number   :
SWIFT   :
Phone
Facsimile   :

Name of Beneficiary   :
Business Address (No PO Box Allowed)   :
Phone   :
E- mail   :
Bank and account used to apply collection and deposit of credit;
Name of Bank   :
Address   :
Account Name   :
Account Number   :
SWIFT   :
Phone   :
Facsimile   :
Amount   :
Payment For   :

Terms and Conditions of Issuance :
The Applicant hereby irrevocably and unconditionally (except as stated herein) undertakes to pay the Beneficiary on their first demand in writing at our counter based upon the pre advised condition which once fulfilled and met allows this credit to become operational and collectable for the sum of;

USD$XXXXXXXXXXXX (XXXXXX XXXXXXXXXXXXXX XXXXXXXXXXXXXXX)

Pre Advised Stipulation to enable collection: Full details to follow.
(1) Upon collection being applied for, the Beneficiary's written and signed notice of demand is to be presented under affidavit or fully notarized declaring that the amount being demanded is due and owing between the Beneficiary and the Applicant.(2) The SLC being presented for collection bears the terms "Original" on its margins and carries an original hand applied signature in blue ink pen of the issuer. The hardcopy courier delivered credit is issued directly to the beneficiary. This document is the ruling operative document.
(3) This SLC can only be paid into the bank account of the named beneficiary with all charges and fees applied for collection to be made for the account of the beneficiary.
This UCP600 standby letter of credit is payable unconditionally upon first demand once the said pre-advised conditions are met; paid from the advising bank as withdrawn from the account of the issuer, and transferred to the account of the beneficiary; the final net sum is transferred to the account of the beneficiary less all transfer costs, any statutory taxes and the likes made enforceable under the law of the country from which the funds are transferred (if any).
This standby letter of credit shall remain valid from XX/XX/20-- until XX/XX/20--. The demand in writing, if any, under this standby letter of credit may be presented to the advising bank counter between XX/XX/20-- and XX/XX/20-- (15 days before the expiration date; both dates inclusive to Australian Eastern Date Line. These date(s) hereafter shall be referred to as the "Presentation Period"). Any demand under this standby letter of credit presented to the advising bank outside the presentation period shall be considered invalid and shall not be honoured by the issuer.
I, the applicant issuing this credit hereby engage with the Beneficiary that their demand in writing is made strictly in compliance with the terms and conditions of this standby letter of credit. As expressly stated herein this shall be duly honoured by the advising bank on presentation in accordance with the terms and conditions of this standby letter of credit as allowed under UCP600 rules of reference.

This standby letter of credit shall be subject to UCP (Uniform Custom and Practice for issuance of a Documentary Credit) Publication 600 as defined By the ICC, Paris France.

Print Name :The Issuer/Applicant: }
Signed: }

Date of signature   }

Figure 19.1   Standby letter of credit: Sample to show layout

About the Authors

Davide Papa has been an international trade intermediary for more than twenty years and is CEO of FTN Exporting, an international import/export business in Melbourne, Australia that buys and sells a variety of exportable commodities worldwide. Davide is also founder of the Academy of Global Intermediaries (AGI), the educational arm of FTN Exporting. It offers a consultancy and mentoring service as well as model documents for use by intermediaries in international commodity transactions. Davide lives in Melbourne with his wife and daughter.

Lorna Elliott is a barrister who writes extensively about legal issues both for businesses and consumers in the UK and internationally. She is the affiliate advisor to FTN Exporting and head of the European Branch of the Academy of Global Intermediaries (AGI). She lives with her husband in the North East of England.

For further details of FTN Exporting and the Academy of Global Intermediaries please visit: http://www.ftnexporting.com.

For online support and updates relating to this publication please go to http://www.itsi.itgo.com.

Index

If you have found this book useful you may be interested in other titles from Gower

Purchasing Performance:
Measuring, Marketing and Selling the
Purchasing Function
Derek Roylance
Hardback: 978-0-566-08678-6
e-book: 978-0-7546-8308-7

A Short Guide to Procurement Risk
Richard Rissill
Paperback: 978-0-566-09218-3
e-book: 978-0-566-09218-2

The Global Business Handbook:
The Eight Dimensions of International Management
Edited by David Newlands and Mark J. Hooper
Hardback: 978-0-566-08747-9

Strategic Negotiation
Gavin Kennedy
Hardback: 978-0-566-08797-4

GOWER

**Global Outsourcing Strategies:
An International Reference on Effective Outsourcing
Relationships**
Edited by Peter Barrar and Roxane Gervais
Hardback: 978-0-566-08624-3

**The Relationship-Driven Supply Chain:
Creating a Culture of Collaboration throughout
the Chain**
Stuart Emmett and Barry Crocker
Hardback: 978-0-566-08684-7
e-book: 978-0-7546-8778-8

**Dynamic Supply Chain Alignment:
A New Business Model for Peak Performance in
Enterprise Supply Chains Across All Geographies**
John Gattorna and Friends
Hardback: 978-0-566-08822-3

Visit **www.gowerpublishing.com** and

- search the entire catalogue of Gower books in print
- order titles online at 10% discount
- take advantage of special offers
- sign up for our monthly e-mail update service
- download free sample chapters from all recent titles
- download or order our catalogue